HOW COULD YOU?

HOW COULD YOU?

Mothers Without
Custody of
Their Children

Harriet Edwards

The Crossing Press
Freedom, California 95019

Library of Congress Cataloging-in-Publication Data

Edwards, Harriet.
    How could you? : mothers without custody of their children / by Harriet Edwards.
        p. cm.
    Bibliography: p.
    ISBN 0-89594-336-0   ISBN 0-89594-335-2 (pbk.)
    1. Absentee mothers—United States—Attitudes.   I. Title.
HQ759.3.E38   1989
306.8'743—dc19   88-36463
                                              CIP

Acknowledgments

I always thought it would be great fun to write the acknowledgments for a book, but I see now that it is a daunting prospect; there are so many people who deserve credit for helping me in various ways and in varying degrees, and I tremble to think I might be leaving someone out. However, I do extend heartfelt thanks to:

The American Association of University Women, for giving me the initial grant enabling me to start my survey, and to its many helpful and knowledgeable members, especially Dr. Alayne Pettijohn, Marianne Huggard Haselgrave, and Barbara Riley;

The Long Island Women's Network, where I first nervously announced I was undertaking this book and found interest, support, and an attitude of belief in my abilities, and especially to Dr. Barbara Brown, and to Marilyn Goldstein of *Newsday* for her hints, leads, and her own writing on the subject;

The always delightful staff of the East Meadow Public Library, past and present, especially Annette Landau, reader and advisor; Sandy Berlstein, who shared stories of her home life as if mine were quite as normal as hers; and Louise Liebold, who invited me to speak on a panel on Alternate Family Lifestyles, thereby offering credibility to mine;

Other writers and researchers of the phenomenon of the non-custodial mother, who wrote with information, suggestions, and valuable leads, among them Dr. Judith Fischer, Dr. Catalina Herrerias, Barbara Kaufman, Ellen Kimball, Jan Koehler, Joan Kuver, and Karen Rosenblum;

Special friends old and new, among them Jan Zimmerman, for keeping me supplied with kind words and the names of agents and publishers; Barbara Kouts, who tried, and Tom Sergiovanni, who did too; Alice Frier and Lee Boojamra, for helping revive a near-moribund project; Pat Heffernan, who understood; and Irene Stevens, who never forgot there was such a project;

Stephanie Becker and Tom Feggeler, support staff extraordinaire, for typing, inputting, and general manipulation of multiple and mysterious computers and printers;

Irene Zahava, for being everything I could have dreamed of in an editor, and much more;

My three amazing "children," who, with their children and spouses, give me more happiness, laughter, and pride than they can begin to imagine;

The more than 300 women who answered my advertisements, completed my questionnaire, recorded tapes, wrote long essays, and simply made the book possible in the first place, especially Shirley Glubka, and several others (who know who they are)—you all have my deepest gratitude, admiration, and best wishes for continued happiness.

Finally, love and gratitude to my friend and companion Rhea White, who lent not only her editing, proofreading and grammar skills, and her office equipment and staff, but who for over ten years has given me unfailing warmth, devoted support, cheerful encouragement, gentle (and not so gentle) prodding, and an unswerving belief in the project and in my ability to do it.

Harriet Edwards
Dix Hills, New York

To
Susan, Dan and Carolyn
and to
Sister Anne
and, of course,
to Rhea

Table of Contents

Introduction

Ten years ago, at the age of 41, after 20 years of marriage, three children, and a life as a typical suburban matron—complete with women's clubs, volunteer work, bake sales, needlepoint, dutiful behavior as a daughter and daughter-in-law, Sunday School teaching, and a genteel part-time job at the local library—I left my husband, my three children, and the home where I had lived for 19 years and began to live a lifestyle that was as much a surprise to me as it was to everyone else.

The decision to leave my home was not lightly made. It was fraught with guilt, fear, and incredible aloneness, mixed, I confess, with unbridled and unseemly joy. I knew of no one else who had taken such a step, knew of no source of advice or support, had no guidance, no guidelines to follow. I was completely ignorant as to how to live without my family, had no idea whether any woman had ever successfully made such a transition, how or what the consequences might be for all concerned. I felt baffled, adrift in uncharted waters. It was terrifying and challenging, full of unexpected despair and delight. Imagine a ball, attached by a long tether to a tall pole, being batted back and forth by unseen players, now circling in predictable rhythms, now swinging wildly, bouncing off the pole in erratic and unmanageable arcs, and never, never, coming to rest. I felt like that ball most of the time.

Now, ten years later, I find I have come through the experience relatively intact, and am living in a new family configuration, sustained by a strong support network, and equipped with a new store of knowledge and insight that I very much want to share. I have met, and talked to, and corresponded with, and heard about, many other women who have also made the decision to leave the family home but *not* to "abandon" the family. All of us agree that we have suffered greatly from the lack of realistic, rational, and concrete information on the mother as non-custodial parent. All of us agree that we would have benefited greatly, both before and after we made our decisions, from an awareness of the experiences of other women in similar situations. All of us agree that our children, our parents, our friends, and our counselors could have helped us more if they had had the information necessary to understand us.

It was this that prompted me to apply to the American Association of University Women's Educational Foundation for a grant to assist in the preparation of a book exploring the worlds of women who have chosen to relinquish residential—that is, physical—custody of their minor children to their husbands, or to other adults, but who continue to parent. I proposed to do so by means of a questionnaire, plus interviews, plus a review of the literature which, as a reference librarian, I already knew was sparse, scanty, scattered, difficult to

1

locate, and often of little practical value. I found that while there is a large and growing body of material on divorce, and on the mother as single custodial parent, and that while increasing attention is being paid to the father as custodial parent, next to nothing is available on the *mother* as non-custodial, or non-residential, parent. I felt it was time to address that lack.

Let me say here that terminology was, and is, a major source of difficulty and frustration. What to call us? Non-custodial sounds janitorial, institutional. Non-residential sounds as though it applies to someone who is homeless. Standard research indexes only offer such headings as "divorced mothers," or "part-time parent," or "absentee parent." A new friend, who gifted me handsomely with her Master's thesis on the subject, settled uncomfortably for "women who have left the mother role." Besides being too long, such a phrase does not indicate an *alternate* mother role, which was what I was trying to describe. I suspect that the word *Mother*, with all its stereotypical, illusory, and unrealistic connotations, should be avoided altogether. Woman parent? Non-custodial parent? Extra-familial parent? The establishment of a national organization called Mothers Without Custody might give us a term, possibly an acronym (Mw/oC?) but what about women with *joint* or *shared* custody? The term "non-custodial" also excludes those women, but I found it to be the term most often used—so "non-custodial mothers" it is, though not because I'm convinced it's perfectly apt or inclusive.

I did receive a grant from the American Association of University Women. My first advertisement seeking respondents for my questionnaire appeared in the July, 1981, issue of *Ms.* magazine:

Noncustodial mothers! I need your help with my book about us. Please write: Mayflower, Box 534, Hicksville, NY 11801.

Within the week, letters began to arrive. Within three weeks, I had had responses from 14 states; after six weeks, from 22 states, the District of Columbia, and Canada. They wrote from New York City and Mabelvale, Arkansas; from Chicago and Calhoun, Kentucky; from Los Angeles, Denver, San Antonio, Indianapolis; from Amherst Junction, Cottage Grove, Florissant, and Kailua. Some were terse:

- In response to your ad, you may contact me at...
- Write or call re your ad...

Some were cautious:

- Your ad piqued my curiosity. Tell me why I should share my experiences with you.
- Hi! What do you want to know?
- I'm curious. What do you need?
- I'm very curious about what you are doing with this.

2

Many were full of outreach and support—and need:

- I know there must be lots of us around but I don't know any at all!
- Glad to hear someone is addressing our situation!
- I wish you success. It's an important and poorly understood subject.
- ...having traveled these United States from one end to the other I have yet to meet even *one* other mother with the same situation.... My main need these past years had been to share these feelings with someone.... Thank God I can now take isolation off that list.
- It is almost revelatory that there really *are* others in my situation.

They generously offered assistance:

- Please let me know how I can help.
- I'll do anything to assist.
- I am at your disposal to help in any way possible.
- I am eager to help.
- Very willing to contribute.

Most exciting, though, were the previews of the stories they would later relate through their questionnaires. These previews were instructive for me in planning my approach to the material. Some confirmed my preconceived notions of what I would hear:

- I have been co-parenting for four years.... It was *tough* at first (family, friends, social stigmas, ugh) but we're all used to it by now and it works well...of course, eyebrows are raised whenever I must explain...
- I am the mother of three children ages 8-16 who live over 2,000 miles away from me. The decision for their father to have custody was mine...
- After almost six years of it, I still find non-custodial mothering very painful (devastating, in fact), and I would value sharing my experiences and feelings.
- Well—I'm "one of us"—an arrangement that suited me—painful at times—but has worked well for six years.
- ...She was nine and he was only seventeen months when I left (six years ago). I have unlimited visiting rights and have maintained a good relationship with their father to insure same.
- I left my eight-year-old son over eight years ago. During this time have been through many good times and bad times...and have generally survived to have a good relationship with my now 16-year-old son.

These were the sorts of replies that I had had in mind—a conscious choice that was proving viable. But others brought home to me the realization that many times the "choice" was really *no* choice:

- I have been divorced since 1968. For financial reasons I had to send my children to their father in 1976. I am still filled with rage and pain.

3

- I relinquished custody of my two daughters in February of 1973 in New York State. I later challenged that custody here in Louisiana and lost.
- I am a non-custodial parent but not by choice...
- I lost custody of my three children to their Iranian-born father...There is a lot of heartbreak (I'm not sure I've learned to cope with it), shame, and loneliness connected with it.
- What else could I do? I had no money, no job, and a two-room apartment. He had a good job, the 10-room house we owned, two cars, and he flatly refused to pay me a cent. How could I make those kids take their chances with me? It broke my heart, but I left them there.

And more and more I had the uneasy feeling that my correspondents were not going to fit into the neat categories I had lined up for them, and that I was probably going to have to redefine my terms:

- Technically speaking, I am not a non-custodial mother. My husband and I have joint custody of our two sons. However, they live in Schenectady, New York, and I live in Chicago...
- I had them for seven years after the divorce and then gave their father custody.
- Two of my sons have elected to come and live with me in the past year and a half and have faced tremendous disapproval and guilt to do so.
- My children lived with me for five years and then moved in with their father for the last three.
- Ten years ago my husband took our three-month-old son and left. I have not heard of either of them since.

Furthermore, I was going to have to expand those definitions:

- My son lives with his grandmother and his godmother...definitely thrives from the love of his "many mommies."
- ...a teacher in his day care center appeared as if by magic in my living room one day and by the end of several hours she and I had agreed that she would try being his mother and I would try something that was not quite being his mother...that was nine years ago.
- I was married for 13 years and have two sons that live with their father. I now live with another woman in a love relationship...
- I am recently divorced and was not able to obtain custody of my one-year-old son due to the nature of my job. I am a merchant marine officer and sail as third mate for an oil corporation.

Most exciting of all, I realized that a gold mine of shared information was opening to me and that I could anticipate quantities of material beyond my fondest hopes. Perhaps my favorite indicator of this wealth was the letter I received from a woman who had made her decision to leave nearly 40 years before. She wrote:

- What do you want to know? I could write you a book full. I am an old woman now, so my version is so very different than recently dissolved families, and I have lived it to its destination.

Astonished and much encouraged by this response, I sent my questionnaire that summer to 97 women. "Who are you?" I asked. "What was your life like when you decided to take this step? How prepared were you? How did you manage? Who helped? Who hurt? How did it feel? Are you happy with your decision? What message do you have for other mothers?"

By the end of the year, 67 percent had returned their questionnaires. Others called to explain why they had not been able to complete them—usually, they said, because the questions dredged up too many painful memories and emotions. Some felt they did not qualify (they always did). It became apparent that I could not draw a neat line between "voluntary" (which ranged from putting a child up for adoption to letting him/her go to avoid unpleasantness and acrimony) and "involuntary" (which began where "voluntary" left off and continued on to bitter losses in lengthy court battles). One irate woman called to chastise me for my "terrible bias" in favor of women who actually *chose*, who *wanted to be*, the non-custodial parent (I confessed guilt to that since it had indeed been my original intention). However, as her own story spilled out, she stormed, "I agreed to let him go to his father; he wanted to, and I let him go so I could keep him!" Technically she, too, "chose" to give up custody, though it was a choice born of no choice. And very often, that was what it came down to; there *was* no viable alternative. And so these women, with varying degrees of willingness and readiness, gave up their children.

I placed more advertisements. I continued sending questionnaires, and the responses continued to arrive, many with additional pages attached, several with accompanying cassette recordings. I was staggered by these women's overwhelming need to be heard, fairly and honestly, by one of their own, a kindred soul, so to speak. I was deeply touched, and not a little saddened, by the self-revelations so generously given to a sympathetic stranger. Many gave me the totally unexpected gift of thanks; gratitude for the opportunity for sharing, and for pressing them to examine their lives and emotions in new ways—often, they said, with rewarding results.

After ten months I reached my goal of 100 representative responses, chosen from among over 300 replies from 41 states (including Alaska and Hawaii), and from Canada, England, and Australia. In the meantime I had joined an organization called Mothers Without Custody and began receiving their newsletter. I obtained transcripts of television shows devoted to the subject, most notably from the Phil Donahue Show. I searched the scanty literature and collected what I could find; sometimes authors sent me copies of their articles when they learned of my interest. I contacted the few researchers I could locate who are involved with this topic, and acted as consultant to some. I tried to find examples of well-known women who shared our situation. I appeared on several panels and gave a few talks (one to a group I expected to be hostile but whose overwhelming support, as it turned out, greatly boosted my motivation). I even, with no small difficulty, filled out my *own* questionnaire. Then, with no further excuses for delay, I plunged into the task of sharing what I had learned.

The writing of this book has been enormously difficult, and yet joyous and rewarding. Wading through other people's pain, tearing open my own wounds and examining my own inner self—and then sharing it—has sometimes been so terrifying it has been immobilizing. On the other hand, rejoicing in the successes of others, learning about stable, rewarding, and productive new family structures, and building my own, was glorious. So is the encouragement and caring of other women—women who were and still are, strangers to me; those women who have become my friends through this research; and those women who have always been and continue to be there for me. Their warmth and support is awesome and humbling.

Throughout, I struggled with a title. I knew that I wanted the book to be upbeat and affirming, not apologetic, or defensive, not self-pitying. Whatever the situation was, whatever the reasons and pressures and pain, the choice *was* made, the deed *was* done, and now the task at hand was to make it work—to make the new way support and help and produce growth for both the mothers and the children. I wanted to help people do that. So I dreamed up many titles that seemed less negative than the one I finally chose. "I Have Three; They Live With Their Father," was one. Or, "Mothering From the Outside," or, "Nora in a New Land" or "After the Door Slammed" (these two with apologies to Ibsen). Or "Alternative Mothering." How about "Defying the Myth"? But I kept coming back to the central question, asked in curiosity, in admiration, in anguish, and in disbelief—by our parents, our children, our husbands, and our counselors, by society in general, and most of all by ourselves, as we, and they, came to terms with our decisions: *"How could you?"* How could an ordinary woman defy the dictates of custom, religion, society, a life-time of conditioning and a bred-into-the-bone expectation of roles and duties and choose to live apart from her children? And moreover, how can it be made to work?

I have tried to answer those questions in this book, in the words of women who have made that decision and who have discovered that it is, indeed, possible to mother a child successfully without living in the same house full time. What follows is the generous self-revelation of these pioneer women who have described fully and with painful honesty the fears and guilts, the joys and rewards, the problems, the processes, and the people they have encountered on their journeys.

They are, of course, all different. They are also very much alike. They have entrusted me with their experiences and I have tried to pass them on intact. I make no pretense about this being a scientific survey or a sociological study, or an objective reporting on aberrant behavior. My goal was and is to offer realistic and practical information about a viable, albeit unconventional, lifestyle, based on the lives of contemporary women who have chosen to allow their experiences to be shared. These are their stories—and mine. We offer them in trust to our families, our friends, and our counselors; to our adversaries and critics; to each other, and to ourselves.

Who Ever Heard of
Such a Thing?

It kills me! What kind of a woman leaves her own baby?
—letter from a grandmother

Indeed, what kind of a woman *could* "do such a thing"? What circumstances could combine to put someone in so drastic a place? And now that *I* had done this unthinkable thing—wanted it, chosen it, and actually *done* it—what did that mean for the woman I was, or thought I was? It had always been easy to define myself; there were so many others just like me. Peers of my own generation; role models from generations past. I was doing just what they had done and were doing, and I could measure myself against them, compare notes, so to speak, exchange experiences, and take comfort in our similarity and, therefore, in my "normality." I had been brought up to admire and seek this goal of similarity. There was a definite set of rules to be followed; we knew what they were and we did not stray. And I never had—until now. Now I was without rules, without normality and, terrifyingly, without identity. How to define myself now? Who, indeed, was I? Against whom could I now measure myself? Because it seemed I was the only one. *Was* I the only one? I thought I must be. I knew of no one else. No one. And my respondents later wrote, "I knew of no one."

But there were others, of course, and we did know about them. They were in the novels we read. They were in the plays we saw. They were in our history books. Their names were in the headlines when their decisions became known. Names like Ingrid Bergman. Happy Rockefeller. Joan Kennedy. Margaret Trudeau. Yoko Ono. They were there, and we knew about them. But we didn't identify with them. They were not like us. They were rich and famous. We were just "normal" women. Everyday, housewife-type women. Surely we had nothing in common with these public women whose lives were so different from ours.

Let's consider these famous women who chose to live apart from their children. First, Joan Kennedy, wife of Ted Kennedy, senator from Massachusetts and member of the most publicized family in the United States. We certainly knew about *her*, just as we knew about all the other Kennedys. A biography written in 1975 was entitled *Joan: The Reluctant Kennedy*, and so she was portrayed to us. "The hardest thing," she said shortly after her marriage, "is learning to keep up with the clan." Later she said, "I tried to be like the Kennedys, bouncy and running all over. But I could never be like that."[1]

Life heaped much anguish on the Kennedys and on Joan too. The assassinations of her brothers-in-law and the resulting terror over her husband's vulnerability, intensified by his near-fatal plane crash in 1964; her three miscarriages in a notably prolific family; and, most demoralizing of all, the insistent rumors of the Senator's womanizing, culminating in the events at Chappaquidick. "Poor Joan!" we all whispered. And poor Joan sought solace where thousands of others have sought it before her, in alcohol. The press kept us abreast of her drinking, telling us about her too-brassy hair, her puffy red eyes, her inappropriate dress, her bloated face. Poor Joan, they wrote. And there was more to be borne. Her son was stricken with cancer; his leg was amputated. Her mother died. Her friend Marvella Bayh died. With this mounting pressure came the news of her separation from Ted Kennedy, then of their divorce after 22 years of marriage. Joan was on her own in Boston; the children were in the custody of their father in Virginia.

Rich, famous, beautiful—and still a lot like us. She had, like so many of us, tried to live her life the way someone else expected her to; tried to be the person she believed she was "supposed" to be. "I was drinking my life away. And I needed help."[2] In 1979 Dr. Joyce Brothers wrote of her, "She has faced the realization that the only one who can rescue Joan Kennedy is Joan Kennedy."[3] It takes some of us a very long time to get to that place, we who have been taught that someone else is ultimately responsible for us—our fathers, our husbands, our children—that someone else should save us or be blamed for what happens to us. Joan Kennedy realized that this is not so, and took the necessary steps to reorder her own life. In the glare of the political spotlight that must have been incredibly difficult.

We also followed the adventures of another political wife; Margaret Trudeau, who at 19 married the Prime Minister of Canada. After six years of marriage to a man 29 years her senior and the birth of their three sons, she fled to New York City, saying she had "had enough of being public property." The popular press gleefully followed her liaisons with the Rolling Stones, her disco-hopping, her jet-set romances, her fledgling career as photographer, actress, author— perhaps we shook our heads at that "flaky, undisciplined, bird that got out of her cage,"[4] as she described herself. And flaky she seemed; beautiful, flamboyant, outrageous, embarrassing. But some of what she said struck a sympathetic chord. She was, she said, "on the edge of not being able to survive."[5] To charges that she deserted her children she replied, "I don't believe that children profit from mothers who sacrifice their own lives and become martyrs.... At the time I left I would have described myself as someone who had a tremendous inner rage, which was very well concealed—but it's gone now."[6]

Her autobiography, published in 1979, gives us a fuller description of her life, as contrasted with the life she wanted and ultimately chose. We begin to feel a great deal of sympathy for that young girl who started out with such high hopes, who made her own wedding gown and baked her own wedding cake and who, when she became a mother, took her nursing babies on state visits all over the world. Finding it harder and harder to cope, she sought help and entered a hospital, but there was no help there:

> They arranged for me to have a round-the-clock shift of private nurses.
> Dr. Boz explained the treatment he had in mind for me. "I want to bore you," he said. "I want to make you sleep. Relax."
> It was all a bit like Alice in Wonderland. "I feel paranoid. I feel everybody is watching me," I said to him.
> "Everybody is watching you. That's not paranoia. That's reality."
> "I feel hostile. I have illusions of grandeur. I think I'm somebody."
> "You *are* somebody."
> One Sunday the hospital priest came to talk to me. His words electrified me. "Whatever are you doing here?" he asked contemptuously. "You should be home with your children."[7]

The problems continued and finally we read:

> Pierre and Margaret Trudeau announce that, because of Margaret's wishes, they shall begin living separate and apart. Margaret relinquishes all privileges as the wife of the Prime Minister and wishes to leave the marriage and pursue an independent career. Pierre will have custody of their three sons, giving Margaret generous access to them. Pierre accepts Margaret's decision with regret, and both pray that their separation will lead to a better relationship between them.[8]

Interestingly, this news of Prime Minister Trudeau's new status as a single parent caused a 17 percent rise in his popularity rating!

Margaretta Fitler Murphy Rockefeller is another woman we might have remembered. On May 4, 1963 the newspapers reported that recently divorced Nelson Rockefeller, Governor of New York and leading contender for the Republican nomination for president of the United States, had married the former wife of Dr. James Murphy. The terms of her divorce, granted in Utah 33 days before her marriage to the Governor, were sealed, but one fact was startlingly clear; her four children remained behind in the custody of their father.

Sixteen months later, after the birth of another child and two days after Governor Rockefeller lost the Republican nomination to Barry Goldwater, Mrs. Rockefeller brought suit in New York Supreme Court to regain custody of her children, particularly Malinda, who was then residing with her and the Governor following Dr. Murphy's remarriage. After 1,000 pages of testimony guided by seven lawyers, and including eight hours of testimony by Dr. Murphy and seven hours by Mrs. Rockefeller, Justice Joseph Gagliardi reaffirmed the original custody arrangement which, he said, "the adult parties themselves determined and their joint judgment was that the father should have physical custody...." The judge ordered Mrs. Rockefeller to return Malinda "forthwith."[9]

Another non-custodial mother we knew about through news reports and a movie was Karen Gay Silkwood. In 1974 Ms. Silkwood was killed in an automobile accident which many believe to be murder. She was on her way to meet a reporter from the *New York Times* with evidence that the Kerr-McGee Nuclear Corporation was manufacturing defective nuclear rods. Two months earlier she had contacted the Atomic Energy Commission with a list of violations at the plutonium plant, and a week before her death she had been contaminated by eating and inhaling plutonium under mysterious circumstances. During the ensuing negligence trial the Kerr-McGee legal staff maintained that Karen Silkwood was so unreliable, so emotionally disturbed, so hooked on drugs, that she had contaminated herself in order to embarrass Kerr-McGee. The major point they brought against her was the fact that two years before her death she had "walked out" on her husband and three children.

Richard Raske, in his book, *The Killing of Karen Silkwood*, gives us some of the background behind that "walk out." While her husband worked, Karen stayed home and had babies. Bill drank, had a mistress, and spent them into bankruptcy. When Karen finally demanded a divorce, Bill agreed, but only if she would give him custody of the children. At first she refused, but after more years of unhappiness she left for Oklahoma City on Bill's terms; Beverly, Dawn, and Michael stayed behind. She saw them as often as possible, and they visited her regularly, but after her death she was accused of abandoning her children and showing little interest in them.[10]

Five years later a federal court jury found Kerr-McGee negligent, and awarded the Silkwood estate over $10 million in damages. Far from being weak and irresponsible, Karen Gay Silkwood's tenacious pursuit of what she perceived as justice and fairness showed remarkable courage. So, perhaps, did the course she took in re-ordering her life.

Dorothy Sayers was, in the words of Mary Brian Durkin, "an entertainer, dramatist, scholar, theologian, translator, and above all else, a Christian humanist whose works epitomize her artistic credo; 'The only Christian work is good work well done.'"[11] We know her best as the creator of the extremely popular detective, Lord Peter Wimsey. She was also a noncustodial mother. It was while she was working on the sequel to the novel in which she introduced Lord Peter that she took a leave of absence from her job at Benson's advertising agency to await the birth of an illegitimate child. She managed to hide the fact that she was pregnant from her parents and most of her friends, and on January 3, 1924 a son was born. She called him John Anthony.

In 1981 a biography, written by James Brabazor with the cooperation of Sayers' son, appeared. In it we learn that two days before the birth Sayers wrote a note to her cousin Ivy, who made her living caring for parentless children, and asked her to take the child, without revealing his identity. Ivy agreed, and on January 27 Sayers wrote again saying she would turn over the child the following week, this time giving what she called the "confidential particulars":

My dear, everything I told you about the boy is absolutely true—only I didn't tell you he was my own! I won't go into the whole story—think the best you can of me—I know it won't make you love the boy any the less. He is really a fine little chap—I can't feel too bad about him myself now, because it will be so jolly to have him later on. I am thirty now, and it didn't seem at all likely I should marry—I shall have something for my later age anyway.... They know nothing about him at home, and they must know nothing. It would grieve them quite unnecessarily. You know, it's not the kind of ill-doing that Mother has any sympathy for. She isn't a man lover or a baby worshiper— so I see no reason whatever for distressing her. So please, not a word of any kind to Christchurch. By the time I want the boy, they will be too old, if they are still alive, to worry much about anything, and they must have these last years in peace....[12]

Sayers never did share a home with her son, but it is clear that she remained well informed of her son's development and well-being, and monitored the care he was receiving. She visited him whenever she could, and wrote to him and Ivy regularly. She paid for his upkeep and made him sole heir to her literary estate when she died in 1957, at which time he was 33 years old.

If our backgrounds in history are well enough balanced we know of the writings, teachings, and life of Charlotte Perkins Gilman. She was, according to Carrie Chapman Catt, the most original and challenging mind produced by the early women's movement. In the nineteenth century she was a champion of the feminist goals held today, the most important of which, in her view, was the economic independence of women. She enumerated her theories in lectures, poetry, fiction, and in several widely acclaimed textbooks, most notably *Women and Economics* published in 1898. In this and other writings she attacked the prevailing notions of the unclouded blessings of home and motherhood and the inevitability of woman's economic and sexual subservience. She deplored the loss to society of the talents of women who were prevented from attaining their natural and fruitful development by their positions as "private servants" to husbands and children. She felt that when a woman who had the ability to enrich society and human growth submerged herself instead in domestic drudgery, she committed true heresy.

One might assume, then, that her decision to give up custody of her daughter Katherine was a direct outgrowth of, and response to, her social theories. It was, I suspect, rather the other way around, and her autobiography may help to point that out.

In 1882 her courtship with Walter Stetson began.

My mind was not fully clear as to whether I should marry or not marry. On the one hand I knew it was normal and right in general, and held that a woman should be able to have marriage and motherhood, and do her work in the world also. On the other, I felt strongly that for me it was not right, that the nature of the life before me forbade it, that I ought to forgo the more intimate personal happiness for complete devotion to my work.[13]

However, they did marry in 1884, and their daughter was born the following year. There ensued an almost total mental and physical collapse, then called "nervous prostration." Finally, in the fall of 1887, in "a moment of clear vision," they agreed to separate, to get a divorce. She writes of this decision:

There was no quarrel, no blame for either one, never an unkind word between us, unbroken mutual affection—but it seemed plain that if I went crazy it would do my husband no good, and be a deadly injury to my child.... It was not a choice between going and staying, but between going sane, and staying, insane. If I had been of the slightest use to him or to the child, I would have 'stuck it,' as the English say. But this progressive weakening of the mind made a horror unnecessary to face; better for that dear child to have separated parents than a lunatic mother.[14]

For the next four years her daughter remained in her care, but:

Then came the end of the Oakland effort. My mother was dead. My friend on whom I had so counted, was gone. I was not able to carry the boarding-house, and there was new work opening for me in San Francisco, but in a place unsuitable for a child. It was arranged that she should go to her father.... I took her to the uptown station in Oakland, where the Overland trains stopped for passengers; her grandfather appeared; she climbed gaily aboard. She hurried to the window and looked out, waving to me. She had long shining golden hair. We smiled and waved and threw kisses to each other. The train went out, farther and farther till I couldn't see her any more.... That was 30 years ago. I have to stop typing and cry as I tell about it.[15]

Casting back even further in time we find a familiar name—the sharp-shooting, hard-riding Queen of the West nicknamed "Calamity Jane." She was, perhaps, "one of us." In 1941 a woman claiming to be her daughter appeared with letters she said had been written to her by Calamity Jane. Deserted by "Wild Bill" Hickok after the birth of their daughter Janey and unable because of the unorthodox ways in which she made her living to maintain a stable home for her child, Martha Jane Cannary Hickok gave her daughter to Helen and Jim O'Neill to raise. She saw her only a few times after that, never revealing her identity, but kept a diary-type correspondence to be shared after her death. Those letters have been published under the title *Calamity Jane's Letters to Her Daughter*. In one of those letters, dated 1880, she wrote:

In two more years I will go to see you dear, then I know I will feel better about you. Perhaps then you will think of me sometimes not as your mother but as some lonely woman who once loved and lost a little girl like you. I shall take you on my lap and tell you all about that little girl. Of course you won't know it's you.... Giving you up nearly killed me, Janey.... You will understand all this some day.[16]

Her last letter, written in 1902, pleads:

Forgive my faults and the wrong I have done you.... I am sick and haven't long to live. I am taking many secrets with me Janey. What I am and what I might have been. I'm not as black as I have been painted. I want you to believe that...forgive me and consider I was lonely.[17]

There were still others. Perhaps we did not notice them or did not remember them. Who, for instance, remembers that when Yoko Ono joined forces with John Lennon she left behind a five-year-old daughter, Kyoko? In an interview with *Playboy* shortly before his death, John Lennon and Yoko Ono discussed this part of their lives:

ONO: I lost Kyoko when she was about five. I was sort of an offbeat mother, but we had very good communication. I wasn't particularly taking care of her, but she was always with me—onstage or at gallery shows, whatever....My communication with her was on the level of sharing conversation and doing things. She was closer to my ex-husband because of that.
PLAYBOY: What happened when she was five?
ONO: John and I got together and I separated from my ex-husband (Tony Cox). He took Kyoko away. It became a case of parent kidnapping and we tried to get her back....Allen called up one day, saying I had won the court case. I said, "What is this piece of paper? Is this what I won? I don't have my child." I knew that taking them to court would frighten them and of course, it did frighten them. So Tony vanished....We had private detectives chasing Kyoko, which I thought was a bad trip, too...
LENNON: It was like we were after an escaped convict.
PLAYBOY: Were you so persistent because you felt you were better for Kyoko?
LENNON: Yoko got steamed into a guilt thing that if she wasn't attacking them with detectives and police and the FBI, then she wasn't a good mother looking for her baby. She kept saying, "Leave them alone, leave them alone." But they said you can't do that.
ONO: For me, it was like they just disappeared from my life. Part of me left with them...we did kidnap her and went to court. The court did a very sensible thing—the judge took her into a room and asked her which one of us she wanted to go with. Of course, she said Tony. We had scared her to death.[18]

Who followed the fortunes of the Dionne quintuplets long enough to know that Marie Dionne's children were placed in a foster home until she died in 1970?

13

Have we forgotten the young Ingrid Bergman, whose flight from her husband and year-old daughter Pia so shattered her saintly image that she was actually censured from the floor of the United States Congress as "a horrible example of womanhood and a powerful influence for evil"?[19] And did we notice another non-custodial mother whose daughter Diana married Charles, Prince of Wales? Lady Diana Spencer's parents were divorced in 1960 when she was seven years old. Lord Spencer was awarded custody of his four children (though in the proceedings each was identified as a "guilty party") and Diana was raised to maturity in his home. The former Sarah Ferguson, now Duchess of York, was also raised by her father after her parents' divorce.

Then, of course, there are the women of fiction: Nora Helmer, heroine of Hendrick Ibsen's *The Doll's House*; Martha Quest, of Doris Lessing's epic three-volume *Children of Violence*; Edna Pontellier, of Kate Chopin's daring *The Awakening*; Mira Ward, of Marilyn French's stunning *The Women's Room*; Joanna Kramer, heroine of Avery Corman's book, brought to the screen in an Academy Award winning film with the same title, *Kramer vs. Kramer*. For self-sacrifice, none topped the favorite radio soap opera queen, derived from a novel by Olive Higgins Prouty and later played heart-rendingly by Joan Crawford—the long-suffering, ever-popular Stella Dallas. There is even Joanie Caucus, a favorite character in Gary Trudeau's popular and award-winning "comic" strip, *Doonesbury*.

So, there were in fact many others. We could have, if we had tried, discovered these women, real and fictional, who had made the same choice we made. We might have used them as examples and guides, if only to help us know that we were *not* the only ones; that we were not so alone as we thought.

But I, for one, did not recall, or in some cases even know about these other women. And I suspect that if I had, I might well have responded that I was not a rich debutante or a beautiful playgirl or an internationally known writer. Nor was I the heroine of a book or a play or a movie. I was a painfully typical suburban matron and I badly needed to find out whether there were other typical, "normal," "average" women out there who were struggling with the same situation.

Who Are You?

Who are you? *Where* are you? I searched the literature, by hand and with the aid of sophisticated computerized information retrieval systems such as *Dialog*, *BRS*, and *Nexis*, and found next to nothing. I decided to try to find somebody on my own. I worked up my questionnaire, advertised it, sent it out all over the country and abroad, poured over the returns, and began to find some answers to my questions.

Let me say here that I am well aware that my sample for this survey is not random; that it does not cover all women of all social and economic levels; that it is a self-selected group who were willing to take a great deal of initiative in sharing their experiences. However, I do not believe that what I write here is less valuable or accurate because of those limitations. I hope that what is shared here will reach those most likely to be in need of it, wherever they are.

Letters began to pour into my mailbox; yes, there certainly were others out there. The answers to my next question, *Who are you?*, emerged from the pages and the tapes and the interviews. It was amazing to realize how similar the women were, to each other and to me, though they came from all over the United States and from Canada, England, New Zealand, and Australia.

The first page of the questionnaire was an attempt to develop a picture of the respondent before and at the time of the separation. I thought the data which emerged from the 100 responses I selected as being the most complete were pretty interesting, especially as they reflected my own circumstances. I set to work and tallied it all up and arrived at a composite picture, looking something like this:

We had all married fairly young (or what I have come to think of as young!): Out of the 100 women, all but seven had married by the age of 22 and most had married at 19 or 20 (I was 21). Most of the women had left marriages of 10 to 15 years' duration; the longest marriage had lasted 25 (I had been married for 20 years). Most of the women had been between 30 and 36 years of age when they left their marriages. (I was almost 42.) An overwhelming majority left first marriages, although five had left second marriages, one had been married three times and one had never married. All but 20 of the women had completed at least one year of college. There was an equal number of women with bachelor's and master's degrees (15 each); (I had a master's degree in counseling in addition to my library science degree.) I heard from one Ph.D., one doctor, and a dentist.

Only 20 of the 100 selected responses indicated that they were actively religious; five wrote in the word "semi-" to describe their religious involvement (I would describe my own involvement that way, too). Interestingly, Catholics or rather ex-Catholics tended to underscore and add exclamation points to their "no" responses concerning religious affiliation. About half the women had sought some kind of counseling (I had not). The women tended to describe their physical health as fair and their mental health as deteriorating. Only a few said they used drugs of any kind, smoked cigarettes or marijuana, or (unlike myself) drank excessively.

Most of the women had one or two children; fifteen, like myself, had three; only six had more than three; four said they had twins. The children's ages at the time the women left their marriages ranged from three months to 18 years. Most were in the "middle years" of six to 12, which I believe reflects the average duration of the marriages and not that these were difficult years for childrearing. My own children were 10, 15, and 18.

Most of the women had lived apart from their children for less than five years; twenty had lived apart for six to 15 years, two for 18 years, one for 26. One woman said she had lived apart from her daughter for 40 years, at which time her daughter had died. For most of the women, therefore, living apart from their children was a relatively new experience.

If we had a common bond it was our financial status or rather the lack of it at the time we left our marriages. Only 17 of the 100 women said that they had had a savings account in their own name, and of these 17 accounts, 14 contained under $400. The top "nest egg" was $4,000; the *sum total* of the remaining 16 was $5,160, an average of $322.50. More of the women had had separate checking accounts, but that seems to have been more a bookkeeping convenience than a reflection of real personal capital. For all but seven the family possessions had been jointly owned; those seven said everything had been in their husband's name. Most of the women had had no assets in their own name alone. Ten reported that they had owned cars (as I had); only one mentioned furniture, and a mere two said they had had their own credit cards.

About half of the women were employed at the time they left their marriages, and about half of the jobs were part-time (as mine had been). Many had gotten their jobs shortly before they left. I had expected to find a fairly large number of career women, but only a handful in fact had worked steadily and upward. Most had worked less than ten years at any job. Of those who worked, all but five reported incomes of $10,000 a year or less. The family incomes were, I thought, surprisingly high: about a third were in the $30,000 to $50,000 a year bracket; the highest was $80,000. These figures are, of course, difficult to summarize and analyze, as there was no common time frame, but I think it could be fairly said that almost all of the women were middle or upper middle class. All but five were white.

This factual data and the statistical analysis, however crude, was interesting and fun, but obviously only prologue. The fuller picture of who these women were when they left their marriages, how they got to where they are

16

now and how they perceive their futures emerged not so much from facts as from the volumes of narrative the women provided in their own words on cassette tapes and in the follow-up interviews.

I wanted history and background; I wanted to know what kind of lives were being led and why they had gone awry. And I got many, many scenarios. "You want to know what my life was like?" asked one. "Go read *The Woman's Room*. That's *my story*. I've been to that party. I've had that same fight. I thought the same things." Another said, "My life? You don't want to hear about my life. It's all so ordinary! You've heard it a thousand times. Just go to any conscious-ness raising group in the world—they've gone over the same territory, told the same tales, felt the same things. Just say 'this one was the same old thing.'" (I was reminded of a friend whose husband left her for his secretary. "His *secretary*, for God's sake!" she used to shriek. "Why did he have to be so damn dull!") And it was true that there was nothing "new" in the stories I read and heard. But that was precisely the value of it, it seems to me. Perhaps even if we can't identify with a Joan Kennedy or a Dorothy Sayers we can with the "ordinary" women who participated in this research. Listen to this Virginia mother of two, who wrote me a lengthy essay, the first half of which follows:

I received your questionnaire today and I promptly sat down and re-sponded. This has been very stimulating for me, for many reasons, and I enjoyed the opportunity to speak my mind. As you can probably tell from some of my responses, my feelings on my status are still mixed. But, they have come a long way from what they were one and a half years ago.

I married my first husband when I was 17 years old. Yet a child myself. He was five years my senior and had what appeared to me to be a stable life. My parents were, as you would say, "supportive" in my relationship with this man.

The relationship between my parents wasn't good. Honestly, I now think they saw this man as a form of "escape" for me because they were discussing divorce themselves and they clearly had enough problems of their own.

This man proposed to me and I must admit I did feel "grown up" while sporting an engagement ring around my peers. My parents had to sign for the marriage, and this they both did without protest. I can remember my Mom telling me I would have a good life because this man was working at a good job, from a good family, etc.

Strangely, I did not dislike this man. He said he loved me and I believed him. In ways I loved him. He was solid, stable, a good provider, and he spoiled me in many ways....

His mother was a difficult person to understand, and I was a bit immature, so I resented her overprotectiveness in trying to give me advice on how to cook, etc.... At that time I deeply resented her and I learned that my husband was very close to her. I resented that also.

Soon, we started building our own house—only a few rooms at first. I felt as though it was a mansion! I devoted nearly all my time to that house. I did manage to complete high school and squeeze in one year of nurse's training, which was good. My husband had very old-fashioned ideas about how a wife should be, i.e. cakes made from scratch, no make-up, etc. One thing that bothered me was I always felt guilty when I enjoyed myself with my friends at school. The reason for this was my husband showed a disapproval of my friends and felt they weren't suitable company for a married woman. Some of these friends have stood by me and are still good and dear friends. The "unsuitable" company turned out to be a lawyer, a dietitian and a school teacher—not that it matters or even mattered then.

When I was 19 years old I became pregnant with my first child. I quit nursing school and stayed home to be a mother.... I was glad to have her and I felt such overwhelming love for her! I also felt very insecure in motherhood. My husband was a perfectionist and he demanded certain things to be in order—such as the house and full-course meals every day. With the demands of a small baby and his demands I felt exhausted nearly constantly. I was alone except for the company of my daughter and my mother-in-law. When my daughter was a year old I learned I was pregnant again. This pregnancy was unplanned. Soon afterwards my parents filed for divorce. My 15-year-old sister ran away from home and got involved in drugs, my mother's home burned in a fire and the relationship between me and my husband wasn't good. He made me feel like a prisoner in my own home. He viewed my friends with suspicion, he resented my hobbies, he allotted me time on the phone, he never gave me money. I had to ask for it and give a legitimate reason for it! As far as material luxuries, I had what I wanted. He would buy them for me, but I had to ask for them. He refused to let me go to the hairdresser or to wear make-up....

When my second daughter was born I suffered post-partum blues. I became deeply depressed and I felt trapped in a marriage and tied down with two children. I wanted to run away and escape. I felt as though the world was passing me by, as though I had never really lived. I began to drink and to smoke marijuana, and that provided a momentary escape. I never developed a habit, but it was a crutch for me. I knew it was wrong and I knew I needed help. My husband was unsympathetic. He constantly ridiculed me for my "inabilities"—always comparing me to his mother.

Our home life was rotten! I would look at those two innocent faces of my children and feel so damn stupid! I loved them dearly but I also had a need to find my own identity. I felt rude, thoughtless, selfish! but deep inside myself I knew I could never be the kind of person my children would someday admire if I stayed in a bad marriage. I would become bitter and cynical. Visions of how a bad marriage had nearly ruined my parents haunted me. My parents were like hollow-eyed zombies and I didn't want that to happen to me. I was a child in a bad marriage and I knew too well the feelings associated with a situation like that.

Another woman also wrote of her high hopes and the life that followed; she too tells a tale familiar to us all:

We moved when our son was three and our daughter six months old. It was the third time I had agreed to a move which my husband desired. My own dream (or one of them) had been fulfilled in becoming the mother of a son and daughter, both much longed for and loved. I had already given up the other important thing in my life— my job as a psychologist— when we left in 1970, feeling it would not be possible to continue with this as well as be a devoted wife and mother...Therein lay the root of my dissatisfaction. My need for development as an intelligent individual had to be constantly buried if I was to commit myself to helping my husband grow vegetables as well as care for two children, a cow, and some chickens. Was this not the ideal environment I had had in mind for my children when I had first agreed to a move? The beautiful countryside, fresh milk from our cow, organically grown vegetables, and bread made at home from whole-meal stone-ground flour.... Yes, the children did wonderfully well, as everyone remarked. I made sure also that I was never so busy with the needs of the farm that I failed to give them the attention they needed, unlike some other mothers I observed who let the physical work eat up all of their time and energy.

But what was happening to me?.... Two years later we both felt demoralized. It was clear my husband could not succeed in business terms because we did not have enough land or equipment. For my part, I was feeling increasingly isolated and lacked the kind of intellectual and cultural stimulation which it seems I badly needed for my well-being.

For a year our friends were aware we were battling with problems in our relationship. The point at which I was made aware that, psychologically speaking, my husband needed the children more than I did was the day when I packed both of the children in the pram with a sleeping bag and set out to walk a mile to visit my nearest friend. My husband was out when I left but returned home sooner than expected. He set out after me and grabbed the pram. He said, "You can go if you like but you are not taking the children." My choice was to go on to Mary's on my own. I returned home but I believe that this was basically the crucial crossroads. It took over a year to carry through on this initial impulse.

From Oregon comes a reply from a woman who feels she married for the reason so many women do—to get away from their parents and out of the family home. She observes:

Had I had the experience of living alone, as I do now, in this apartment that I wrap around me like a cocoon, it would have been very different. When I was 20 or so I had a friend who was working as a beauty operator; I was working for an insurance agent. She suggested we could share an apartment, which we quite easily could have done. My mother hit the ceiling. "'Nice girls' don't ever do that. They don't *ever* do that. They stay home until they marry." That was the one and only time I tried to get away from home, on my own, and eventually I married, to get away from home.... For many years I have been conscious of this missing link, this need for a growth period, and in a marriage you can't have it. Without it I was still an adolescent, I married as an adolescent, and I looked at the world through adolescent eyes. I never grew up until I walked out that door. I now enjoy the kind of autonomy that goes with adulthood; without it, I could never *be* an adult.

One after another my respondents told stories that followed a very similar pattern: high hopes, willingness, enthusiasm; disillusionment, loss of support and companionship in the marriage; a growing self-awareness and a widening world; ultimately, an impossible conflict and a place of hopelessness. But few, if any, come to that place of conflict without trying hard to keep it from happening, often at great cost to themselves. They spoke of blooming, enjoyable careers that had been sacrificed:

I had been employed—owned the weekly newspaper in our town. "Had" to sell it (approximately three years before the split) because *he* said it took too much time away from house, kids, him, his clients, etc. *And I sold it!* That's one regret.

Others quit college, or even high school, to devote themselves to their husbands and children. But for many, despite heroic efforts to "make it work," the struggle was taking its toll. A Michigan woman wrote to explain:

We always had fights and problems. All the old cliches used to go through my head: "You must try harder. You have to work at a marriage." But though I blamed myself, I could never see how life would get any better. Yet it wasn't until my daughter was 13 or 14, when I saw her going out and developing and having a life of her own, that I got the push I needed. I saw the potential in her life, and it made me look at my own life and wonder. I didn't feel depressed, yet I felt I might just as well be dead.

Many wrote, or spoke, in varying ways, of the steady, almost invisible destruction of spirit, the dragging down of the essence of the woman that used to be. A New York woman had been college homecoming queen, president of her class, "most likely to succeed," and winner of several other awards and honors. She, too, married with high hopes and a great willingness to accommodate herself to whatever the marriage required. She wrote:

He told me early on that I made him feel inferior, stupid, and that he didn't like it. Well, who would? So I was careful not to use words he might not understand, literary allusions he might miss, historical references he might have forgotten. This is not a stupid man, mind you. He had two degrees and a good job he was doing well at. But he just couldn't bear the thought that I might be smarter—at anything! He seemed completely unable to find and enjoy his own strengths—the things that *he* was smarter at.

The only way I could think to help (and of course I took that as my duty), was to deny my own strengths, to crouch. Lower and lower, be less and less. I would slink and slouch physically, too, trying to be tiny, tiny—in body, in mind, in spirit—you can't imagine the energy it takes to be nothing! Whenever the kids would do something special I would say, "Oh, wait until Daddy sees! Wait until Daddy hears! Oh, Daddy will be so pleased!" Never mind that *I* was pleased, that *I* was proud. Who was I? It was *Daddy* that was the important one, it was Daddy we were all working for. I didn't even teach them to be pleased for *themselves*, which was one of my big mistakes. And even when I knew I could do something better than he was doing it, I didn't.

When it came time for my daughter to go to college it turned out there was no money. I was horrified and asked what happened. (He always took care of the money, of course.) He said that I must be crazy to think there was any money and that if I had wanted a college fund I should have gone back to work, and it was *my* fault that there was no money!

And he was right. It *was* my fault, for being so stupid and so naive and so mealy-mouthed. I think a lot of women do that, though—they hope against hope that the man will turn out smarter and wiser and more mature than they themselves are, just like the books say he is supposed to be, and they just go along pretending that it is true when they know full well it isn't. I guess that is what I finally gave up—that hope that the pretense was true. Anyway, I finally realized that if I kept making myself small I was going to disappear altogether. There was no way I could be myself and stay in the marriage, so I felt I had to leave.

A Southerner wrote more succinctly about that dissolution of self:

You go through the motions until your limbs ache, your mind's numb, and your heart only beats on special occasions.

When I first started investigating for this book it did not occur to me to try to find women in other countries, but they found me. I wondered whether their stories would be very much different from those of American women; it turned out that they were not. I joined the British organization for non-custodial mothers, which is called MATCH, Mothers Apart From Their Children. The following story appeared in an issue of the MATCH newsletter:

Breda is 43 now. She was 22 when she married, and at first neither she nor her husband David wanted children. But though the first pregnancy was unplanned, the couple was delighted. Breda gave up her secretarial job without regret when Duncan, now 11, was born. She settled down happily to motherhood. Within two years her second son, Patrick, came into the world. "I loved being with the children and felt much richer for being a mother," she says.

In time, however, she began to feel that this wasn't enough. She went to evening classes, studied for O levels and joined a women's group. "I wasn't bored at home, but there was a gap in my life which needed to be filled.

To say I wanted intellectual stimulation sounds rather grand. I just needed an outside interest and I suppose I hoped to get some kind of qualifications so I could go back to work when the children were old enough.

Gradually, the women's group became increasingly important to me. I liked being seen as Breda, not as David's wife or the children's mother. I became a stronger person with a greater sense of my own identity. I became more decisive and more independent from David.

There were other changes in Breda. She stopped wearing make-up and abandoned dresses and high heels for jeans and sneakers. David disliked the new look and what lay behind it and said so. "There is no doubt that in the end I was not the woman he married," admits Breda frankly. "I looked different and I was different. At one time I had been quite happy being the woman David wanted me to be.... Now I knew I had the right to be myself."

As the new, more assertive Breda emerged, the rows became more frequent and the truces shorter. Home life became increasingly intolerable until, with sudden and total clarity, Breda realized she had to leave. "My knowing that I had to go was like a hundred things dropping into place at once," she says, and even now the tears come as she remembers being aware that her marriage was over.

I began corresponding with several of the members of MATCH, and in 1982 I had the opportunity to interview several of them, including a woman who related the following:

I had been married for 25 years, so for me it was a tremendously big decision. I was a sort of typical wife; I followed my husband around with his job and I'd never really entertained having a career of my own. I think the main thing for me was the death of my brother. He died about three years ago, and it makes you sit and think about your own life, and all sorts of things came up. I had never been particularly happy about having the last child. I have five; I hadn't wanted the fifth one. We were living up in Cumberland, which is a rather remote part of England, and it was difficult even to think about an abortion. I did actually go and inquire about one. (My husband wasn't too keen on the idea but he left it up to me.)

Anyway, I did go ahead and have the baby, but after that things changed. I didn't cope nearly as well as I thought I would. I had coped very well with four, but five was just that one too many. But I jogged along and we actually had our 25th wedding anniversary and it was all sort of down hill somehow. I was getting very discontented for the last five years of the marriage. I joined evening classes and started to study. I got very political and joined the Labor Party. And I suppose I just wanted more. It wasn't any longer enough to be home and just a mother. My marriage hadn't been all that healthy for a number of years and I suppose when my brother died I really sort of thought I wanted to change. But I really felt quite helpless about changing my life. I didn't feel there was anything I could do about it. I saw all the negatives. I hadn't got a decent job.

I hadn't any place to live, and I just didn't entertain the thought of leaving until I guess about my wedding anniversary. I had decided by then that I did want to leave, and I told my husband. And actually he didn't persuade me to stay. I think he was heartily sick of my behavior as it was anyway.

My own story is not, as I have said, very much different from those that have just been told, and the outcome was very much the same.

"You know what they'll say," said my sister, referring to our parents. "You made your bed, now you must lie in it." That *had* been among the rules we all went by, but now that I had broken them so radically, I saw clearly the need to reexamine—to go back and review the choices I had made, the paths I had taken, the roles I had accepted, and why. How much of that bed had I really made? How *had* I become the woman I was?

"Pin a rose on me!" wrote my mother, later, when it became clear that my little "on-the-side" job was now providing not just pin money but enough for food, rent, doctor, and gasoline. "Aren't you glad I insisted you go to college and have a career in case you never married?"

I have little doubt, now, that that was what she meant to do; I just don't remember it quite that way. I *do* remember moments of choice and decision, but the surrounding assumptions and expectations guided those choices inexorably. I remember being in high school, at the terrible moment when it was time to decide what would come next. We had sent away for, and received unsolicited, heaps of material on possible career directions. I remember two in particular. One was from the Navy—the WAVES. What a glorious picture appeared on the cover! A bright, smiling, obviously upwardly mobile young woman, so trim and neat in her snappy uniform, hat perched smartly on her bouncy curls. But...the military? Don't be ridiculous! You can't be *married* in the military! And you'd have to travel! True, and obviously those were conditions to be avoided. I had always been fascinated by my father's cousin, who was a captain in the Women's Army Medical Corps, but I *did* know that in my family she was considered very odd, and certainly deprived.

The other brochure was from Katherine Gibbs, *the* school for secretaries, picturing brisk, efficient, productive women bustling around big city offices. But...no college? A *secretary*? They work nine to five! And only two weeks vacation! What about the *children*? No, that's not a good idea at all.

My career counseling continued. "I always wanted to be a librarian or to work in a school," said my mother. "How about a school librarian? That sounded pretty good to me, and would certainly please my mother, which I heartily wanted to do. So I agreed, and off I went to library school.

That there *would* be children was never in question for a moment. And if there were to be children, there would also be a husband. I knew what *he* would be like, too. Not Catholic. Not Italian. Not Irish. He would not be Jewish, or black, or of "the laboring classes." He would be "respectable." He would have a "nice name." He would be "like us."

He was, too. Four years older than I, out of college and out of the Army too, with a good job in New York City, a graduate student—what a catch! Lucky me!! (Years later, when I had been told how "lucky" I was hundreds of times, I finally figured out why that phrase made me so angry. "Lucky," as though without the benevolent intervention of some kind knight, I would have ended up a bag lady on the IRT. But I may have believed it myself, at the time.) We married shortly before I graduated from college.

That first summer was a disaster. I went from days and nights filled with friends and fun and work and excitement and responsibility—to nothing. My three-room apartment required no care to speak of. My husband left for work at 7:15 a.m. and, since he was going to graduate school four nights a week, got home around 10 p.m. (Why four nights a week? I wonder now. Why did I give up everything and he not change a single thing in his schedule? At the time, though, I was very impressed with his industry and dedication.)

Never have I spent such endless days. I forbade myself to turn on the television until at least nine in the morning. I went to the store every day, sometimes twice. I found no friends in that old, established neighborhood. (I see now that I did not know how to look. Friends had always found *me*.) I thought I might go back to school, but everyone said, "What on earth for? Take a rest!" I thought I might spend some time with my family out on Long Island. But how could I do that with a brand new husband? What would they think? So for two endless months I endured. And began, even then, to change.

My job (as a school librarian, of course) started in September. Shattered by the summer, I was nervous and unsure. My principal was notoriously tyrannical; every book I read to the children had to be approved first by her; every bulletin board had to be sketched out and OKed before it could go up. The rest of the faculty took bets on how long I would last; I was the third librarian in a year and a half. (I learned later that one of my predecessors wound up in a sanitarium, which at least made me feel a little better about my own desperation.)

And I didn't last long. By October I knew I was pregnant. Hooray! "Guess what?," I asked my mother. "I suppose you're having a baby," she replied flatly. "Well, yes," I said, crestfallen. "Aren't you glad?" "Well," she replied, "I had hoped you would work for a little while, at least."

That was certainly news to *me*. I thought having a baby was the *point* of it all. Working was just something you did in the meantime. Much abashed, I quit my job in January (we had to leave before we "showed," of course) and there I was at home again.

We moved to a little house in the suburbs. The baby was born. Three years later (*much* to my chagrin, since I had planned to have my children, heroically, a year apart) another baby came and, six years later, after I had gotten my master's degree, a third. I had gone back to work (part time, of course) after each of the first two babies, but quit cold each time; no one suggested a leave of absence and I never thought of it. After the third baby there was no more choice; no jobs in the schools were to be found. But I really didn't care; I already had my "real" career.

My husband and I made friends with the neighbors and exchanged baby-sitting. We went to church, taught Sunday School, and joined the PTA. We were dutiful about birthdays and holidays and visiting relatives. My folks "just happened" to be in the neighborhood every Sunday, and would stay for dinner. I had my volunteer work, my needlework, my household chores, my normality. I had successfully (or so I thought) shrunk to fit the "bed" that I had "made."

When eventually I left my home I had to assess how much of that bed I had really made and how much I had just tumbled into, so to speak. My son asked me, shortly after I left, if I had ever been happy there. And of course I had. I truly loved my children and thought they were a splendid trio. The older they got the better I liked them (still true). I liked my home and my activities, too. And most of all, I was secure in the knowledge that I was doing "the right thing." And I certainly did everything that I did freely, consciously, and with enthusiasm. But I don't believe, looking back, that I ever seriously realized there was anything else *to* do, so steeped was I—were we all—in what was "right" and "normal" and "nice" (and oh, the horrors of being "not nice!"). Doing what is expected and not rocking the boat do have their own rewards, after all; so perilous was non-conformity, we had learned, that we could hardly have done otherwise than toe the mark. And most of us did toe that mark and stay in line. "How could we have been so stupid!" mourned a friend of mine recently. "We should have known!" But how could we know? Who was there to tell us? Just the other day my mother was musing about possible lost opportunities in her own life. "It just never occurred to me to try to do anything. I just never thought of it at all." And that attitude was passed on to many of the women of my generation, too. "My family," an Irish Catholic friend of mine said smugly, "always expected me to marry an Irish Catholic." "But you *did*!" I said. "Well, yes," she replied, "but not because they pressured me into it. It just happened to work out that way."

It "just happened to work out that way" for a lot of us; we found ourselves doing what was expected and felt very righteous, and happy, doing it. But now, in this time of questioning, many of us are saying, "I think it could have been worked out better." And many of us, with extraordinary difficulty and against heavy odds, are trying to do just that; to work it out better.

Our reasons for so drastically changing our lives derive directly out of who we were, how we got there, and who we wanted to be. Sometimes it was a matter of mere survival that made us take the step. Sometimes it was a drive and a desire to fulfill the potential we knew we had. Sometimes it was because we had grown, often even against our wills, too large for the spaces we were in. Sometimes it was a real need, cliche though it may be, to find ourselves. Our *selves*.

Listen to some of those reasons.

Why Did You Leave?

"You know what Grandpa will say," said my daughter. "He'll say, *women's lib!*'"
He would, too, and he'd be right. The women's movement did have a powerful
effect on me; how could it not? I heard, and I understood, when feminists spoke
and wrote about equal pay for equal work, and shared housekeeping, and access
to shop classes for girls, and home economics for boys. I heard them when they
questioned my protests: "What do you mean, he 'helps you' with the baby?
What do you mean, he 'lets' you go to graduate school? What do you mean,
he 'gives' you money for groceries?" Yes, those questions caused me to reassess
my past and reconsider my future, to see that I had contributed far less than
my abilities warranted, that I had given up far more than I had gained; they
raised my consciousness and ultimately led me to conclude that spending
another 30 or 40 years in the same situation would be madness.

It is impossible to understand the underlying motivations of a woman who
opts to live apart from her children without also understanding the discontents
and disillusionments that have spurred the so-called new feminism. It is not my
intention to review the role of women historically, or the impact of the women's
movement in our time; others have done so, thoroughly and well. But it is
essential to realize that as more and more women shared their discontents
and disillusionments—the dismay they felt in their stagnating and unsatisfying
lives—the rest of us began to feel very much like the spectators at the emperor's
parade. He really didn't have any clothes, and the lives we were leading really
didn't have much substance. It was not our fault—the clothes and the substance
just weren't there. So it is with the " myth of motherhood." Betty Friedan's
definitive analysis of "the illness that has no name," as reported in her 1964
book, *The Feminine Mystique*, is crucial to an understanding of what happened
to strong, viable, capable women, how we bought into a myth and discovered
how that the living of it required Herculean efforts to diminish ourselves, to
keep ourselves small, less, secondary. One shudders to think of the human
resources so needlessly squandered as we struggled to fit our narrow molds.
" 'Dwindling' into a wife takes time," says Jessie Bernard."[1] We took the time,
and we dwindled.

Much has been written about this phenomenon in the 20 years since Ms.
Friedan's pioneering work. There have also been many volumes written on the
realities of motherhood and mothering, most notably Adrienne Rich's *Of Women
Born*, Jane Lazarre's *The Mother Knot*, Elisabeth Badinter's *Mother Love: Myth
And Reality*, Jessie Bernard's *The Future of Motherhood*. It is fair to say that

the "myth of motherhood" has been exploded—intellectually. Emotionally, the surface has hardly been scratched. It is all very well to say "you don't have to feel that way." It is quite another to stop feeling it. Women who admit they don't want to be full-time wives and mothers, *and who do something about it*, feel enormous guilt. Even with external reassurances that ambivalence toward motherhood is perfectly all right, the guilt is not noticeably assuaged. Griping and complaining is allowed and even useful. There is a wonderful caption on a map distributed by the *National Geographic*, informing us that the women of the Peruvian Mapuche tribe "released feelings of domestic discontent" by singing allegorical songs "sanctioned by custom." American women, too, have been "sanctioned by custom" to express our complaints about "domestic discontent"; we just weren't supposed to *do* anything about it. When we *acted* on our complaints, we were not able to take comfort in the words of a Rich or a Bernard or a Badinter. How *can* it be all right when we have learned from the cradle that motherhood is our highest and noblest calling? To turn from that illusion is probably the most difficult, most wrenching experience a woman can undergo. But for some of us, that turning was essential. To preserve what was left of ourselves; to rebuild our mangled spirits into the women—and *mothers*—we wanted to be; to become, as Charlotte Gilman wrote, mothers worth having, we had to take that turn.

I designed one section of my questionnaire to elicit the reasons why women left. I wanted to learn whether my respondents had left primarily because they didn't like mothering or because they wanted to flee their marriages and could see no way to do so without also leaving their children. Women in the latter category predominated, although there were many in the first as well.

The questionnaire listed 27 possible responses to the question "why did you leave?" As many as applied were to be checked. The answer most often selected was "no longer loved my husband," which was a reason suggested by one of my early interviewees. Close behind that was "mental, physical health declining" (all but two who chose this answer chose *both* physical and mental). Equally popular was "felt stifled, wanted my own lifestyle" and "felt, from husband, no sense of stability, support, caring, interest" (again, almost no one separated those four reasons instead of selecting the entire answer). They said they "felt no future" in their marriages and their lives. About a third said they felt inadequate as mothers and believed they could be better parents from outside the marriage. Only about a quarter said they left because they no longer wanted to mother. Only six said they left in order to live with or marry another man, and even fewer (four) said they had left to live with a woman lover. Although several others did in fact follow one of these courses after they left, these women made a point of saying that it had not been the primary reason, or even an important reason, for their leaving. Over half said they left to live alone and reported that the solitude was eminently satisfying. Very few (six) mentioned wanting to return to school as a reason for leaving, and only five said they had left to pursue a career.

Many, of course, did go back to school and then on to careers of some sort, but again, that was not felt to be the *reason* for leaving.

There were 20 cases of physical abuse in my survey, but an overwhelming number cited "mental abuse" as a precipitating cause. In one instance the woman cited physical abuse by the children; another said that the children asked her to leave; eight said that their husbands had asked them to leave (I should have used the word "demanded" in that last question, as that was most often and accurately the case.)

Once again, though, their written comments fleshed out the short answers summarized above to provide pictures of real-life women coping with difficult and often impossible situations. My respondents and interviewees shared generously and in details the sequences of events that led them inevitably to relinquish their roles as full-time wives and mothers. Their reasons came directly out of their experiences, of course, and if one can empathize with *who* they were, as expressed in the last chapter, then it should not be too hard to proceed to the stories of *why* they felt they had to leave. There is really no way to separate the two.

It was difficult to separate the stories of women who opted out of mothering from those who primarily left the marriage. I used their own definitions and self-analyses, although it was clear that many of the reasons for leaving overlapped. In the first group—those who left because they didn't like mothering—several women wrote very powerfully of their experiences as mothers. One of these women was Shirley Glubka, who in response to my advertisement sent not only her completed questionnaire but a copy of her master's thesis entitled "Women Who Have Left the Mother Role." Ms. Glubka had herself "left the mother role" four years before. To gather material for her thesis she had worked with a group of thirteen women for over a year, using small group discussions and her own questionnaire. Her subjects, including herself, fell mainly into that first category. She wrote:

> We left the mother role for many reasons. Each of us has lived this out in
> her own style, responding to her own set of circumstances. For some of us,
> those circumstances revolved around the institution of motherhood and its
> failure to support us as we grew beyond its boundaries. Others of us felt
> unsuited to the work of mothering. Others had difficulty relating to the
> children. For most of us the three aspects of motherhood were so firmly
> welded together that we experienced our difficulties as coming from
> "being mothers" or "being married and having children."

Ms. Glubka began with Katherine, who "could not, or would not, continue to live within the confines of the institution of motherhood," finding the rules too constricting and limiting. Katherine, says Ms. Glubka, felt good about her relationship with the children. Feeling good about her children and liking the work of mothering, she might have kept on living with both her children. But in creating a life for herself she violated some prescriptions of the institution

29

of motherhood. "Katherine feels that she 'chose' to leave the mother role," Ms. Glubka writes, "only in so far as she chose to create for herself the life that she wanted—and to suffer the consequences this society imposes on women who take their lives into their own hands."

Glubka says that another woman, Ellen "also left because she would not live within the confines of the institution. Ellen married at the age of eighteen. In two weeks she was pregnant. Within five years she had three children. When the third child was born, and she realized that meant 'that I would never have a chance to do anything else ever for twenty years, I started feeling really angry.' When she finally left, she says, 'My own life became so interesting that I hardly ever thought of my children, much less missed them.' Ellen now spends some time each summer visiting her children."

Another woman is described as "ambivalent about her decision. She is drawn toward her daughter, likes her, wants a close relationship. Sometimes she thinks she wants to live with her again. But then she thinks of the work of mothering—and how she doesn't have the energy to be both a therapist and a full-time mother. She concludes that when it's put up against her work, there is no question."

Ms. Glubka also writes of her own situation:

> I was doing work I hated—the work of mothering a small child. I hated many aspects of the work. I was a rotten disciplinarian. I didn't like playing children's games. I was not good at child-level conversation. And I struggled painfully with every situation that called for a decision about values. Should I teach him non-violence or the art of self-defense? Should I encourage him to question my commands or respect my need to have things done a certain way? Should I demand that he maintain order in his room or allow him a measure of chaos? My own ethical stance and value system were still in the process of being reconstructed after the blitz of the late sixties; I felt absolutely inadequate to the task of building a strong structure for a preschool child.
>
> I don't know if my hatred of the job of mothering was made more or less painful by the fact that I found Kevin to be the most attractive child I had ever met. I liked him a lot. He was (and is) bright and beautiful. I liked being related to him. I was proud to be his mother. My affection for him was powerful, tender, and could well up in tears easily and often—still can. It was not Kevin I disliked—it was the work of being his mother.

This last observation brings up the opposite possibility, one that is absolutely taboo: the possibility that a mother might just not really like her child very much. We do not like to think that this could possibly happen, but we know, from observation and sometimes experience, that it does. Consider these two women, both discussed by Ms. Glubka. First, Sierra, who says:

I never really have liked my kid very much. There's parts of him that I enjoy a lot and that I think are really clever but he drives me nuts.... Sometimes I just hate him.

Then there is Jeanne, who has two children, a son and a daughter. She likes her daughter and doesn't like her son. Both children live with their father. Jeanne would like to raise her daughter, but doesn't want to separate the children. She cannot imagine explaining to her son that she doesn't like him. Jeanne does not live easily with her dislike for her son, but she has had to accept it, and has chosen to act on it.

I also heard from women who wanted relief from the burden of full-time mothering. For some, the gap between the myth and the reality was just too wide to manage. In a long, hand-written essay, a woman from Wyoming wrote:

I had wanted children, babies in particular, since I could remember. When I was growing up the big news story was always abandoned babies being found in garbage cans and in the fields, etc. My day at play usually consisted of going out looking for babies in the field. I needed something to be mine and to love and to love me back.

It took two years to conceive and carry to term. When she was born I was elated, until I found out all the other things that babies represent: dirty clothes, diapers, spitting up, etc. The biggest jolt was the fact that she could not *love me*, just depend on me. I could hug and kiss, she would blow bubbles and dribble. I had absolutely no patience when it came to teaching her the simplest things. Eating, potty training, cutting with scissors, etc.

At times I had to lock myself in the bathroom so I would not get near her during her whining sessions. Such was my fear of beating her. She was a beautiful child and I hated those feelings. *There was no one to talk to about it.* My husband was always working or sleeping or doing some project of his own in the garage. He never had anything to do with the care and coping with the baby. He told me I was going through a phase when I tried to tell him how I felt about the baby.

The marriage started to fail. My first thought was to have another baby, for God's sake. I don't know how I could have been so naive, but there it was. She was even more beautiful, and good as gold. Well, if I thought it was difficult to have one child, guess what it was like with two. I loved them with all my heart and still do, but all I am really capable of is loving them—not caring for them full time. Raising children cannot be done on love alone, in my opinion. If they had stayed with me, sooner or later they would have been taken away. I could not cope with them, even being my own flesh and blood. It is evident that the advantages they have had cover a lot of the hurt they may have had over not being with their blood mother. The regrets I have are strictly selfish. Now I sometimes wonder if I am ready to finally to be a mother, but dismiss the thought after less than an hour with someone else's children. I guess once not a mother-person, always not a mother-person.

I found her phrase "mother-person" to be particularly apt. No one questions someone who says she is not a "nurse-person," "teacher-person" or "engineer-person." To announce that one is not a "mother-person" is seen as quite another matter, though one has to wonder why. Certainly many women are not cut out to be "mother-persons." Unfortunately in this society there is no good way to find that out until you are already a mother.

A woman from Oregon wrote to discuss the ways in which she felt her past affected her future and that of her children:

> I had the opportunity to observe the damaging parenting skills that were passed from my grandmother to my mother and then to me, and I saw I was inevitably making the same mistakes. We parent as we were parented, so I guess you could say I did a Harry Truman and decided the buck stops here, and I got out before I could do any more damage than had already been done.

Some women had to accept the fact that they had very real aversions to motherhood that were leading them in threatening in directions. They took steps to avoid catastrophe:

> We were high school sweethearts, married at young ages. I was 19, he was 20. My youngest son (age seven) presented a myriad of complexities and problems. He was difficult to manage when he was young and to relate to him positively at all times seemed an insurmountable and draining task that extended beyond the bounds of motherhood. I began to dislike my children, and myself. Feelings ran quite high during the times I disliked my children...for, isn't a mother always giving, always there, always steadfast? But I did not want to be a martyr to motherhood!

Other women wrote of more serious damage:

> Was depressed, hated husband and could not express that hate and anger so abused my son, then four, by banging his head on the floor, etc. I told my husband I needed help. He said, "Help yourself. Think happy thoughts." I knew it would take more than that to save my son from me.

This last letter reminded me of a letter that appeared in an Ann Landers column some time ago. It read in part as follows:

> Dear Ann,
> As I write this my little boy is lying on the couch under an icebag. His face is as red as a beet and the skin is broken in places where I slapped him. When he gets stubborn or has a tantrum, I become so angry I can't control myself. I have hit him like this several times before, even though I know it is wrong.... When this boy was born four years ago, I really didn't want him but my husband was crazy about kids and insisted that I have a

family. I have always hated this kid, which is a terrible thing for a mother to admit. His Daddy died two years ago and thank God I don't have any others. I am a rotten mother. Many times I have thought of giving up the boy for adoption. I know there are many couples out there who would love to have him. He is very smart for his age and darling looking. But just when I get ready to put my hand on the phone I tell myself, "Don't do it. Keep him and learn to be a good mother." I live 1,500 miles away from my own family. I have a good job and work 50 hours a week. Please tell me what to do.

In her reply, Ann Landers counseled this woman to contact Parents Anonymous, a group that counsels abusing parents; that is fine advice, of course. But wouldn't it be just as fine if turning her child over to "someone who would love to have him" were an *acceptable* option for this woman? And to know that in so doing she was also being "a good mother"? Surely the answer is yes. Perhaps that is why the following letter touched me so deeply.

Right now my son is still in my custody but my brother and myself are now in the process of making legal arrangements to have my son go and live with my brother and sister-in-law in New York. He will be legally in their custody and if all goes well will be adopted by them. In any case, he is not coming back to me, ever. I have tried for six years and I just can't make myself into a mother. I feel so alone and torn up in this! The guilt is incredible! Overwhelming!

How can we not wish for this woman a world in which she could make this arrangement with a happy heart? My letters to her have been returned as undeliverable, so I have no way to know how she is, but it strikes me that there is a depth of caring in this woman that must have been transmitted to her son even as she gave him up.

While I was working on this section of my book, I read a news article that brought home to me the attitudes that are often held, deep down, about motherhood and the talent that it requires. It concerned a woman who survived a grisly accident. While she was working in a fast food restaurant, a three-inch long nail, propelled through the wall by a .22 caliber cartridge, struck her in the head. That she is alive at all is considered nothing short of miraculous. Her doctors described her as shy and socially awkward, her thinking as slow and difficult, and she is paralyzed on the left side.

"She will be able to lead a reasonably happy life, as long as her expectations are not too high," said Dr. Lawrence Friedman. "She can make someone a very good wife. She can be a mother. But she has memory and thought problems, and to work she would have to be in a sheltered workshop, doing simple repetitive tasks."[2]

Expectations that are not too high. A sheltered life, doing simple, repetitive tasks. Able, in short, to be a wife and mother but not much else. It is all too clear how Dr. Friedman sees the role of wife and mother; I suspect that he is far from alone in his evaluation. We women are told that motherhood requires, among other things, the highest levels of creativity, intelligence, personality. Many of us find it, instead, stupefyingly dull. "I was so bored!" wrote a woman from Massachusetts. Interestingly, both Margaret Trudeau and Joan Kennedy used that same word when when discussing their choices. Ms. Trudeau wrote:

> As Pierre settled down to married life and no longer felt he had to court me, he returned to spend more and more time at his work, leaving me alone. I waited, and waited, and waited all day for him to come home, devoting the last hours to putting on my make-up and prettiest clothes so as to look beautiful for him. When he came home he took *off* his best clothes and climbed into old, baggy slacks. When I told him how bored I was, he looked disgusted. "How can you be bored when life is so full, when you have so many options?"[3]

And Ms. Kennedy noted:

> I find I always function better under stress. I find I can't cope with boredom, not having a purpose in life, not knowing what you're going to be doing. I think I was bored all those years...[4]

Shirley Glubka observed in her thesis:

> Much of the work of mothering consists of being present for another, being ready to respond to emergencies, being ready to appreciate accomplishments—being there for long periods of time with nothing, really, to do but watch and wait.

It is this waiting, this requirement that the mother be ready at all times to drop whatever she is doing in order to respond to someone else's demands, that is so maddening to so many women. Rather, said one, like being a toll collector on a not-busy highway. Can't leave, but can't function either. Having to snatch little chunks of time for herself when she is safe, or relatively safe, from the demands of others—while the children are in school, or at a neighbor's house, or sleeping. That "eternal vigilance" makes doing anything really worthwhile virtually impossible. It was this that prompted Virginia Woolf to recommend that a woman have "a room of her own." But that option is no more acceptable, or feasible, for today's woman than it was for the woman of Woolf's day. So women all across the country try to make a life out of a task that is casually compared to functioning in a sheltered workshop. It is seldom enough. A woman from the Midwest said:

> I had a nice eight-room house with a smallish yard and garden, and three kids in school. Maybe this sounds conceited but I am bright and energetic

and well-organized and there just wasn't enough to *do*. I *know* it is enough for some women and I say "fine, be happy." It just wasn't enough for *me*. You know, one of the things that you hear most often when a group of housewives get together is how to get out of the house. Getting out of the house is a really big goal. The trouble is that they have to find a way to get out when everyone else is out too. It is OK to be out bowling or playing cards or drinking coffee or going to some ladies' meeting, but you'd better be back when it is dinner time or bed time (theirs *and his*). There isn't a whole lot that you can find that meets those requirements, not that's going to be any kind of a challenge, any kind of real fun, and I would say nothing that is going to pay you money.

Getting *all* the way out of the house is the answer for some of us for whom housework and child care and volunteer activities just don't provide adequate outlets:

This will probably sound very egotistical and make a lot of women very mad, but frankly I was too good for it. My skills, my training, my native abilities, my intelligence just weren't challenged by dusting and cooking and washing little faces. Oh, they could have been challenged by child care, all right: I could have hounded those kids to do what I said and be what I said and wear what I said, go where I said. That would have been a great outlet for my managerial skills. And unfortunately I saw I was doing just that— couldn't help it, in that insular setting. Now, I do have a salaried job where those skills are necessary and productive, which they certainly weren't when I was manipulating my kids. And not surprisingly, they are doing much better with some space to follow their own bents, and I am enjoying seeing it. I'm confident that I made the best choice for all of us; for me, being a good mother meant being a not-every-minute mother.

Another woman wrote of the impossible conflict she discovered between who she was and who she was "supposed" to be:

It just wasn't for me. You hear all the time about "individual differences" when you go up to school and talk about your kids. Well, those "individual differences" don't go away when the kids (us) grow up. But the trouble is, no one acknowledges that for the girls. Women are *all* supposed to like housework and kids, *all* do it well, with grace and charm, and do it *forever*. That staggers me. How does it come to be? We raise and educate children and the boys are supposed to explode into a million different careers and interests. The girls, I guess, are supposed to *implode*, and all crowd into one career, housewife. And to love it and find contentment in it! Well, I tried, but I couldn't do it. I *really* couldn't. And when my chance came to get out, I took it. I truly believe that if I hadn't, I would have died. Shriveled up and died. I know that sounds dramatic, but there it is.

She was not the only woman to use that analogy. Many, many of us said we felt we were dying, dead, going to die; many a woman said that leaving "saved my life," "brought me back from the dead," or "was truly a life-saver." Many of us saw our home situations as truly life-threatening, and our moves away from those homes necessary to maintain our very lives. Margaret Trudeau writes:

> From the day I became Mrs. Pierre Elliott Trudeau, a glass panel was gently lowered into place around me, like a patient in a mental hospital who is no longer considered able to make decisions and who cannot be exposed to a harsh light. The result was that for five years I lived in cotton wool, uncertain about whom exactly I was fighting against, but increasingly convinced that this artificial life was slowly crushing me to death.[5]

These, then, were the women who discovered, too late, that their expectations regarding motherhood and mothering were not founded on fact, and who realized that continuing to try would benefit neither themselves nor, more importantly, their children. They realized they were not equipped by "Nature" to do the job, and that they were not willing to undergo the self-sacrifice required for traditional motherhood. They decided to give up their roles as full-time mothers not because they did not want what was best for their children but because they came to realize that *they themselves* were not what was best, no matter what society was saying. I believe it took great courage to risk censure and scorn to come to that realization, make that decision, and remove themselves from their children's everyday lives, in whole or in part, rather than continue in patterns destructive to themselves and to their children.

Nor do I think we can dismiss these women as "abnormal," as lacking in the normal attributes of the human female. According to the books on motherhood, there is almost certainly no biological or psychological foundation for the theory of instinctive motherhood in humans. When Ann Landers asked in her popular advice column, "If you had it to do over again, would you have children?" a staggering number said "no."[7] Ministers, psychologists, grandmothers, fathers, and other mothers rushed in to explain this unheard-of response. But I for one think those answers can be trusted as the heartfelt and truthful opinions of despairing parents. So those women who realize that, given adequate and accurate information, they would have made a different choice, and who *make* that choice, are far from abnormal; they share their feelings with the thousands of parents who answered Ann Landers' question in the newspaper.

Finding that motherhood is beyond their desires and/or capacities is a major reason why women leave their children and husbands. Many more of my respondents, however, were women who wanted to leave what they perceived as intolerable marriages and found that the only way they could do so was by leaving the children along with the marriage. I place myself in that category.

With the divorce rate currently figured at one marriage in three and rising, it should come as no surprise to find that it is often the wife who wants to end the marriage. But apparently this is a truth difficult to accept and when the wife is the one to *leave* we are even more astonished. It is estimated that over a million women in the U.S. live apart from their minor children (not even counting those who surrender their children for adoption), but we are still shocked and surprised when we hear of such a case.

The reasons given by the women in my survey for the breakdown of their marriages are not startling in themselves; to read them, however, is to understand again how often we drift into relationships, how tormented we are when they go awry, and how difficult and painful it is to change or leave them even when that is clearly the best course of action.

Sometimes the marriages were doomed from the start:

- He was on a scholarship (football) at college—big man on campus. I met him the summer before he was a sophomore. Pregnant from our three weeks together. I lived in Florida, he in Ohio. I informed him he was to be a father—thought he had a right to know. He wanted to marry. I said OK. I worked when I could, paid a sitter for the baby (he had to get his sleep). It was obviously going nowhere.

- I did everything I could. But it wasn't enough. I was pregnant when we got married. I didn't want to get married just because we were going to have a child. We never mentioned marriage to each other before, so why now that I'm pregnant? We had never viewed our relationship as a permanent one—nonetheless we got married to please parents and friends and tried to convince ourselves that it was all OK. I suppose my ex-husband was willing to settle for that, but after a few years I felt I was missing out on one important thing in my life. That was real love. I thought I loved my husband. But I realized it was only pity—he isn't attractive, doesn't have much of a personality. I felt pity for him and I dated him; I mistook pity for love and I married him. Pity wears off and is a poor substitute for love.

Many of the marriages described to me had started off all right, but as the passing years brought changes the partners found they were facing insurmountable difficulties. Here is one such story:

If I had remained as I was when I married at 21, as a dependent, immature girl, Bill would have been able to cope with me better. I became seriously ill with asthma.... My body was acting out what my psyche was unable to express: "I'm smothering, I'm dying, help me." Finally I listened and went into therapy as a very confused, dependent, desperate woman. The year that was to follow was the most painful and emotionally wrenching time in my life, as I came to know myself clearly for the very first time. In the first trusting environment I had ever known, I was forced to face myself honestly, openly, to know my unattractive, needy, manipulative and frightened self. But in the process I discovered a woman I hadn't known was in me, a woman who emerged cautiously yet persistently and with courage. It was this woman who ultimately caused the fissure to widen between my husband and myself and who precipitated the final rupture.

Bill was unable to reconcile himself with this woman. In bitterness and confusion he wondered what happened to his dream of eternal happy marriage and desperately attacked me: "This is my house and my children, if anyone is to go it won't be me! I'll take you to court and prove you an unfit mother!" That's almost laughable now...but at the time it held enormous impact.... There we were, two bitter and disillusioned people with the fate of two children to decide as sanely and amicably as possible. Bill was willing to drag through the court any dirty linen he could uncover in his determination not to let his children go; I, unwilling to fight though I knew I could win, was aware of a growing sense of strength and a life I wanted for myself, and the realization that having the children stay with Bill suited me and that life. Guilty, selfish, irresponsible woman—all those feelings flooded me for a time, but I knew it was the right thing to do for all of us. The vision of that life, as I would design and live it, became impossible to push away.

Other changes occurred in these marriages, too, changes that could not be accommodated. The partners found that their expectations, and their values, were growing further and further apart, until there was no way to bridge the chasm between them. I chose these five as examples:

- My husband resented me, felt isolated and betrayed because I was not able to measure up to his fairy tale expectations of romantic response and household tidiness. These expectations were socially and religiously confirmed and enforced, and I believe they eliminated any possibility of his coming to terms with me as a human being. In fact, I was a totally domestic, reasonably efficient, highly conscientious and committed mate. But he was never able to recognize this.
- My husband was stifling. Felt school (which I desperately wanted) was a waste for women. Although we both worked 40 hours a week, I was responsible for *all* cooking, cleaning, and child care. I could not survive the pressure.
- The marriage got to be such an adversarial relationship—we were always combatants, never partners or friends. I wanted so much to be friends and companions and we just never were. Maybe he was still trying to get even with his mother—I suspect that was at the root of a lot of it—but that did not make it any easier. I suspect he is glad to be out of that rivalry also. He helped me to move and never asked me to come back, not once.
- My husband and I were miles apart on everything. He was a wham-bam man (not even a thank you) and went right to sleep after sex. He didn't want to even try anything that might please me more. He consulted his mother on every decision we tried to make. Even the private ones. He thought the kids at Kent State got what they deserved. I really hated

him when he said that. I didn't want my children growing up with arguing in the house and no real love. My husband refused to help with the housework or the children. I would come home from the restaurant at midnight and have to wash diapers. He never bathed or fed the children, not even one time. I felt as though I was doing it all alone, and I might as well be on my own for real, because it wouldn't make any difference than what I had. My husband said he would kill me or himself if I took "his" children.

- My older sister had two children, mulatto. She had some problems.... I advised her to come to Ohio and I would help all I could. My husband's grandmother lived next door. She said "no niggers" were allowed in her house. My husband sided with her, as usual. While we were discussing this one, I clicked: "I want a divorce." Calmly...he cried,...he begged.... I didn't budge....I always said I divorced his family, first, and then him for standing with them and not with me.

I think we might characterize the problem in these situations quite accurately as "irreconcilable differences." Others of my respondents saw two possible courses of action, which were truly irreconcilable; for these women, the bitter choice had to be made:

- Decided, with much agony and real questioning about how he could love me and still ask me to leave my children, to move to Los Angeles with my new husband. *Yes*, his job was more important than my wish to stay near my children. I love him. I had to accept that.
- My ex-spouse was insisting that I pick the family (him and the kids) over law school. This was an impossible choice (he could not see parity) and, coupled with other marital problems, I left.
- My jobs were a sore spot in the marriage. My coming independence, which I could not give up. I believe that to be among a list of major factors.

Well over three-quarters of my respondents mentioned "mental abuse" as one of their reasons for leaving. The foregoing stories describe a sort of mental abuse—the diminishment of one's sense of worth and self-respect. Twenty others did, however, mention physical abuse, these two among them:

- I was a battered wife. Had there been shelters or some help ten years ago I would have seen my children growing up. It was quite necessary for me to live alone...and it was my only choice. In the end his lawyer asked me if we couldn't "take out all that stuff about knives and guns and being tied up"...in case he (my ex) wanted another job and they happened to look at the separation agreement. I still want to scream! I agreed! I was so *afraid* I couldn't get a divorce! Such fear!
- He had literally thrown my clothes out of the house twice before. This third time he threw me out physically, too. I refused to go back again despite his pleading and the advice of "friends."

It is well worth one's time to read the literature on battered women. I was amazed at the parallels between women who suffer terrible abuse physically and those who stay in spiritually and emotionally abusive, unrewarding, unproductive relationships. The two kinds of destruction suffered by women—physical and mental—seem nearly identical to me, and are endured for many of the same reasons. Why is it, then, that people can cheer for the woman who finally breaks out of a physically destructive relationship and yet condemn the woman who escapes a similar destruction of her mind and spirit? Because we can see broken bones and black eyes but not wounded hearts and battered souls, we sometimes do not accept that the damage is just as extensive and painful:

> I even envied a neighbor whose husband beat her up and broke the windows and threw her clothes out of the house. Everyone could *see* what she was going through. I felt every bit as hurt and beaten—and demeaned—as she did, but on me nothing showed. My husband was a "nice guy" who "let" me do whatever I wanted. He didn't run around with other women, or drink, or gamble; he just squeezed the life out of me in other ways. I needed to escape as badly as she did, and yet when we both left, people were happy for her and shocked at me.

And then, of course, there is sex. Despite the reams of medical and psychological advice being churned out, we are not so far, after all, from the days when brides were advised to "close your eyes and think of England." Lately, much attention is being paid to the phenomenon of "marital rape," which used to be a legal impossibility but is at last being viewed as one of the more insidious forms of battering. It *is* a form of battering, and usually accompanies the forms of battering we tend to think of as "real" violence, like punching, kicking, whipping. Somehow we do not consider unwanted sex in marriage as being abusive; we think of it as *necessary*, as part of the job, intrinsic to the married state. "It comes with the territory." A wife is not taught that she has the right to refuse her husband. I dare say many of you who are reading this right now do not believe that wives have this right. So when women find themselves forced into unwanted sex, they are extremely reluctant to say so. A woman quoted in a book by Diana Russell called *Rape in Marriage* explains:

> But women do not like to admit it's happening. It is not easy to admit that the man you once loved and trusted could do that to you. It's the worst sort of violence—but the bruises don't show.[6]

Additionally, the ambivalence that is aroused in the woman who finds her husband undesirable can hardly be overstated. A man's right to have sex with his wife is, in our society, a given; it is part of the package. We can almost understand the genuine puzzlement of a U.S. Senator who asked, in a discussion of a court case on marital rape, "If you can't rape your wife, who can you rape?"[7]

A wife might be wondering the same thing; since monogamy is *also* the rule, what else is he supposed to do? So she submits, or tries to. But the contradiction can be overwhelming. Ms. Russell notes:

> Mrs. Selby's description of her role as being "little more than an unpaid hooker to a drunken, violent husband" highlights an interesting contradiction. In most societies prostitutes are looked down upon for their ability or willingness to have sex with men they may find revolting, obnoxious, or immoral;…wives are admonished if they *cannot* or *will not* perform for husbands they find revolting or immoral.[8]

Consider the importance placed on this aspect of marriage by suffragist Lucy Stone, who in 1855 wrote to Antoinette Brown:

> It is very little to me to have the right to vote, to own property, etc. if I may not keep my own body, and its uses, in my absolute right. Not one wife in a thousand can do that now.[9]

When we consider the passion that Lucy Stone devoted to those other causes, we cannot help but be awed by the stress she put on physical autonomy. One wonders why we don't hear more about this aspect of her crusade.

Almost all of the women quoted in Russell's book on the subject of marital rape (she puts the figure at 46 percent but it seemed higher) answered the question "how did you stop it?" by saying "I left." That was the answer of many of my respondents, too. The following, fairly lengthy account makes clear the conflict felt by a self-respecting woman who finds herself caught in a destructive sexual relationship:

> Well, the worst was the sex. He called it making love, but I can tell you it was plain old dirty sex. We were about two months into the marriage when I realized we were in bad trouble. We had both been "technical virgins" if you remember that phrase—lots of panting and wrestling around but not "going all the way"—don't these phrases sound ridiculous? Anyway, once society gave us the go-ahead it was a disaster. Wham-bam-thank-you-ma'am, as the joke says. When I protested he became furious, said I was frigid, etc., etc.—you've heard it all before, I'm sure.
>
> Now, a child of the '50s did *not* complain about sexual unfulfillment— not this one, certainly. So we went along, saying to outsiders that everything was fine, he leering and me blushing in the prescribed manner. I knew that if he would just take a little time—and give me some time off once in a while—I would be fine. But there was no hope for that. So I settled.
>
> Not gracefully, I must admit. We spent years with me screaming too much and him screaming too little! We couldn't even go to a movie without my having to "thank" him afterwards. Well, I won't go into the gory details—I'm sure you can imagine. He would always say, "What

possible difference could it make to you? It's no skin off your nose—just spread your legs for five minutes and stop all the fuss!"

So for years that is what I did. It might not have been any "skin off my nose" but it sure did whittle down my soul. I felt I was a masturbation machine—now wouldn't you say that should be called a whore? I *did* get room and board for it. He *did* let me have a lot of outside involvements, politics and such; I just had to "give him his," as he would say, after I went out—sometimes before, too.

Of course after a while I began to be really revolted with myself. So—here's another old story—I began to drink, more and more, and soon I realized I was heading for even more trouble. Drinking in the morning, and alone, and having blackouts—you can't *imagine* how terrifying that is until you have experienced it. I used to spend a lot of time on the telephone at night and the phone was right next to the liquor cabinet. I would call people and make arrangements and plan meetings and the next day I wouldn't even remember what I had said or what had been decided. I tried to take notes but in the morning I couldn't read them. Once I keeled over in front of my daughter. I told her I was ill and I guess she believed me—all my children were very surprised when I told them what a battle I had had with the booze. Yes, of course my husband knew—and he liked it. I would say, "Please do not fix me a drink tonight." But there he would be with a double Manhattan saying, "Oh, just one won't hurt." And then he would "freshen" it—that way you really don't know how much you've had. It all seems like the same one drink, or so you can tell yourself. And of course I would drink it, and it would feel *so good*, all warm and fiery and blurring the night ahead and the command performance at 11 o'clock—so I just kept on drinking.

What did he think? He thought it was just dandy. With me passed out he could do what he wanted with, as he put it, no hassles. "What's wrong with that?" he'd say. "This way everyone gets what he wants." Well, even as far gone as I was I could see how revolting that was, how destructive, and not only to me but to *him*—can you imagine trying to live with yourself? But for a long time I did go along with it—I would wake up in the morning and realize what had gone on and be so *repelled*, by both of us—it makes me sick to talk about it. But he would come in with a cup of tea, all smiles, and I would think I *must* be losing my mind.

And there was no one, no one, no one to tell—how could I confess such perversion?

One night, when things were particularly repulsive to me, I said that if he continued with what he was doing I would leave in the morning and never come back. *He* said, "Fine, I better get what I can while you are still here." And he *did*, so *I* did. To my dying day, no matter what the consequences of my leaving are for any of us, I will rejoice that I had the nerve to get out of that slime— that I did not allow my children's mother to continue to be so horribly used. And I must say that this is one of the reasons that I came out of the marriage without my kids and with practically nothing of material value—I refused to tell that story in public, ever, and he knew it. I've never regretted it.

It was clear to me, from hearing that story and the ones that went before, that the main motivation running through all of them was an overwhelming instinct for self-preservation or, as Shirley Glubka wrote, a powerful impulse for personal survival. There were dramatic examples:

- I would not eat much, and would drink too much. I slept little, and cried a lot. I wanted to remain alone all the time, and considered suicide as the "out." I would take allergy pills, as they tended to make me drowsy, and I appreciated that feeling.
- I knew the time had come to make a decision when I would come home from work and go into the bathroom with some wine or a six-pack of beer and sit on the floor for hours at a time.
- I was suffering what felt like suffocation seizures: I would wake up in the night feeling I couldn't get any air and would have to rush to throw my head out an open window.... I had no idea what this meant but felt instinctively that it was related to the way I was being "forced" to live.
- I finally realized that my kids having a mother in Bellevue was not the role model I had in mind.
- I had to leave to save me. That took years to accept.

Joan Kennedy used this same image:

I was advised by all the doctors that I try to get some time, some space as my college kids call it. I needed that for my *life*! It was a medical problem...[10]

Charlotte Gilman describes her mental and physical state; that condition called "nervous prostration":

I, the ceaselessly industrious, could do no work of any kind. I was so weak that the knife and fork sank from my hands—too tired to eat. I could not read nor write nor paint nor sew nor talk nor listen to talking nor anything. I lay on that lounge and wept all day. The tears ran down into my ears.... I went to bed crying, woke in the night crying, sat on the edge of the bed in the morning and cried—from sheer continuous pain. Not physical; the doctors examined me and found nothing the matter....A constant dragging weariness miles below zero. Absolute incapacity. Absolute misery. To the spirit it was as if one were an armless, legless, eyeless, voiceless cripple. Prominent among the tumbling suggestions of a suffering brain was the thought, "You did it yourself! You did it yourself! You had health and strength and glorious work before you—and you threw it all away. You were called to serve humanity, and you cannot serve yourself. No good as a wife, no good as a mother, no good at anything. And you did it yourself!".... The baby? I nursed her for five months. I would hold her close—that lovely child!—and instead of love and happiness feel only the pain. The tears ran down on my breast.... Nothing was more bitter that this, that even motherhood brought no joy.[11]

43

And there were other, less dramatic but no less powerfully compelling impulses, from women who felt the time had come to repair themselves:

- It was just time in my life to make a decision. To stick it out, forget that there could be some other way, or just make my break. Before, I felt I was dying in place; now there's challenge and vistas of myself that I could never explore before. I am sorry that people were and are being hurt by my decisions, but then no one worried about me so much. I know that must sound cruel and hard, but, you know, there comes a time... [her ellipses]
- I had spent my entire life being told I should be grateful that someone provided for me (first my father, then my husband). I desperately needed to prove to myself that I was an independent person.

It is apparent that for the women in this survey the decision to leave was never a case of a lazy, irresponsible slattern tossing aside duty for selfish pleasure (although many of us tormented ourselves with that image). In addition to the instinct for preservation of self and soul, the decision came from a perceived need to shatter the structure completely and start from scratch—using the same pieces, perhaps, but in a new configuration. Once in an interview I used the image of one of those three-dimensional puzzles which when completed form a cube or a sphere or a dog. If you have started to put the thing together incorrectly there is *no way* you can jam all the pieces in to fit; you have to take it completely apart, re-study the pieces, and start over. My interviewee replied, "Yes, and then you may find you were trying to make a cube out of pieces that were meant to be a sphere."

So, many of us took those pieces and rearranged them into new shapes, ones that took into account the diversity of pieces and of possible outcomes:

- Certainly I felt an obligation to my children—a commitment—a sense of duty and obligation in addition to the love I felt, and feel, for them. But that commitment, that obligation, did not, I came to see, include allowing myself to disappear completely. If I had, indeed, continued to allow myself to become what I perceived as simply a drunken whore, what kind of a mother could I be? Staying and allowing that to happen would be no favor to them, certainly. Whining and cringing and shrinking away to nothing—that was not included in the vision of the commitment I had. *My* vision was of being for them a strong, cheerful, loving, caring, sharing, self-assured, achieving, friend and guide, worthy of their admiration and respect. There was *no way* I could meet that commitment within the confines of my marriage. Unless I could find a way to see *myself* as that kind of mother I could not *be* that kind of mother. So I chose this way of meeting my commitment. It might be an unusual one, and one that the "experts" say cannot be done, but for me it was the *only* way, and I had to try it.
- One of the homilies, I guess you'd call it, that I was taught to use as a

guide was Polonius' advice to Laertes in *Hamlet*: "This above all, to thine own self be true." I knew I wasn't being true to myself in any way, living as I was—living, in effect, a lie. So I trusted that the second half of that advice was also true; that if I was true to myself I couldn't be false to anyone else. I think that has proved to be true, as so many of those old cliches are; I guess that is how they get to be cliches, eh? But that is why I left—to be true to myself, as I saw it.

And what of my own story? When I try to analyze my reasons for leaving it becomes clear how complex those reasons really are, for me and for the others. There is an element of my story in almost all of the foregoing ones: falling short of expectations, strict role adherence, clash of values, mental pain, unrewarding sex, and the "dying in place" sensation. I felt a great sense of being more, deserving more, *owing* more, to the world around me—a need to expand. There was a terrific sense of loss that I at last recognized as a sense of the loss of self.

Not that there was no outlet for this stronger, more capable self. I found myself rising to leadership positions in virtually all of my volunteer activities. I reveled in the responsibility and challenge inherent in these, and other, positions. I loved feeling I could offer something unique; I loved feeling capable; I enjoyed the feeling of making a difference, of being needed and sought after for advice, opinion, judgment. I liked using my skills and creativity; I liked, frankly, the feeling of power.

There was little of that in my home life. Perhaps that was as it should be; I do not know. What I *did* know was that it was becoming increasingly difficult to return home after my "outside" involvements and become diffident, obliging, quiet, less powerful, subservient. I sometimes forgot my "place," and of course trouble invariably ensued. More and more I felt I was living a double life: one where I was leader—capable, efficient, strong, self-sufficient; and one where I was, or tried to be, a follower—needy, dependent, lesser. And I began to confuse those two roles, and to be confused by them. The summer before I left I was appointed by the governor to a state commission. With great delight I told my husband. He said, "You mean you took it? Without discussing it with me?" I realized that for the first time it had never entered my head to discuss it with him. My autonomy was getting the better of me, even when I was not aware of it. Clearly that would continue to happen— and I was not willing to give it up.

And oh, the women I was meeting! Congresswomen. State senators. Corporate executives. Women who owned their own businesses. Who managed their own finances, who traveled alone. Some were single, some were not. Some had children, some did not. They were *doers*. They were making a difference. They seemed to think I could, too. They inspired me. I envied their poise, their sureness, their sense of power and place, their independence. I wanted that for myself. I knew that if I had made different choices, my life might be very much like theirs. As it was I found myself feeling apologetic. I remember meeting a young woman at a conference at the United Nations. She asked me what I "did." Hard pressed for an answer, I launched into a description of my volunteer assignments, my children, my substitute teaching, hoping to paint an exciting picture. She seemed impressed. I asked her the same question. "I am one of the prime ministers of my country," she replied. Oh, yes, I wanted more for me.

I had also become fast friends with one of my colleagues at the library where we worked. She was, quite clearly, my "road not taken." I discovered with fascination and astonishment where that road had taken this person who seemed so much like me in drive, intelligence, goals, values, and sense of the spiritual. Eagerly we exchanged life stories, outlining the very different lines along which our lives had developed, she with clear and concise explanations of why she had acted as she did, her rational thought processes, her carefully planned blueprints for her progress; I with many shrugs and blank looks and "that's what I was supposed to do" sorts of answers. She had a future with goals and dreams; I had a vast void of sameness ahead of me and no clear idea of how I had gotten where I was, or why, or what I was going to do next.

She asked me to help her with a book she was writing; I agreed. We met fairly regularly and our discussions ranged far beyond the manuscript. I felt my mind creaking into action. It was rusty with disuse, but to my delight I found that it still retained a vocabulary not used in twenty years: ideas from literature and philosophy, theories of religion and psychology; stories from art and nature and mythology. I was challenged and inspired, stimulated and irked, infuriated, bewildered, delighted. I was, in short, alive again. I saw again the self I had put aside, and I wanted it back. I saw what I believed I could and should be, and a way of life that was too extraordinary to be incorporated into the traditional life I was leading.

"Please," I said to my husband. "I am changing so fast and so much—we *must* make adjustments. We *must* restructure our life together. We *must* set new goals. We *must* get help. I don't want this to be happening but I am powerless to stop it." He merely shrugged and said *he* was satisfied; he had no intention of doing anything differently. The grimmer aspects of our relationship surfaced and took center stage. I continued to protest. He observed that if I didn't like it I was free to leave any time. I had never thought in such terms. I began to see that I might have to. And, in the end, this was *my* impossible conflict, my irreconcilable difference.

It was this confusion of influences—the consciousness raising of the women's movement and the marvelous, achieving women I met through it; the call of power I felt in my outside activities, and the yearning toward inner realization, as clarified by a special friendship, together with the hopelessness, degradation and stagnation of a moribund marriage, that combined to offer a vision of a future toward which I was irresistibly compelled.

"OK," said a man in one of my audiences. "I can buy all of that. The bad marriage and the problems and the wanting more and all. But what I *can't* accept, what I *can't* understand, is why didn't you women take the children? How *could* you leave them behind?"

Why Didn't You Take the Children?

I think this question is on the minds of most people when we try to describe our lives and situations: what of the woman who wants out of her marriage but not out of mothering, yet leaves anyway? Why doesn't she take her children with her? Why doesn't she fight for them? We think of those stories of mothers' incredible sacrifices to protect and defend their young. Surely nothing, nothing, is so bad that it can't be borne "for the sake of the children." Surely any mother worthy of the name will, like a tigress, fight to the death to keep her children by her side. Can there really be any decent reason for a woman who protests that she loves them to let them go without a fight?

The answer is yes. There are many reasons, and good ones. To begin with, when a marriage breaks up decisions must be made about the future of the children involved in that marriage. And there *are* situations where, after a carefully reasoned analysis of what is truly best for the child, it seems preferable to give over primary custody of the children to their father. This decision is sometimes arrived at with the cooperation of the child and with good feeling between the parents and the child. Such was the case in the situations described below:

- The child was only 30 months old and very attached to his father, who was with him constantly while I provided the family income...
- It was very hard to leave my dear child. But she had cats and dogs and she did not want to leave the farm. She begged to stay. She did not want to change schools, and I really had nowhere to take her.
- The psychiatrist said my daughter needed the security and stability of her brother and her familiar home, school, and friends. We felt this would be weighty testimony in court. My daughter was unable to deal with the conflict and she couldn't state a preference; indeed, we didn't want her to. So she stayed with her father.

It is often possible to consider the welfare of everyone concerned and to realistically assess the situation as it actually exists as opposed to how it is painted in the ideal. When this appraisal is done, custody by the father may be the wisest course:

- My husband was just as good a father as I was a mother. He told me he would never have other children or be able to love more children than just these two. Someone had to leave—I didn't feel it should be him just because of his sex.
- I wanted to live apart from my husband but I didn't *ever* hate him. Leaving him for another man hurt him deeply. Ultimately I felt I couldn't take away his home and his children too. He was/is an excellent parent.

Admittedly, this kind of cordiality and cooperation was rare among the families described by the women in my survey. In most cases, many other issues clouded the decision:

- Although I could have fought the custody thing and probably won, I would have ended up without support (financial) and I didn't want to put the kids through the whole ordeal. The situation is awkward in that I don't want to say bad things about their father—they have to live with him. In adulthood, they will understand, but meanwhile...there are a lot of years in between.
- I felt the all-day custody battle would be terribly damaging, especially to my children, and I loved them too much to do that to them! I also doubted I would win in the white male dominated court system. I was involved in school an hour away from their home, neighborhood, school, supports. I knew I didn't want to live there any more, but I felt it was wrong to uproot them. I had no job, no money. I also felt empty. I'd been a fantastic mother to my children and never got re-supplied (nourishment-wise) by my husband. I therefore felt like a dry sponge—totally depleted, with nothing left to give.
- What had I? No promise of a silver lining. It was like bracing into a violent storm and not knowing the outcome.

One of the "outcomes" that was quite apparent from these observations and many others that came my way was the financial problems that lay ahead. Many of the women who wrote to me would not have chosen to relinquish custody if they had had any choice. But often—in fact, usually—they did not, and the primary reason was economic.

I have described the financial situations of the women in my survey. They had, as they had been taught to do, and as society dictated, hitched their economic wagons to their husbands' stars, so to speak. And when the crunch came, they found that those stars were not theirs to share. They had sacrificed (*there's* that word!) their earning power, their schooling and education, their economic independence, for "the good of the family."

When they did work, before divorce, they made, as we know, 59 cents to a man's dollar. A recent survey conducted by 9 to 5, the National Association of Working Women, was reported in *Newsday* in May, 1988. It states that 84 percent of working women have incomes of less than $19,000 a year. Women with college diplomas still generally earn less than men with high school diplomas, and women with high school diplomas earn about the same as men who never made it to high school. The average annual income of a single working mother was $10,076 in 1985. In regard to child care, the survey reported that annual costs for child care average $3,000 per year. Only 3,000 of the nation's six million businesses, or .0005 percent, offer employees any form of child care assistance.[1]

For a woman to raise her children alone requires enormous economic sacrifices on the part of the children, too— sacrifices that many women are not prepared to ask of them. A recent report by the U.S. Commissioner of Labor Statistics stated that one out of every twelve families headed by a woman lives in poverty. The median income for such households is $6,179; the Census Bureau lists $8,414 as the poverty level for a family of four. "Women who maintain families on their own have a very difficult time in the labor market," the commissioner said.[2] This is hardly news. It is a fact, and one that must be faced during the decision-making process. The idealized fantasies of Marmee and her Little Women exist only in books. Poverty is rarely genteel. Most women want more for their children.

Russell Baker, the popular *New York Times* columnist, describes in his autobiography, *Growing Up*, how, after his father died, his mother faced the bleak prospect of caring for three small children and having no way to make a living. The youngest child was an adorable blonde infant, Audrey. When Baker's childless Uncle Tom and Aunt Goldie arrived in their big car and expensive clothes and proposed that they take and raise Audrey in their luxurious home, the decision seemed inevitable. A few days later Audrey was bundled up and sent on her way to her new home. Even though this was so clearly the best opportunity for Audrey, Baker writes that years later, in her old age, his mother was still worrying that she had made a terrible mistake when she "gave up" her baby. It was, he writes, the only deed of her entire life for which she ever expressed any guilt.[3]

The end of a marriage is very like a death, as has been noted many times, and the foregoing situation is not unlike ones we faced at the end of our marriages, when similar decisions had to be made. It was often preferable to leave the children in familiar surroundings with their middle class comforts than to see them exist hand-to-mouth in some two-room flat on the wrong side of the tracks where, as we will see in the next chapter, many of us found ourselves at first. Coming to such a difficult, though valid, conclusion does not negate our basic love for our children or our concern for their welfare. As one woman expressed it:

> I believe in motherhood, the flag, and apple pie—but what if the mother
> 1) hasn't got a degree and can't earn enough to take care of her children;
> 2) doesn't want welfare; 3) doesn't trust her husband to pay child support;
> 4) can't take the stress of children seven days a week with no support from
> the husband?

It is interesting to note that approximately a quarter of the women in my survey did initially have custody of their children. They decided at a later time to relinquish that custody. Sometimes, there was no economic factor involved and a decision such as this one was made:

> Rob was having some problems, although none really serious, and his father felt he was in a much better position to take over. He had remarried, had a younger child, was much more stable than I, and had a much greater income. After much discussion and soul searching I felt also that it would be an advantageous move for my son, as he needed time and direction which I couldn't give successfully. In many ways I had just "run out of gas" at that point in my life.

Generally, however, matters were not so fairly arranged:

- After 17 plus years of a good marriage my husband left very abruptly. I lived in the family home with my two children for over a year. I chose to give up the children when I realized what keeping them involved for me physically, financially, and legally. I *wanted* to keep them but felt I could not do it in view of the situation I was in. I am interested in helping other women know that they have a choice about single parenting. Not everyone is equipped to be a custodial single mother.
- The children lived with me for two years when, due to dire economic need I allowed them to live with their father. When I reopened the custody case he brought criminal charges and used all of his wealth and influence to twist things. Out of personal fear I let the matter drop, and gave him custody.

There are also cases where the children themselves, as time passes and they begin to mature and to better understand and direct their situations, are the ones to precipitate change:

> My older son chose to live with his Dad two years ago. He had lived with me for the first 14 years of his life. His father has always maintained some sort of visitation, and I felt this might happen one day but it shattered my self-concept at first. After 18 months I can see it was a successful move and therefore accept his decision. I still have legal custody of both my sons but I can't see going back to the court system…to help our family control private matters.

Mention of "the courts" has crept into several of these accounts. I think that "going to court" is the course of action most people are referring to when they ask why we "didn't fight." The presumption is that in the courts that we could find comfort and restitution and a confirmation of our motherly "rights." And indeed,most women, faced with the loss of custody do consider legal action, but most decide against it. A little careful reflection should help the reader to understand our reluctance.

You will remember that we were, for the most part, traditional, typical, housewives and mothers, for whom "going to court" would be an alien, drastic, and potentially disastrous course to take. For any number of reasons, a court "battle" was, for us, unthinkable. Lawyers are expensive and we had no money. Trials are often public, and messy, and potentially damaging to the psyches of the children, to say nothing of our own. We were unfamiliar with the labyrinthian court system and we had been brought up to believe that only criminals and low-lifes got caught up in it. "Decent" people like ourselves did not.

Furthermore, the spectre of charges and counter-charges flung in open court, of children called as witnesses to testify or closeted with a strange judge and asked to choose between two parents (or even to consider some third alternative) is so repugnant that we often reject it at all costs.

We had also seen and read enough to know that the "good guy" does not always win. We did not want to take that risk; going through it for nothing was a possibility too dreadful to contemplate.

Finally, as the traditional women we were, our desire to avoid acrimony and combat was so strong that many of us chose non-custody instead. Better, we decided, to take our chances with what we could work out in private, and to trust that our genuine love and concern for the children would win out in the end. In the words of a woman from California:

> I could *not* put my children through the hell their father was inflicting on them because I was in a custody battle with him. They were bones in a war between two dogs. By giving them up I gave them peace.

These motives are understandable and, I think, reflect a common and very classic motherly desire to protect the children from unnecessary stress. I heard variations on the same theme from the majority of my respondents.

Other decisions were made out of woeful ignorance; some out of misplaced trust. As I have pointed out, we were unfamiliar with the legal aspects of what we were doing, and of the possible ramifications. We were all too willing to let our decisions be guided by someone else, as we had been conditioned to do:

- I had no money and no hope of winning a contested settlement, according to my lawyer. He advised that the best I could do was every other weekend and two weeks in the summer, which I accepted. I learned too late that he did not give me the full facts.
- My husband and I agreed that he would take care of the children. It never occurred to me that he could pay me alimony and/or child support and I could keep the kids. It never occurred to me that *he* could leave. It was all his or his family's, the place we lived and everything.
- I relied too much on the verbal promises of my husband. He promised much but yielded little. I was undergoing emotional stress at that time and I really felt this was what I wanted.
- My husband, being a lawyer, handled the divorce.

The last situation, incredible as it seems, was the case in *four* other instances. We were trusting souls, and we often paid the price for that blind trust.

There were other, uglier, stories—instances of pressure and power plays that bordered on, or were, blackmail:

- My husband refused to let me out of the marriage unless I signed over custody. I did not think I could start over, find myself, and care for two young children. He vowed *no* money would come.
- My husband told me he planned to lie about my mental stability. He was determined to win custody and scared me out of going to court. In retrospect, I should have gone to court to fight for my child, but at that time I did not seem to have the strength mentally or physically, and he knew that.
- My husband called all the shots after I filed for divorce. He said if I took, or even asked for, the children, he would take an $8,000-a-year job and I could have my support out of that. He would have, too, at least long enough to prove his point. I could not have supported them through all of this. I could not have provided a home and the other things they had become accustomed to.
- My husband found some letters written to me by my woman lover. He said that unless I signed over *everything*, including the children, he would make the letters public, or at least implied that he would. At the time I was scared to death to have anyone know about my relationship with this woman, so I signed.

I have made reference once or twice to the lesbian mothers in my survey, who most certainly must be included in a section on these women who opted not to undertake a court battle. The woman last quoted above went on to say that after having lived openly with her lover for five years she wondered why she had been so afraid. I think her fear was well founded, though perhaps slightly misplaced. I did spend some time investigating this aspect of non-custody, with no small reward.

I think that many of us, if we have even thought about it at all, would consider those two words "lesbian mother" to be mutually exclusive. The consciousness raising of the women's movement let lots of us in on the news that many women married and had children in an effort to conform to the "norm" and later found that such enormous deception was beyond them. Others, women who had had no previous experience with or inclination toward physical relationships with other women, found that their special, close, and deepening friendships with other women demanded expression and commitment beyond the bridge table and the peace march. When these women reached their crossroads, their decisions involved delicate and special considerations not shared by the majority of divorcing women.

Some lesbian mothers declared themselves openly, battled publicly for custody, and actually won. An example is the case of Madeline Isaacson and Sandy Schuster, who "threw the diaper pail and the sleeping bags and our

52

clothes into a van and took off" for California with all six of their children. Their husbands brought suit against them, but Judge Norman Ackley ruled that "the mothers have shown stability, integrity, and openness," and awarded them custody. Not, however, without a rather major caveat; they were awarded custody on the condition that they live apart. They abided by that stipulation for two years, living in apartments across the hall from each other.[4]

The fact that these women and their families were written up in a national magazine and appeared on national television is an indication of the uniqueness of their story. Far more typical was the case of Mary Jo Risker, reported in *Ms.* magazine. Ms. Risker was described in court as a "warm and loving mother," albeit a lesbian. A Dallas jury, however, awarded custody of her son to his father, a man who had "broken Mary Jo's nose during a fight, had a record for driving while intoxicated, and had paid for the abortion of an 18-year-old who accused him of impregnating her."[5]

Love between women is probably as compelling an emotion as any found in the human experience. It is also true that a woman who is called to another woman, and answers that call, makes herself more vulnerable than almost any other class of citizen. A wife beater, a thief, a drunk, a child abuser, all have a better chance at gaining custody than a lesbian mother. She has placed herself under a double burden of societal disapproval; she has left her children (shameful!) and chosen to live gay (shocking!). The lesbian mothers in my survey *knew* that society is still so far from accepting their chosen lifestyle that legal action for custody has almost no chance of success. While there are open lesbian women who have obtained court-ordered custody of their children, there are so few that the bottom line for contesting custody for most lesbians is "don't try it." Most of them have taken that advice and gone outside the system altogether, and have met with a good measure of success.

The responses from the women in this category were, I found, the only ones with any real humor. They seemed the most joyful, the most settled, the most self-accepting, and the most thoughtful. I theorized that these women, having come into full acceptance of themselves as they are, are then more able to relate to their children, former husbands, parents, other family members and friends in an open, honest, and human manner than many of the mothers who continue to search for some identity outside their old roles. One may speculate that throwing over the old roles in so radical a fashion may possibly have made the lesbian mothers more accepting and open to the struggles of their children as they, too, attempt to gain self-definition and maturity. Having relinquished all claims to being deemed by society "normal" mothers, and no longer feeling required to teach their daughters to follow in their footsteps, as it were, into a traditional family role, they seem better able to sort out what is important in their roles and relationships and what is illusory, and to emphasize the positive and wholesome. That, at least, was the impression I had from the few women who wrote and identified themselves as gay and living with women partners.

They further wrote that their relationships with their partners are known to their children and to their former husbands, and often to their parents, friends and co-workers as well. (Perhaps lesbian women who are not "out" would not have written to me in the first place. There were, however, two or three who asked that I not use their names because not everyone "knew" and they would just as soon keep it that way.) They spoke of their partners as "co-parents" and as far as I could tell, in terms of the adjustment of either the women or their children to the non-custody situation, there was very little difference between the lesbian and heterosexual women who responded. Many of their problems were the same and their solutions were the same. As I have observed, the only difference seems to be an apparently greater self-acceptance on the part of the lesbian women. *None* of the lesbian women tried to gain custody in the courts, and most of them said the major, if not sole, reason for that decision was their sexual preference and their awareness that such a preference has almost always precluded success in a custody contest:

> Sure that's why I didn't contest. How would it all have sounded in court? Now, my husband knew about this relationship—yes, affair, we'd better admit—and in fact he encouraged it. That happens sometimes—they don't take this kind of sex seriously, and as long as he "got his" he wasn't complaining. But he had some of the letters she had written to me. Actually he had told me he found them and burned them, but as it turned out he had put them in his safe deposit box "just in case," as he put it. When we decided on divorce he told me he had lied and that he still had them, and he outlined his "terms." He got everything, including the kids, and I got my clothes and his silence. I think it was realistic of me to have decided not to try for anything better, at least in court.

It was not only the almost certain fruitlessness of a court session that prevented these respondents from contesting. Lesbian women were reluctant to face the possible loss of jobs, of friends, of supportive parents—all the things *all* of us feared losing and which they might lose on an even larger scale, so to speak. Further, they did not want their children to have to defend their life-styles, should they become public knowledge:

> • My children know the full extent of my relationship with Terry, and they have no problem with it, but I do not want them to have to fight this particular battle in the school yard or with their grandparents. Let's face it; it can be embarrassing, to say the least, to have a gay parent, and even more so when it is your mother who doesn't live with you. Someday I hope to be completely out, but for now I think it is best for us to be "good friends" to the outside world.
> • No one, not my children or parents or friends (except a few) really know the full truth about the relationship—which amazes, me as we live together in obvious harmony and affection, and it should not be too hard to figure out. But I think not saying anything for certain gives everyone that "out" to believe as much, or as little, as is comfortable for them. This way,

if someone asks my child flat out if I am gay, he can say truthfully that he doesn't know. He won't have to either lie, or fight for me.

- Well, I was brave enough to move in with her, but I sure wasn't brave enough to say why. I also knew that if I got to court and was asked what was what I could never deny her; I care too much for her to lie. So I figured it was best not to take the chance. It's much easier for the children this way, I think. They say as much as they like to each person that comes along, depending on how close they are to that person. I know my daughter's best friend knows, and she has been here many times, and my son told one or two of his friends. I like the fact that while *they* know the "whole truth" they can decide how much to reveal, and not have some court record or newspaper clippings telling the whole story to the whole world.

I think that it is also important, when we discuss the reasons why some women decided not to undergo the rigors of a court scene, to realize how much of our power—mental, physical, emotional, financial, and spiritual—we had relinquished in our efforts to conform and adjust and be "good helpmates." By the time we felt we had to leave there was just enough strength left to set out, but rarely enough to do battle. A few lines from Fay Weldon's book *And The Wife Ran Away* seem to sum up the feeling of enormous pressure and helplessness we felt:

"Marriage is too strong an institution for me," said Esther. "It is altogether too heavy and powerful." And indeed, at that moment she felt her marriage to be a single steady crushing weight, on top of which bore down the entire human edifice of city and state, learning and religion, commerce and law, pomp, passion, and reproduction. Beneath this mighty structure the little needles of this feeling which flickered between Alan and her were dreadful in their implication. *When she challenged her husband, she challenged the universe*[6] (italics mine).

It was as if marriage, that heavy and powerful institution, had worn us down, reshaped us, made us so much less than we should or could have been, that when we most needed our strength, our intelligence, our common sense, we found that we had buried them too deeply. We had had to learn dependence and we could not unlearn it in time. We were weak and fearful and very, very weary:

- I was terrified of some unknown judge appraising my personality, life style, fitness.
- I was virtually alone, with no role models, and I did everything in a reactionary manner. If my ex-husband fought with me or tried to demoralize me, I fell to pieces.
- Why didn't I fight? Well, I had already spent nearly 20 years fighting every natural instinct I had to change and grow and expand and *act*. And that habit can become ingrained. Patterns of behavior wear deep, deep ruts,

too deep to climb over; bowing out becomes second nature. I just rolled over and played dead, as usual.

• I was so poor, and so burned out, and so afraid.... I knew and he knew that I hadn't the means or the nerve to go to court...it was a pointless farce.

And, the simplest answer, this one from California:

I was too tired to fight.

Clearly, then, for many women and for many reasons, contesting custody is not always in their, or their children's, best interests. It is often not only unwise but impossible. But what of the women who *do* go to court? How do they fare?

It would be too monumental a task to analyze the results of the thousands of custody decisions that are made each year, and to remark on the justice of those decisions. It is not difficult, however, after reading books on divorce, and on women and the law, and on the court system in general, to arrive at an overview. As in so many areas of life in our society, women do not fare very well in custody battles, contrary to popular belief. One such case even drew the ire of the *New York Times* editorial staff:

The Fitter Parent

In New York State this month, a woman lost custody of her children. She was deficient in her religious duty to them, shared her bed with the man she later married, stayed out too late and allowed her male friend to violate the Sabbath by turning on television. Their father, who presumably can give them a better home, has them now.

"This is going to open a Pandora's box on custody battles," his happy lawyer said about the Court of Appeals rejection of the need for "extraordinary circumstances" to justify changes in custody agreements in divorce cases. "This will open a floodgate," he said. Pandora's box, floodgate; why not a can of worms?

Is it really in a child's best interests to be raised in a world where a parent is under constant pressure to prove herself fit? (One uses the feminine pronoun because to do otherwise might be politically correct but a factual lie.) Where having to work overtime, or the occasional overnight male or loud party could be construed as evidence of iniquity? Where a last discharge of marital venom can be cloaked in parental concern and have a far better chance of hitting its target?

This is, after all, a world in which not every woman should have custody of her children but in which all women suffer opprobrium if they do not ask for it. In which the working mother is often assumed to be selfish, the welfare mother sluttish, and the spouse-support ed mother lazy. In which women are made to feel guilty for having too many children—or for having none. One reason women have been responsible for child-raising in the first place is that men haven't exactly clamored for the role.

Maybe more men should have that role, but several years after the divorce and on possibly specious grounds is not a reassuring basis for the switch. "This is really a very special treat the parents of this state are getting and it will benefit men in the long run," said one enthusiast of the court's ruling. But since when has benefiting men—or women—been the point of a custody suit?[7]

While the courts are often baffling to the novice, in the case reported above, and in several reported to me in the survey, even experts might agree that they are nearly incomprehensible. Two cases in point:

• I was quite naive about the law. It never occurred to me that a judge would award my husband custody because of his history of violence and my history as essentially sole caretaker of the kids, but I was told by my attorney, by the social worker, and by the attorney *ad lisem* for the kids that since my husband was *in possession* of the children and living in another state, that would be the sole deciding factor.
• The agreement was that the children would be with me. They stayed with their father for three to four weeks while I found living space. He then refused to let them live with me. We went to court for custody, which he was granted because I left. The fact that he was an alcoholic, an abuser, and had had an affair with my younger cousin which produced a child made no difference to the judge.

Decisions of this sort are not as unusual as one might think and hope, according to an organization recently formed to assist mothers who have lost custody. This organization attributes this new phenomenon to a change in the courts' attitude toward awarding custody to the father if he has superior financial resources; normally the mother cannot hope to match those resources. Called the Committee for Mother and Child Rights, the organization is co-chaired by Beth Green and Kerstin Salk, former wife of Dr. Lee Salk, one of the most celebrated custody-winning fathers. This organization reports that a survey conducted in 1979 showed that fathers are awarded custody in contested cases *two-thirds* of the time[8].

This argument is rebutted by John Roessler, vice-president of a group known as Equal Rights for Fathers of New York State. He claims that it is only because the consciousness of the courts has been raised that fathers are getting more consideration in matters of custody awards.[9] This may be true, but it is also true that it is a rare father who cannot offer more financial security to his children than can their mother. If income becomes a major consideration, fathers may gain an edge that cannot possibly be remedied in today's economy, and that is a frightening thought. In most of the cases I surveyed for this book, it was economics that dictated the final decision. Not the depth of care or love, not the mental and emotional stress, not the wishes of the children, not the past history of the family, but the economic facts of life. Running through every woman's story was the thread of no finances, no economic security, and no immediate prospects for any. There were other reasons, to be sure, and I have and will outline many of them, but in the last analysis those women who reluctantly gave up custody when their marriages ended, or who did so shortly thereafter, did so in large measure out of economic necessity.

Did our British sisters fare any better in their courts? I did some inquiring on this subject and found that they did not. A woman from Seaton, Devon, recounted this experience:

> I found that during my children's custody case I was not informed of any hearing date, sent no documents, and found out about it by sheer accident the day before, in conversation. I attended the hearing, naturally nervous and confused as to how a hearing could be held without my knowledge. I was not asked anything by the judge, there were no welfare or school reports and custody was automatically given to my ex-husband with access to me. The hearing lasted four minutes. I was so shocked I could not have spoken if I tried and besides I did not know courtroom procedure. I never received in writing that my husband was awarded custody or billed for costs. It was as if I never existed. At a subsequent hearing 18 months later the judge glossed over previous events as irrelevant. The children are now settled into a routine and it was such a drawn-out affair that I withdrew the case in the end, the effect on the children was too much. I don't think I will ever believe in British justice again.

Another British woman might well say the same thing, given her experience with the same courts. Her story, like so many, is convoluted and complicated and difficult to summarize; here is part of what she wrote:

> The court had promised to make our case a special one and try for an early hearing.... I saw my beloved children, if I was lucky, about seven hours a week, or even less, and for only half an hour on Christmas Day, despite their pleas. Finally after two months the new case was heard. The first welfare officer (we had two) was reprimanded for not being able to give sufficient evidence for her recommendation that the boys stay with their father. The judge described me as "a gentle, cultured, cool, calm, collected person...[who] has completely restructured her life." He also said that young children must never be separated from their mother except in the gravest circumstances.
>
> Five minutes later we were called back. My husband had lodged an appeal because in this last statement the judge had 'misdirected' himself. Two months later another appeal was heard based on a new affidavit I had never seen. A large proportion of its contents were either totally untrue or grossly exaggerated. I was not allowed to speak, and my legal representative said very little in my defense.
>
> The result was that two appeals judges reversed the care and gave the control order back to my husband. I was broken, shattered...I was told that because I had lost the appeal I should now expect to pay another seven hundred pounds in court costs. Until I did so he refused to hand over

my legal file, thus preventing me from taking any further action.

Why didn't we fight? Not because we didn't care, obviously. Not because we didn't want what was best for our children. Not because we felt no pressure to do so, or because we felt no pain at the thought of parting. We came up against hard reality, and made our choices.

I, too, experienced that same pressure and pain, harsh realities and hard choices. I had, to be sure, been able to arrange for myself much more fortuitous circumstances than most of my respondents, at least as far as living quarters were concerned. My friend and colleague, of whom I spoke earlier, lived alone in a very spacious, very beautiful, but very expensive home. It would, we decided, be mutually advantageous to join forces. We were, we thought, compatible enough to make such an arrangement workable. But we had, as I have said, lived entirely different lifestyles. She had lived alone for 13 years since the death of her mother. She had been an only child, she had never married; her only relatives were two distant cousins. Assimilating me would be a huge adjustment.

Conversely, for me to adjust to living in someone else's home, after twenty years of having my own, would be arduous too. I had friends and relatives and children who would expect to visit. I had my own ways of doing things, my own patterns and rhythms. There was a great risk involved for me, too. If this plan did not work out, then what? A tiny apartment somewhere? A rented room? Or even, possibly, a return in defeat to my former life? There was no way to know. I had leaped off into who knew what kind of life, a complete unknown, with an old station wagon, a couple of pieces of furniture, $350 and a part-time job that paid $5.10 an hour. Obviously I was not going to be able to make a fair financial contribution to this set-up, even if it was just myself. How could I expect my friend to subsidize three more? It was crazy enough for *me* to attempt such a move, without dragging my children into it, too. They had their schools, their friends, their father and the financial security he could offer, in the home where they had lived for their entire lives. They had their grandparents, their cousins, uncles and aunts, with whom I was not at all sure I could continue to have any relationship once they found out what I had done.

And I, too, was staggering under the burdens described by my respondents: the guilt, the shame, the fear, the emptiness. I, too, had no money. I, too, was afraid of the courts and all that they represented. I, like the rest, felt selfish and undeserving and presumptuous in my quest for self-development and affirmation. I was horrified at what I was doing and terrified at the effect it would have on my children. There was room in my new home for them to visit me, should they wish to do so. Surely that was all I could expect or require of them—a visit. In truth, weak and fearful as I was then, I could not have insisted that they come with me even if I had wanted to. Sometimes I wonder whether I could have been more forceful, but it is the woman I am *now* that is wondering. For the woman I was *then*, it was truly impossible.

Whether my reasons, or those of the other women in my survey, justified our decisions remains a point to ponder, I suppose. My own internal censor is as effective as the most virulent member of any "Moral Majority" and I can hear it scoffing at these stories with scorn and disdain. "Bunch of selfish, greedy, immature, women's libbers, up and quitting when the going gets a little rough, don't care who gets hurt, walk out and leave their babies crying…" I heard that inside, and I heard it in actuality. After I left, my mother signed her first, devastating letter in response to my news "sickened and shamed." Part of the reason that hit so hard, despite my conviction that what I was doing was right and inevitable, was that some part of me, too, was "sickened and shamed." I, who had always tried so hard to be "good," was now "bad." I, the achiever, had failed miserably in this most important of tasks. I, who had tried for their whole lives to protect my children from hurt and harm, had caused them their most grievous hurt and harm. It was a burden hard to bear.

But I also knew that to remain where I was would do grievous harm to *me*, had *already* done grievous harm to me. Selfish or not, the loss of self was too high a price to pay. I do not think that in the long run my children would have demanded it of me. Nor would they, I think, have demanded of me a life of sham and illusion. In a story found in her book *You Can't Keep a Good Woman Down*, Alice Walker wrote:

> Well, she was a fraud anyway. She had known after a year of marriage that it bored her.… "The Experience of Having a Child" was to distract her from this fact.… He seemed to know, as she did, that if anyone packed up and left it would be her. Precisely *because* she was a fraud and because in the end he would settle for fraud and she could not.[10]

Jessie Bernard, in her book *The Future of Marriage* says, "…to be happy in a relationship which imposes so many impediments on her, as traditional marriage does, a woman must be slightly ill mentally.…"[11] If that is the case, the woman who perceives that she is "ill mentally" and takes steps to get better is clearly acting in *everyone's* "best interests." Almost all of my respondents described their mental and physical health as deteriorating. If marriage was indeed the cause of their illness, then removing themselves was, as many of them said, life saving. "Through it all," wrote one woman, "through the pain and the fear and the unknowing, I felt, and even said to myself, 'I am getting well. I am getting well.'"

Was there any other way? For the heroines of fiction, there was. Edna Pontellier walked into the ocean. Anna Karenina threw herself under a train. Madame Butterfly stabbed herself fatally rather than have her son "feel the torment when you are older that your mother forsook you!" But for my respondents, who were searching for less dramatic and more productive solutions to their dilemmas, there was not. This woman speaks for many:

> Actually I believe I had *tried* every other way. But if there is no coopera-

tion, and no understanding of your torment, and no help, no, there *is* no other way to work it out. I would love to have had a normal, peaceful, fulfilling home and family. But you can't do that by yourself. I really believed I could work it out better from outside—that is, be a better mother when I was a better woman, a better self. Clearly that was not possible for me from inside, and where else is there *but* outside?

And so we chose to leave—leave our homes, our children, our ways of life. We did so after long and careful deliberation. But while we may have come to our conclusions and reached our decisions rationally and thoughtfully, it appears that when we finally did act, we did so in alarmingly irrational and self-punishing ways. Far from rejecting the stereotypical role of wife and mother we seem to have clutched at it in a final, last-ditch attempt to convince at least ourselves that we were indeed "normal" after all. Let's consider what we did when we left.

What Did You Do When You Left

How did you do it? What did you actually *do*? Where did you go? What did you take with you? How did you manage housing? Finances? What did you tell people? I asked about these things in my questionnaire. Some of the answers were downright scary. I was awed by the chances taken and the desperate measures necessary to make the decision stick:

- I went to the YWCA with $200, the *New York Times* ads, and the well wishes of friends who helped with free meals and $10 when I needed it.
- Sold my engagement and wedding rings, and with the money I received from the sale and a few dollars I had saved ($300), I had some spending money.
- I made "friends" with men who could provide necessary services around the apartment, stole food from the hospital where I worked.
- On December 29 I took my $90 and found an efficiency, one-room furnished apartment, utilities included, no deposit, and rented it on the spot. The apartment was like one big room, with a bathroom that was really a closet. I could sit on the toilet and brush my teeth in the sink at the same time. There was a kitchen in one corner, a table and two chairs, a bed, a dresser, a night table, and two or three cupboards. I put up a lot of contact paper to cover the walls, which were some institutional green color. Sounds bad—it was—but it was mine. I worked double shifts when I could at the all-night diner where I worked for 90 cents an hour and tips. Tips were good if I got two or three dollars a day. I worked weekends at a pizza shop after I got off at the diner. I did babysitting. I hustled drunks at pool for food sometimes. I wore tennis shoes in knee-deep snow until a highschool kid at the diner bought me some boots.
- I had a total of $100 to my name, no job, no car, no furniture, in an apartment that I rented with money I borrowed from my mother. I had to sleep on the floor for months, and find a job within walking distance.

Others did not find themselves in quite such dire straits, but their situations were certainly not enviable:

- I moved in with a friend and then later with an uncle who is handicapped.... He gave me support in ways he wasn't even aware of because of his handicap. In his own way he is a "reject" from society, so to speak, and so was I. I learned a lot of things from him—one being the will to go on.

- After a weekend of "thinking it over" I decided to leave. We were living in a small town which I didn't like living in. My children had spent all of their lives in this town and my husband's business was established there. I had "tried" to leave several times in the previous three years (once with both my kids and once with just my daughter) but when confronted with three crying people, I stayed. My husband told me he would never pay child support to me and if anyone was to leave it would have to be me. I felt numb at the time I left (on a Sunday night). I came to Fort Worth (30 miles from our home), the city I had grown up in. I stayed with my sister for two weeks until I could move into an apartment of my own.

- Although we talked about separation between ourselves and in therapy, the counselor seeing us advised against it. However, things escalated and without the right skills we found ourselves in a situation where I had to leave suddenly and immediately. I was fortunate to have friends to stay with for a few weeks. Then my aunt and uncle, who have always been surrogate parents, took me in for a month and a half. I then sublet the friends' (mentioned earlier) apartment while they were away. Upon their return another friend took me in for a week, during which time I found my own apartment. Is this wandering typical of those of us who leave abruptly?

I think the answer to this question is yes, it is fairly typical for us to move from one inadequate place to another until we get some sense of balance. An interviewee in London said:

> I've found that when you move out on your own you tend to move around a lot. Several of the girls I've met have done the same thing. I've had six bed-sits in the time I've been away, which will be two years next month. That's quite a lot of moves. And I had some lousy experiences—I was beaten up by one landlord, and all sorts of things happened. I never imagined I would be able to cope—and yet I did.

Quite often we lived with relatives or friends at first, and quite often they were reluctant hosts. Unwilling to become burdens, we went from one household to another until we could manage something of our own. Rarely did we plan our moves very far ahead; in fact, we rarely planned them at all. As I worked on this section of the book, I found I was getting a stronger impression of flight than of mere leaving. Certainly I did not read or hear much about plans and arrangements; the emotion of the moment was paramount. When we decided to leave, it seems we did so most precipitously:

- I had to leave in a hurry and didn't want to take too much to my friend's apartment and be an extra burden. I was very scared and confused at first and didn't even know what I wanted to take.

- I left and went to a friend's house with just some overnight things. The next day I went back to the house to get my clothes and things. The whole time I was packing up I was screaming, out loud, "What are you doing? You're crazy! You'll never get away with this!" And all this time I was throwing things into boxes—only my own things, *everything* from my bureau and closet: scraps of fabric, old pencils, buttons, odd notes, just everything. Later I threw out about four cartons of stuff, including my maternity clothes, which I had also taken (I gave them to a church bazaar). That first day I just wanted to grab everything and run, before I got caught and stopped. It was *not* a good day, and it did not get better for quite a while.

I can empathize with that feeling of frantic haste and blind panic. When I was interviewed by another author she asked what I remembered about those early days. I had to say that all I really remembered was a lot of screaming (inner and outer) and a strong sense of moving in total darkness, blindly, sort of how I imagine it must be to run across a field of battle during the height of shelling. I felt desperate to get to safety, without a clear notion of where safety might actually be.

Fleeing in this way seemed to have made us behave in strange and atypical ways. We seemed to have forgotten all our hard-won skills when we set out. Women who wouldn't dream of going to the grocery store without a list and a pocket calculator leapt off into a great financial unknown with absolutely no preparation. Women who had efficiently run large households with ease and grace found themselves completely at sea when faced with the simplest decisions. Women who had always talked openly and honestly with their children found themselves mute. "I can't believe I did so many stupid things!" said one women from Oregon. "I just couldn't think," recalled another, from Vermont. "There seemed to be a block between me and what everyone else was saying, and I just agreed to whatever it was with no idea of how it would affect me later. It's hard to believe that with my talent for planning I let this happen in such a totally no-planning way."

And so it went. We were ignorant and trusting, and naive, and unrealistic—as we had been conditioned to be:

- He promised me $2,000. It seemed like a lot of money.
- We didn't have enough money to be concerned about and I was totally uninformed about what little we did have.
- I didn't want to disrupt my son's home—and never realized my husband could and would afford to replace things more easily than I can *yet* manage. The total settlement was $3,500. *Arghh!!*
- I only wanted total possession of me. Material possessions meant little to me.
- My husband paid for my apartment (ghetto-ish, at my insistence) until I was able to take over for myself (two months). I was overly proud and refused all other help from him, and was much too old to go back to Mom and Dad. I was determined to pay my own way, a combination of idealism

and naivete. I will say that there is nothing like pretzels dipped in peanut butter to inspire one to find a job. Luckily I was able to find one within hitching distance of the kids.

I decided to go back a bit in the sequence of events and ask *when* they knew they wanted to leave. For some, of course, the dawning came over time, the reasons unfolded slowly and pressures built steadily, until the decision was clear. For others there was an explosion of insight, a revelation as it were; once enlightened, they said, there was no going back:

- One day I was walking around the yard, in the fall, with the baby in my arms and my little boy holding my hands, and suddenly it was like I "woke up," and I thought, "what am I doing here in this apron and this ugly housedress? How did I get here? This isn't where I should be. There must be more." That was when I knew I couldn't stay much longer and stay sane, too.
- I had been involved in a number of "values clarification" sessions of various kinds, and in various capacities. My top value was always *honesty*, and I was comfortable with that, and knew it to be true, and felt I lived in harmony with it. One summer night, though, as I as walking with a friend and explaining about this value and what it meant to me, it came *flooding* over me that my whole *life* was *dis*honest. I did not want to be a wife. I did not want to be a dutiful daughter. I did not want to spend my time and energy putting others first all the time. I did not want to be second best. I was honest within that framework, all right, but the whole *framework* was false. My *life* was false. And it was crystal clear how drastically I had compromised that top value of mine. From that cataclysmic moment on, I knew I was going to have to get out and start over.

In the main, we didn't reach out for much counseling or consulting while we were deciding to strike out on our own. Only rarely did we talk over our decisions with our parents, mainly because we were pretty sure what the reaction would be:

- My mother would have gone right through the roof if she had known what I was planning to do, and I have a feeling that her shock and anger and disapproval would have caused me to back down. Even after I left I had a hard time telling her (I wrote a letter) but I know I wouldn't have gotten any objective advice or sympathy if I'd asked her beforehand to help me decide.
- I never had the kind of relationship with my parents where I could talk over my inner discontents and fears and insecurities. They are very straight-laced and conventional and have *no* sympathy for anyone who acts in the least bit different, so I knew they would have nothing to offer in the way of help and advice. I had to do this by myself, and I did.

- A couple of times I had tried to tell my mother how unhappy I was and how unsatisfying my life was, but she would just say, "well, we all make the best of what we have," and "life is never perfect," and things like that. I knew she felt we should just settle for whatever situation we found ourselves in, and the thought of taking action to change that situation was really outside her ability even to consider. There didn't seem to be much point in making a real effort to make her see my side, since she didn't think I had a right to *have* a side.

A few of us, not many, sought advice from lawyers before we left, but for the most part lawyers entered the picture only after we had already left and had found that we needed to untangle what had already been done. A few more of us went to counselors and therapists for advice. Those of us who turned to the clergy found the least help of all, and in fact when I asked who or what had been the *least* helpful both before and after the departure, the clergy was mentioned the most frequently:

- Religion has a big stake in keeping things the way they are, in preserving the patriarchy, in teaching us to "endure." My minister was shocked that such impure thoughts were even in my head, and advised me to repent, and to emulate Mary and sacrifice all. He didn't say what to do if your child doesn't turn out to be Jesus, and mine wasn't!
- You really can't expect that a minister is going to tell you that divorce is OK, and leaving your kids that God sent you from Heaven is OK, that breaking your vows is OK. I *had* hoped for a little more personal sympathy and understanding, though, and I felt very deserted when he said he didn't want to discuss it at all.
- I think he [the clergyman] knew perfectly well that my decision was a right one, but he couldn't very well say so. He just said I should go for outside counseling, by which he meant someone other than him. He was the only one I could afford (free!) of course, so I just went it alone.
- I had gone to this church for about fifteen years, and when I moved of course I stopped going. He never called to find out why. I went back once and told him the whole story, and he said did I want to talk about it. At the time it was pretty raw, so I said "not right away," but I did give him my address and phone number. He never called, and when I went back to a church service a few months later he said, "Well, well! You never know what's going to turn up!" I didn't go back after that.

We didn't say much to the children, either; 65 percent reported that they'd left after no discussion with, or only "vague hints" to, the children. In some cases, of course, the children were too young, but in the cases where they were old enough to understand, only about five percent of the women offered a "full explanation" prior to leaving. This was probably the hardest part of the whole experience, and we did not meet the test very well. There were many reasons for our reluctance:

- I really didn't know for sure that I *was* going to do it until I had actually done it, so I didn't tell the kids. And I don't know what they thought; I never had the nerve to ask, and they never really said.
- The children and their father left for a planned vacation (I had to begin work). While they were gone I found an apartment and moved out. He was supposed to tell them while they were away but he didn't, so we did not break the news to them until they returned and I was already gone.
- I didn't tell them before I went because I was so sure that I would never have the nerve to leave after. Just one tear, just one hug, just one "Mommy, don't go" and I'd be stuck for another ten years and I just couldn't take the chance. It was bad enough as it was, telling them after.
- I simply could not think of one thing to say to them that I thought they would understand and accept. I was having trouble with my own sense of whether I was justified—all that guilt and doubt, you know—so I was pretty sure I couldn't make much of a case to them. You can't describe a feeling, or a knowing, and you also can't start telling them what a rat you think their father is, when you are about to leave them in his sole custody.
- I can't think of a right way to tell a kid, "hey, I don't want to be stuck with you all day every day," to say, "you bore me, you tire me out, you don't give me back enough for my investment." I *did* and do love him, so I thought I'd better find a way to show it in a way that I *could* show it, and that was to leave him and just see him part of the time. He thinks I was too poor to keep him (which was certainly at least partly true) and I don't think there is much point in telling him anything different.

When it came to material things, almost all of the women reported that they had taken with them "less then I would have liked." The most frequently cited reasons for this were "thought I could take more later" (34 percent), "husband wouldn't relinquish more" (53 percent), and "didn't want to strip the children's home" (81 percent). Those who thought they could "take more later" were usually disappointed:

- My husband said I could get other stuff when I had more room. Eventually I did get my rocking chair, some of the dishes, pans, etc., but that was two or three years later and not without a struggle.
- I left my personal belongings—clothes, typewriter, sewing machine—no furniture except a rocking chair. I wanted what I absolutely needed and that was all. That was also a mistake, because my ex, soon after the separation, "changed his mind" about sharing things like the camping equipment, much of which I had made myself.
- Before I left we made lists of things I would get and he would keep. After I left he said that I had no legal right to any of it. I believed that, so I didn't make any protest.

This phenomenon of the husband "changing his mind" came up fairly frequently. Somehow the marriage-related habit of trusting the man to provide persisted and carried over into the verbal agreements we made at the end of the marriage. We believed that verbal agreements were enough, and found later that we had been quite unrealistic:

> My husband told me I could get other belongings later. But he changed his mind. I ended up with only my car and a few clothes. All my family heirlooms were kept by him and are now being used by his present wife.

This feeling of trust, of being able to reach amicable arrangements later, after the dust had settled, persisted despite quite concrete evidence to the contrary. A story that best exemplifies this phenomena of misplaced trust is the truly startling case of a battered wife who left for the first time after a beating that led to a miscarriage, and left finally after a severe beating on Christmas Eve over the expenditure of $15.75 to fix the furnace. She wrote:

> All I was concerned with at the time of leaving was safety. I found more clothes—there was no need for furniture because of the living arrangement. I did return and get some more clothes, toys, and personal things when my ex wasn't home. I didn't even take my car. *I assumed that a fair settlement would be made later.* (Italics mine.)

One can only marvel.

"What did you take?" I asked next. They replied:

- I took my clothes, etc. Two blankets, two towels, two sheets…etc. I really only took what I had come with to the marriage. I didn't want "his" stuff. I even left my diamond engagement and wedding rings, but I took my plain wedding band. I took two plates, two forks, etc. Just enough to get by. I didn't even take all my clothes or my sewing supplies. I didn't take the sewing machine or other appliance-type things. I didn't take any furniture.
- A TV, a chaise lounge, pictures, pillows, ceramics which my mother made. I asked for nothing in the way of furniture except the piano, which I will get in two years.
- I took a small amount of furniture, some kitchen stuff, personal things. I also took stuff from the old family home and had the pieces of me in one place for the first time.
- I only took the barest of essentials, buying my own (second-hand) bedroom furniture. Most of our furniture had been paid for by me, so my husband had no complaint over what items I did take and he even stated that I was *quite* fair in my division of property. He gave me no money whatsoever, and I didn't ask for it (I guess in repayment of my guilt feelings).
- Ex-husband to this day is angry that I took the stereo with me. I left and never asked for: a brand new washer-dryer, electric range, color television, two-year-old Pontiac Catalina, wedding gift appliances, linens, etc. Yet he had an hysterical fit over a cheap four-year-old stereo. There were

several pieces of furniture I would like to have had, but he put up more hassle than I could deal with.

The impulse "not to strip the children's home" was very, very strong, and appeared, in one form or another, in most of the responses. Feeling that our own absence would be enough of a jolt, we wanted to minimize further change in our children's surroundings. We wanted them to continue in as "normal" a way as possible. We tended to leave furniture, home decorations, household goods, etc. even when we keenly felt their loss, and even when, as was pointed out earlier, our husbands could have easily replaced anything we took. Family heirlooms, special personal gifts, and family treasures such as baby books, school drawings and papers, and vacation trip mementos were among them. Photo albums were frequently mentioned. Sometimes albums were split up, sometimes it was possible to make new copies of old pictures, and sometimes photos became the focal point of as much bitterness as money:

- I was the one who had taken the pictures, had them developed, and organized them into albums over the years. But when I said I wanted them my husband insisted on keeping them "for the children." I said they could easily see them at my house if they wanted, but he refused. And there they are still, gathering dust I suspect. The whole history of my years as a mother is there in those photographs and I still resent losing them.
- It is almost always the mother who is the family historian, I guess you'd call it, and I had loved saving their little school projects and report cards and such. He threw them all out as "clutter." I think that was a tragic loss.

We were, it is clear, a sentimental bunch; I, too, wince at the loss of that "clutter." Some of us, who would not think of battling for money or furniture, felt that these souvenirs were worth retrieving:

- I snuck back into the house one day and took all the old baby things, school papers, little kid gifts, etc. I have them all packed away here and I am pretty sure he does not even know they are gone. It's nothing to him where they are and it means a lot to me to have preserved those baby years in some way.
- I am always glad when the kids say, "remember that igloo I made in the fourth grade?" and I can say "sure, here it is." I am sure their father wouldn't even know what they were talking about, as he never paid much attention to their school projects, at least then. Sounds silly, I know, but I am glad to have them.

Perhaps this is one of the reasons why we retrieved those items:

I think the fact that I took all those souvenirs and baby things made them realize that I did still love them and care about them and felt they were important to me, even if I didn't want to live with them anymore. That the times we had shared were precious to me and that I wanted to remember them and not put them out of my life.

There was also an impulse to maintain a presence in the former home. Perhaps we thought we might return someday:

> I felt, I don't know why, that he'd feel the reduction of stress, see I'd made an effort to set up my own home, and would offer furniture, kitchen supplies, maybe money (?). Or he'd contact me and ask why I had been so Puritanic and suggest I take more. Somehow I suspect, nine years later, that I'd hoped he'd ask me back, on *my* terms, so why slog up and down stairs with books, records, furniture, when there was an outside chance it might all be moved back!

There was also (and we have seen this reflected in the foregoing cases) a desire to forget, to block out the "old life" and start over:

- I didn't want anything more to remind me. I wanted a fresh start. I was feeling too weighted down with material possessions. At the time I wanted only basic necessities to try to determine what my real priorities were.
- I took minimal furnishings (an old couch, a chair, a sofa bed, and an old TV) largely because I wanted to set up my own household and did not want any "baggage" from my marriage.

Other, less clear-cut, more sinister reasons emerged, too: guilt, desire to avoid a "hassle," self-punishment. These have been alluded to in the foregoing quotes. Often we did not take more because *we did not feel we deserved more.* Consider the following:

- Everyone involved, including myself to a large extent, felt I deserved practically nothing. Whatever I was allowed to take was seen as a generosity (even my clothes).
- Strong feelings of guilt stopped me from being assertive.
- I'm sure much of my reluctance to take more stemmed from feelings of guilt, from wanting to just get out and start over. Had I not had a good attorney I would probably have agreed to much less than my legal right to half the property.
- Because I was the one who wanted out, or at least I was the one who first said so, and did something about it, I didn't think it was fair for me to take what we had earned together. Even though I knew that a lot of the fault was his, I knew that a lot of it was mine. And besides I was the one who was leaving, so I didn't think it was right to take anything but what was mine.
- In our initial agreement I gave away much more than was reasonable, due to guilt. My lawyer pointed out my errors and appropriate changes were made.

• Felt guilty about leaving and felt I was not worthy of taking anything. My freedom was my legitimate amount of things to take, something I frequently told myself for a couple of years.

All of this led me to conclude that despite the wildly unconventional step we were taking, we were acting otherwise in solidly traditional, "feminine" ways, and we were paying the price. We did not want to appear greedy and grasping, so we stepped aside. We continued to trust our husbands to be fair and supportive, as they are in the myth, despite every evidence to the contrary. We remained ignorant about finances and about the law, which are traditionally masculine provinces. Our wants were sentimental. We took souvenirs and mementos and left the money and goods. Understandably, sentimental items are often of great importance and support, but in times of stress it is not very practical to leave it at that; sentiment does not help much when you are "dipping pretzels in peanut butter." We continued to try to spare everyone's feelings. We constantly apologized, even to ourselves. We took most, if not all, of the blame for "our" failures. We accepted punishment, as it were, through the losses we often inflicted on ourselves. We took only what no one else wanted. We cringed and we fled. All in the manner of traditional women.

I must plead guilty to these charges, too. Knowing that I was leaving for *me*, because *I* wanted more, because *I* wanted something different, filled me with such guilt that I couldn't consider making an effort to obtain an equitable settlement. I knew, also, that my husband could and probably would make any contest extremely unpleasant and damaging, and I did not want to provoke him.

So when, three months after I left, he presented me with a formal separation agreement giving him the house and its contents, the vacation home, the savings bonds, the stocks, the newer car, *and* custody of the children, it seemed somehow right. He agreed to continue my medical and automobile insurance for one year, and to pay $1,000 a year for five years into an IRA account (no ready cash). It seemed wildly generous to the guilt-stricken side of myself. He asked what I wanted in the way of furniture. I gave him a list, which he marked with notations like "yes," "no," "maybe later," "perhaps loan," and the like. I was "given" the stereo, that had been a gift to me, my sewing machine, a hand-carved chest and a what-not table that had belonged to my grandmother, and a desk I had rescued from a house demolition. I had title to a six-year-old station wagon and I had $350 in the bank. It seemed more than I deserved. (My parents observed, when they saw that the stereo was no longer in the house, that "the one who leaves should get nothing." Having been brought up under this philosophy, I agreed. My hard-won assertiveness, my social conscience, and my self-esteem all in retreat, I could not help but agree with that hard-line judgment.)

My husband's lawyer advised him that I *must* have counsel, since the agreement we were contemplating was so obviously coercive that it would never survive a contest. I contacted a lawyer friend who was active in government and hence unable to represent me. She gave me the name of another lawyer and wrote me, "I *urge* you to contact her *as soon as possible.* Review of your papers makes it clear that negotiation should take place." I contacted the new lawyer, but refused to let her negotiate, insisting that no "fuss" be made, that it was all agreeable to me as long as I got out without confrontation. "Why don't you at least go for joint custody?" she urged. In my ignorance, I had never heard of joint custody. When it was explained I decided that I would at least try for that. My husband, against the advice of his lawyer, agreed to the language, though the mechanics would remain the same as in the original draft of the "agreement":

> The parents shall have joint custody of the unemancipated issue during their minority. Notwithstanding the foregoing, it is agreed that the Father shall have physical custody of said children in that the children will reside with the Father.... Both Father and Mother shall equally share the responsibility regarding decisions pertaining to education, religious training, vacations, health care, trips, and domicile. The Mother shall have the right of visitation at all reasonable times, including overnight and weekend visitation, subject to reasonable notice to the Father....

I could hardly bear to read these words, let alone consider their import.

By the time the "no-fault" year was up, I was sufficiently stabilized to realize that I was being, in the words of my son, "stiffed." But the most vigorous protest I could muster was a refusal to sign the final document. This made it necessary for my husband to actually appear in court. Since I did *not* appear, the divorce, complete with agreement on custody, went through by default. I consoled myself with the righteous thought that I had not actually *agreed*, but even I could see how thin that argument was. As much as any of the women I surveyed, I had caved in to fear, guilt, self-blame, and self-effacement; to an habitual and deep-seated desire to placate and soothe; to a palpable, albeit child-like, desire to be "good," to be "nice," to be "helpful," to be "acceptable." Unrealistic as that might have been, it directed my decisions and actions.

In our actions and decisions we revealed our deepest beliefs about our roles as wives and mothers, and it was this realization that most astonished and confused me. One woman said she left, after 12 years, to set up her "own" household. What had she thought she had been doing for those 12 years? Over and over we said we took, after five or ten or fifteen years, only "our own things." What about the "things" of the marriage, then? Were they not ours also? Did we not feel a sense of possession, or ownership, of belonging? Apparently we did not. What does this say about our perceptions of ourselves as partners, co-workers, co-contributors, helpmates? What did we believe to be our rights and benefits? Had we accepted that part of the myth that minimized our rights, along with the rest? Did we not see ourselves as major contributors to the family structure and the family welfare, as the myth had told us we were? Apparently we did not.

I wondered whether we had actually let the "system" deal us this final blow, whether we punished ourselves, and allowed ourselves to be dealt with unfairly, because we had been taught that what we were doing was "bad," "abnormal," "sinful," and therefore worthy of punishment. I concluded that, to a large extent, it was so. We *did* feel horribly guilty; we did feel sinful; we did feel callous and selfish and self-serving, in large measure because we allowed society to impose its judgments on us. And we were caught between these negative judgments and our feelings of rightness and self-preservation and budding power. And we expressed another overwhelming need and desire: to *start over*.

That need is stated over and over, in questionnaire after questionnaire and interview after interview, as we have seen in many of the foregoing answers. "I didn't want any 'baggage' from the marriage." "I wanted a fresh start." "I left with only my personal belongings." "I took only the barest of essentials." "I really only took what I had come with to the marriage." It is as though we knew we had been living a life of illusion, and when we left that life, it somehow no longer seemed real. We realized that we had set off on the wrong course from the very beginning of our marriages and that in order to remedy our mistakes we had to go back and begin again; we felt a deep need to start at the beginning, as fresh and unfettered as we had been the first time around.

One wonders how much this need to start over influenced our decisions to set off without the children; they, after all, were not there at the beginning and in certain ways were also "baggage" from the marriage. But in exploring this possibility with my respondents, I discovered no desires to renounce the children along with the furniture and the washing machine. Rather, we wanted to become the persons we had once imagined we could become. To do that, we often had to go back to where we last felt ourselves to *be* ourselves; for many of us that was before we were married. As we saw in the chapter on who we were, very often we were women who had been "nipped in the bud," who had had no chance to try our wings, to "find ourselves," to use a cliche. So the need to expand was a major motivating force, along with the others we have identified.

Ultimately, I believe we left in most instances in the same manner as we had lived—as traditional women doing traditional things in traditional ways, exhibiting traditional feminine behaviors, preserving traditional feminine appearances. Our economic predicaments and our self-effacing postures reflected the realities of our society and the traditional values in which we were taught to believe implicitly. These traditional mores led us to put others ahead of ourselves, to allow our husbands the leadership role, to place material comforts for our children ahead of any emotional and spiritual benefits we could offer them, to remain ignorant of "masculine" provinces like money and law, and to place ourselves in less advantageous positions in order to avoid conflict. And given those traditional, "womanly" values and goals, it is no surprise that in most cases we did not even consider precipitating meaningful conflict, or else did not fight hard enough or knowledgeably enough when we did.

Whatever our actions, and whatever the reasons, motivations, and pressures leading to them, we took a monumental leap into the unknown, for good or ill. And we began to discover the answer to the question that had haunted us from the first moment we contemplated leaving our families, "What will people say?"

What Did People Say?

One of the concerns that most often keeps us from acting as we would prefer to act is the question "what will people think?" Certainly for the woman who is contemplating giving up custody, this concern looms large. How will my friends react? My co-workers? My parents? My children? Will they care? Will they support me? Will they hate me? Will they ever speak to me again? Will society condemn me totally? Will I be able to stand it? *What will happen*?

If I were to sum up the responses I have received from other women, and to add my own experience, I would reply: you will be pleasantly surprised. Not immediately and not predictably, but it will go better than you think. And adding my own observations on others' responses, I would say: it depends in very large measure on you and your *own* perceptions of yourself. The days of the scarlet letter are gone; hellfire and brimstone are no longer the watchwords of mainline religions; public scorn and humiliation are no longer routine forms of punishment. Tolerance for, and acceptance of, individual choices and differences are goals for which we are taught to strive, and that has led to many changes in what most of us now find acceptable. Teachers are no longer fired for smoking; single people bear, or adopt, and raise children; alcoholics receive treatment; gay couples live and love openly together; priests marry.

The merits of individual freedom versus strict adherence to the prescribed dictates of society can be endlessly debated. To my mind, at least, such rigidity is destructive, unproductive, and causes untold damage to the general welfare. So I applaud the new acceptance of the individual, I rejoice in the blossoming of the non-traditional, and I support the new emphasis on self-realization and development. Perhaps that is why I insist that one's own perception of oneself is critical to others' perceptions of oneself. This is not a new thought; it is often called the "power of positive thinking." And it is essential to anyone, including a non-custodial mother seeking to live a non-traditional lifestyle.

But I am getting ahead of myself. We *do* care what people think. We want to be thought well of, to be admired, to be sought out by people we care about. These are basic and primary needs—and ones that have not been met in our marriages and/or in our mothering roles, when we decide to leave. That much we are sure of. What we are *not* sure of is how *other* people will react to a controversial course of action. We *hope* that those who have known us and accepted us as wives and mothers will continue to accept us in our new roles, but we have no way to know for sure whether that will happen:

Mostly I can say that the people who loved me were extremely supportive and always there for me. It's just that I didn't really know until the final hour who really loved me for what I was and as myself. Some of the people I thought really cared didn't support me, and some people I didn't or wasn't sure of were there through it all....

Books on divorce warn us that there will be changes in our social and familial relationships when we divorce. Some people will stand by, often those you least expect to do so. Others, again sometimes those you would least expect, will fall away. People's initial reactions may be temporary or they may be permanent; they *always* are complex. People respond to the actions of others according to their own needs and desires and subjective perceptions. This makes it difficult, if not impossible, to judge accurately the support and sustenance you can count on from any one person. I asked in my questionnaire, "Were you surprised by the reactions of the people around you?" The answer almost always was "yes," but for varying reasons:

- Yes, the friends who supported me. I didn't think I deserved it.
- The only reactions that surprised me were the ones that expressed that it was OK for a mother to leave her children. I was torn apart emotionally and expected *everyone* to hate and judge me, *no one* to understand. But most people were kind and supportive or matter of fact accepting. They still are, and it still surprises me sometimes.
- People were more supportive than I expected.
- Yes, a "churchy" married woman friend was quite supportive when I expected her condemnation. (She seemed envious)....
- Yes, when friends thought what I was doing was revolutionary, and defiant, and admired me more so. They were very supportive and gave me much encouragement. Many felt my move was daring and bold and aggressive.
- Yes, the people who were so insensitive that they thought it was easy to give up a child! They would say, "Oh, you're a real women's libber!"
- Yes, the clergy. I understand their views of women leaving the home but what amazed me was that they were so outwardly disapproving and unaccepting of me.
- Yes, my mother. I expected her to be more open. My father— I didn't expect he would. My kids—I thought by now (five years) I would have lost their love and respect. The world—I didn't expect so much hatred.

These comments, particularly the last, illustrate my point that people's reactions will be surprising and unpredictable. They will also be mixed; it was extremely rare to hear a woman say that the reactions were uniformly bad or uniformly good. The following comments are typical:

- I felt envy from some, to understanding from others, to definite criticism from one who thinks my kids need me badly. I tend to discount her view a bit, though, because I think it is heavily influenced by her personal experience.

- Good friends remained good friends. Some had trouble taking sides—him or me. Oddly enough he continued with the married circle, I did not.
- Many couples who had been our friends continued contact with my husband but not with me. On the other hand, individual friends, male and female, were very supportive of us both.
- Some people changed their opinions of me, mostly couple friends, a number of whom terminated our friendship since I had left a "good thing"—better than what they had.
- Two women friends, of whom I had been fond and whose children had been my boys' friends, broke off all communication with us. Both were well educated, stuck in housewifery and frustrated much of the time. I believe they felt directly challenged by my move and couldn't handle it. So I felt sorry about it, but wasn't really wounded. Some other women respected me more and were wonderful. My male friends were without exception supportive and seemed to treat me more as an equal.
- People admire my outlook and my taking responsibility for my life and for getting out (finally) of a situation that would never have gotten any better.

My respondents mentioned frequently, and were particularly sensitive to, the reactions of other women. Perhaps we felt that it was them we were deserting, them and their traditional roles and the beliefs and values they still held dear. Therefore it was especially rewarding to discover that other women not only supported but admired us; often they made us feel that, rather than abandoning them, we were in fact setting an example:

- I thought my colleagues would be more judgmental, particularly the mothers among them. Two or three of my women friends said they admired me, particularly in view of my age (46).
- Women kept saying to me, "I wish I had your nerve." That surprised me. They were actually jealous. I went and acted out their fantasies. I kept saying, "It doesn't mean it is right for you. Think about what you want."
- My women friends seemed awed by what they perceived as "courage" and have said to me, "You are incredibly brave."
- I had a good woman friend who was always supportive of me— did not approve, particularly, but was concerned for me.
- It was actually embarrassing to have other women raving about how "brave" and "courageous" I was. I didn't see myself that way at all, and coming from my expectations of scorn and rejection, it was astonishing and hard to adjust to. I will say that once I *did* adjust to it, it was helpful and very nice.

Our friends' surprisingly supportive reactions were not only heartening and comforting, but eased our adjustment to our new lifestyles. Our friends and colleagues helped us to discover new dimensions in ourselves and to depend on those new-found strengths as we grew. The following comments make this clear:

- I was really surprised at the acceptance I got from my co-workers. Even the older women whose whole lives revolve around their children and grandchildren treated me with kindness and sympathy and enormous understanding. I had really expected to be scorned as some heartless monster, but I felt none of that. They seemed concerned about how everything was going, asked after my children, but at no time did I feel they were condemning me, or even judging me at all. And believe me, I was on the lookout for it. It was very comforting. It made me feel I was accepted for myself and not for my role.
- I was absolutely amazed at the support and affirmation I got from many of my friends. I even got letters from some, congratulating me on my "courage" and expressing admiration for my strength in carrying out what I felt was right. There were *many* words of encouragement. They had a lot more faith in me than I had!
- It was such a surprise to me to have so many women drop their masks, so to speak, once I had in effect dropped mine. So many of them came to me with their fears and anxieties and dissatisfactions. It was as though I had opened a door to a place where they could really be themselves with me and not the wife-mother-clubwoman-volunteer we had all been so busy being for each other. They seemed to feel I was some sort of pioneer in self-actualization. And while they either could not or did not want to do anything so drastic, they could at least cheer me on. And they did cheer me on. It really gave me the strength to persevere when I lost heart and thought I couldn't possibly carry it off. They apparently saw much more in me than I saw in myself, and that helped me to discover myself more freely.

At the same time, my sample included women who felt they had received unremitting condemnation. There was so much sorrow and bitterness in their responses, so much loneliness and pain. They wrote as follows:

- Everyone's attitude towards me changed. Everyone said they couldn't believe I had done such a thing. They thought I was a "good mother." "Those poor babies, their mother left them"—things like that. Everyone seemed to think that I was the worst criminal on earth.
- I couldn't believe the reactions. I still can't believe the reactions. People really take the thought of a mother leaving her children at a gut level and personally. It's like I single-handedly tore down the fabric of the whole society. I still can't believe some of the things people said to me: "Well, you must not love your children." "Some women just aren't cut out to be mothers." "You shouldn't have had the kids." "Your children will never forgive you."
- All these people let me down when I needed them most. It caused me to become bitter and untrusting.
- Women were harder on me than men. Even those with bad marriages.
- Everyone scorned me, as if I were a criminal. How could I not feel scorned? I still get that reaction occasionally, but I've learned to ignore

it pretty much. People who feel that way generally aren't worth my time or energy. I have my own inner sense of worth now, so I don't care what other people think about me like I did at first.

- Most relationships established over a 16-year period went down the tubes. Very few people reached out to me then or acknowledge me to this day.
- Some churchwomen friends now have reason to criticize me, as they always saw me as insufficiently submerged for a Christian woman.
- Only one of my four closest friends stood by me. The other three have not spoken to me again.
- Everyone changed toward me. I never allowed anyone to see or hear about our unhappy life and when it was out in the open they were shocked that I had done such a thing. Since I moved out, everyone blamed me, so I was shunned by my family, friends, etc.
- The silence was the worst. No one wanted to hear my side or how I felt. People my husband and I had known would look away, if they saw me in the store, as though I didn't exist any more. It was as though I had quit existing to my family and friends when I quit being a wife and mother. Some said it, some implied it, but they all thought I was abnormal, a bad person, and best forgotten, except perhaps as an object lesson. And I was alone, more than I had ever been.

I was very much interested in the reasons for the diversity of experience. What made the difference in these reactions? Could it be that some people just have fewer decent friends and family than others? I asked the women why they felt they were experiencing such hostility and anger. One answer that came up fairly frequently was that we had rocked the boat, so to speak, made waves and upset the local equilibrium:

- Perhaps one of the things that prompted such totally negative initial responses to the divorce itself, as well as our "bizarre" arrangements, was that we were so...normal (her ellipsis).
- Although some people distanced themselves, I felt it was more because they felt threatened by my decisions than because they hated what I had done or disapproved of it.
- In everyone's opinion I had the perfect marriage, husband, and life. I had no right to be unhappy or discontent. As long as I did what everyone expected of me and never voiced an opinion, it was OK. But when I couldn't deal with my life as it was any more, everyone felt I was going off the deep end and couldn't possibly know what I was doing. In other words, I wasn't the person they thought I was or wanted me to be.
- I had shared my unhappiness in my marriage with a few close friends, but most people thought everything was fine and were shocked and disappointed with me. Also, most of our friends were church-goers and we were actively involved in the Christian community where divorce is totally unacceptable.
- They all thought of me as "sweet, quiet, and uncontroversial." But when all this happened it shocked some people. I liken it to the feeling some

people have about gays. It is a fear that we all have that we could be like that too, God forbid. It is easier to hate and condemn them than to try to understand something a little different.
- I did ask a couple of women to come and see me, but one didn't come because her husband objected. Their marriage isn't very happy and I think he was afraid that there was a risk she would do the same thing. I find that by and large men are more hostile than women. I think they are afraid the same thing could happen in their marriages and I would be responsible. And in fact I lived on a road where three other women have gone since I left, which may be a coincidence but it seems unlikely.

These women had clearly disturbed the comfortable and uncontroversial image of themselves held by those around them— held, one might point out, for others' *own* comfort and sense of stability and normality. When people's comfortable perceptions were disrupted, they reacted with surprise, chagrin, disbelief, and, since there was inevitably fear, with hostility. Change is very disturbing, and changes that require one to re-examine and re-evaluate one's own situation and constructs are especially disturbing. I found this to be a reasonable explanation, in part, for the hostility.

Another reason for hostility is jealousy. This is a fairly well-documented reaction to change and growth on the part of one member of a family, workplace or other context where people interact. You will recall that some of the foregoing answers included perceptions of envy and jealousy (for instance the woman who said she felt she was acting out other wives' fantasies). Others remarked on the same phenomenon:

- I think some of our friends were jealous of me because they didn't and don't have the guts to take a stand in their own behalf—especially females.
- I have found that people think I am selfish. I gave my daughter to her father because I felt she would have advantages with him that I could not give her. As a consequence of this, my life was made financially better. I find that those around me regard my happiness over my improved situation as a selfish attitude.
- I sensed a lot of envy in the reactions of friends. The ones who were the most horrified kept saying, "I could *never* do that, *never*." But they said it so vehemently that I began to realize that it was not because they didn't *want* to, just that they didn't have the nerve. And because I did, and because I was obviously better off, they hated me.
- Well, if they had agreed that I did the right thing, that would mean that it was OK. And that would mean that they could consider it too. And they didn't dare. So they rejected me so they would not have to admit that this was a possible option, not only for me but for them.
- I guess no one really likes to hang around with someone they envy. I was "free," and they were not, and they envied me, so they just dropped me.

While envy is a plausible explanation for negative reactions, I was still puzzled by the diversity of answers to this question, and I wanted to investigate other, subtler reasons for the bad experiences suffered by some of my respondents. Included in my questionnaire was a section in which the women were asked to complete statements like "I believe my own circle views me" with a check mark anywhere along a scale between "negatively," "indifferently," and "positively."

It was in tallying the answers to this section that I found my first clue. My respondents consistently checked the high side of the scale, near "positively," on lines that read, "I believe my own circle views me..." and "I believe my children view me..." and "I view myself...." But when asked to rate the reactions of society in general, they chose a lower point along the scale. (This was true of most respondents, including those who reported predominantly positive reactions.)

Why, I wondered, if their experiences with the people closest to them were positive, did they still feel they were viewed negatively by "society"? What did they perceive society to be? Why would some amorphous mass out there carry more weight than the real support and caring of their friends and families? Perhaps, I mused, I should have called this section "perceived" attitudes of others. And having shifted the focus from others' reactions to the women's perceptions, I found that a whole new light was shed on the subject. I re-examined the answers of those women who said they had been scorned, shunned, rejected, ignored. Had they really been? Or were they seeing their *own* negative perceptions of themselves projected onto those around them?

On closer inspection I found in the negative reports many phrases like "I thought," "it seemed to me that," "I just knew," "they didn't actually say so but..." Rarely did they have anything concrete to report. And I thought about those women who said that people's attitudes had, with time, become more positive. Had they really? Or was it the *women* who had changed? Consider these answers, first from those who felt they were badly treated. The italics are all mine, to emphasize my point:

- *I feel they were thinking* that I must be a terrible person because I left my child. *I don't know if anyone actually did....*
- People *sure look twice* when I say my children live with their father.
- I found that when acquaintances found I had children, but not with me, there was a *period of silence. Almost like they were thinking* "what did she do to lose her children?"
- Basically *I still feel* most people do not understand children not living with their mother(s). There is an *automatic stigma*. "What must be wrong with her so that her children can't or won't live with her? She must not be a very loving or dedicated person or mother.... She must be a drunk or a prostitute or something evil." *Most of this is unstated*. In a way, I wish I could have had more of a dialogue on the subject, even negative. Most people *seemed* to turn in the other direction unless I brought the subject up myself. And in that case *I heard myself* offering either an apology or, later, as I knew people better, a pathetically sad account of my sadness and longing for my children.

Moreover, these feelings of insecurity carry over into new situations, even ones that are meant to be supportive (italics again are mine):

- Most of the women in my group (for divorced women)…have custody of their children. *I feel very reluctant* to discuss my children because *I fear they will be judgmental* and I don't need that. *I especially fear their condemnation* for the fact that I am realizing my basic satisfaction with the situation. I am bitter.…
- Basically I've been surprised at the acceptance and non-judgment I have received from new acquaintances. But *I am always ashamed* to admit that I am a mother without custody.
- Some of the people at work were discussing another woman who gave up custody of her son. They were very understanding and were nodding and saying that she had probably thought it was better for them and that it was very brave of her to make that choice. I just sat there and listened. Somehow *I still felt* that they would not be so understanding of me *if they knew* I had done it too.

I looked at the answers of the women who had been apart from their children for a number of years, to discover whether the passage of time had had anything to do with improved attitudes, and I found that, indeed, it had:

- The *immediate* reactions of other people were more negative than positive. When they saw that I was still a loving mother, a committed parent to my children, the same person I had always been, the negativism receded rapidly.
- I would say that most people's attitude at the time of my separation was neutral. As time passed, however, people seemed to develop a new respect for me as I tried to go on with my life, develop a career, and discern what was in the best interests of the children despite the anger I had toward my spouse.…
- Reaction from others was something I feared and dreaded. Many friends expressed surprise at first, but later were supportive and expressed respect for my courage to do what I thought was best for my daughter.

Many of these women were able to articulate their own participation in imposing this stigma, and to put things into better perspective:

- I told people I was divorced, but was slow to disclose that I had children. I was defensive, tended to be a "loner." One male friend made me feel comfortable with it, so I gained courage to discuss. In time, as I gained new confidence and told more people, there was curiosity, but I lost no new friends. Some traditional family members remained at the Christmas card exchanging level. They were confused, I later found out—not knowing how to react, so did nothing. I expected to be confronted, I was defensive—and we both lost out!

- I think some acquaintances changed their opinions of me—they thought *surely* something must be *wrong* with me. Many friends backed off. However, I may have induced some of this behavior due to the *big* guilt trip I was on at that time.
- I think a lot of my being cut off from other people was my own fault. I tended to anticipate that they wouldn't want to see me.
- At first I felt totally rejected. After about six months I realized that everyone was treating me about the same as they always had. My mother, who had always had about as much faith in my common sense as she would have had in a half-witted six-year-old, was confirmed in that opinion (in her mind), and continued to treat me as such. My husband supported and resented me by turns. My children shrugged and said, "whatever you want, Ma." My friends really reacted according to prior closeness—close ones held me closer, peripheral ones nodded from the sidelines, co-workers maintained the same level of cordiality and expectation of performance. Only *I* had changed my view of myself, at first to something much less than anyone else saw and accepted. When I realized that, I was able to improve my self-image considerably. I could see that I had not become the pariah I had feared I would be.

No one can ever be fully prepared for divorce, and less so for arrangements as radical and unpopular as ours. And if *we* were not fully prepared, how could anyone else be? For us, it was not a question of right or wrong—either way *someone* had to leave and someone had to be hurt. Those who have never had to face—or never dared to face—that fact will always judge us negatively.

There were even those who were able to take the responses of their friends, positive *and* negative, and find comfort and peace in the truth that emerged:

> A situation like mine reduced things to skeletal simplicity. Half-hearted friends fell quickly by the wayside. People who had always found fault with me finally had perfect cause to hate me. Those who were true friends remained steadfastly loyal. In the end, there were only a few people standing by my side. The chaff blew away in the wind and truly my life is better now.

With several women I was able to explore in some depth this business of friends' reactions. We came to the realization that friends' reactions often had more to do with their own issues, and with what our actions forced *them* to deal with, than with what we had done. In other words, there were times when our friends *needed* to react negatively in order to preserve their own equilibrium. While I was writing this chapter I came upon an article written by Herbert Gold for *San Francisco* magazine, excerpted in *Newsday*. Mr. Gold has kindly given his permission to reprint it here:

> Let me tell you about the two friends whom I lost. One is a deeply sympathetic and loyal man, a man with a commitment to friendship, a gift for expressing it. I say this with no irony, although he abandoned me.

In the pain of a foundered marriage, I, like others in the same situation, became demanding, petty, childish, repetitive, weepy, with a reduced sparkle of blood to the brain, dulled by anxiety, sleeplessness, doubt, guilt, shame, loss—and I probably smelled sour besides.

Surely I was no fun, but I was in need.

Because of my friend's depth of responsiveness and our long feeling for each other, I laid my burden hard upon him, and he replied over the months with an outpouring of reassurance and companionship. Naturally, in my tactless state of confusion, I exhibited my worst qualities. Perhaps I even borrowed a few I don't normally have.

With each contraction of my stomach, I felt a response of contraction in my brain. I was giving birth to stupidity. His loyalty and—I'll use the word—love endured.

Yet as I struggled to survive, and seemed to be surviving, the idea came to his wife that I was an example to her husband. If I could do without a wife, so could he.

My friend's wife made abandoning this wicked creature a condition of their marriage, and since my friend is loyal, has a primary loyalty to his marriage (another of his virtues, I think), he could not merely cut me away for the sake of a greater tie. He had to see me as his wife saw me; he needed to cut me away willingly, with judgment. It would be a growth experience. How much closer it would bring him to his family. It would be Good. And so he did.

He wrote me a cold and dismissing letter, and, when I telephoned, his voice was cool and dismissing. For a long time I was hurt and angry. Now I am touched by his painful retreat, so necessary to him. He still has the gift of loyalty and friendship. It has limits, but not in patience, insight or generosity, which are the usual borders of friendship. The limits are those that his wife can bear, but, after all, a wife too is a friend.

The other friend I lost, a more banal case, is also more typical and modern. He's a psychiatrist, a longtime companion, a lover of food and theory and mutual flattery; a man adept and knowledgeable about trouble; a man who perhaps hides confused depths of feeling but has thick protective walls to keep out the stormy waters. He likes music. He likes to laugh and check out the action. He was fun to be with.

Perhaps because he is a psychiatrist and professionally interested in marriage, and we had often talked about the matter, I now asked his attention as I suddenly oozed spleen and real blood. I thought he might be entertained by my nosebleeds (usually in the morning after not sleeping). To my surprise, however, I noticed that our association was suspended. He wanted nothing of me. His voice on the phone was brisk and professional, as if I were a patient, not a friend. He was too busy. Sometime soon we must meet, but he wasn't sure when.

As time went on, a year, maybe two, I occasionally received messages from my psychiatrist friend. On his official stationery he noted very formally: "Just because we don't meet, don't think you are not in our minds. We think of you often...."

Despite the royal We, I realized he had his own troubles, and although he dealt professionally with suffering like mine and worse than mine, he was incapable of dealing with mine in a not-professional way. As a suffering friend I was more than he (or We) could bear, a menace to his comfort.[1]

I was particularly moved by the account of that failure of friendship. I, too, had had such a friend, of many years standing, who had shared my activities and problems and goals and heartaches. When her husband left her, shortly after I left my family, we became even closer, and for nearly a year depended on each other for our souls' comfort and our hearts' ease. She enjoyed my fullest confidences, which, she said, she treasured as jewels. But when I left for a week's vacation she became, as she put it, "lonely," and to assuage that loneliness she phoned—can you guess?—my former husband, who was of course more than happy to oblige her. And despite an agonizing year during which I tried to salvage our relationship, in the end she chose to turn away from me. And, like Herbert Gold's friend, she could not simply turn away, but chose instead to believe that we never *had* been friends, never *had* been dear to each other; I had simply, as she explained, "used" her as a worker, a side-kick, a foil, and now that she saw the light she could break away from my overbearing dominance and stop being my follower (she who then followed me in such spectacular fashion!). I grieve, naturally, not only for the loss of our friendship but for her self-deception and her loss of the memory of a relationship that had been, despite her protestations, special and rewarding. And I *knew* (and this is why I tell this particular story) that my loss of this friend was not due to my inadequacies but to her own deep need for the traditional, the ordinary, the known, wherever she could find it.

In the case of less intense relationships, I have come to the conclusion that most people couldn't care less what we are doing with our lives, as long as we don't upset theirs. This is unsettling, to say the least, but it nevertheless appears to be a fact. With the exception of family, what we do is a matter of great indifference to those around us, and it is in large measure only insofar as we interpret people's reactions through the prism of our fears that they wound us.

Observing this basic disinterest, I am infinitely relieved to know that no mob will come thundering to my door to pin a scarlet N-CM, for "non-custodial mother," to my bodice. On the other hand, I am more than a little bewildered to realize that people in whom I invested decades of my life, countless hours of my time, and huge doses of my energy seem able to let me fade out of their lives without a murmur. I feel a gratitude for, and yet a dis-ease about, this unconcern for my personal trauma. I feel ambivalent about these emotions. I wonder what it is that I expected, or want. Surely it is foolish to imagine that my former mother-in-law would wish me well, or keep in touch (though many do). Yet how is it possible that this major figure in my life has not a word to offer, of praise *or* blame? Does she miss seeing me? Is she thinking, "I knew it all the time?" Should I try to find out? Do I *want* to find out? And what are my former neighbors thinking? I disappear after 19 years; does anyone wonder how I am doing? Does anyone think of calling me to say my children are doing fine or that they are running wild? How about the minister of the church I attended faithfully for years, where I taught Sunday School and where my children were baptized and confirmed? Isn't he supposed to inquire after my absence? How can I have been so minor to people who were so major to me?

And is no one outraged for me? I am glad, most of the time, that my divorce was so "civilized." I am almost always content to have mutual acquaintances "not take sides," and to remain cordial to both of us, to be "modern" and "with it." But, oh, sometimes I do yearn for a partisan! For someone who *did* take sides—*my* side. I do not want to demand that of anyone, but sometimes I do imagine how lovely it would be to have such a champion. A "civilized" divorce can mean some very watered-down relationships with former friends, and unless the partners are on an extremely amicable basis there is, or was for me anyway, a sense of people "consorting with the enemy."

Part of my readjustment, reassessment, reordering involved coming to terms with this inescapable fact that I was, indeed, extremely expendable. I suspect this truth is brought home to everyone, at some time. The effect of accepting this fact was, for me, two-fold. It was, as I have said, extremely disconcerting to discover how little I seemed to be missed. On the other hand it is very helpful to realized that we are much less responsible for the psychic survival of those around us than we generally think. Rather like carrying one end of a heavy load and finding that when we let go, the other carrier strides on with hardly a misstep.

In this vein I cannot resist including an anecdote that caused great hilarity among my confidantes, and for me also, though not without some pain. My former husband called not too long ago to say that a political newsletter distributed in his neighborhood featured a story about the Long Island Fair. The article was, he said, illustrated with a picture of me, tasting cakes in my colonial garb. He offered to save it for me and indeed, the next time I had occasion to stop at his house, the newsletter was there, along with a merry note about my notoriety and exposure. I opened the article and saw, with disbelief and yet resignation, that this man with whom I had lived for 20 years, whose bed and table I had shared and whose children I had borne and nurtured, had saved for me a picture of somebody else.

Aside from that last vignette, however, an attitude of disinterest on the part of others was extremely welcome. For instance, I was deeply grateful to my colleagues at work for exactly that stance of unconcern. I can't believe that I didn't figure in some coffee-break discussions here and there. But when I was present it was as though having one of their colleagues up and leave her husband and children and move in with another of their colleagues was a most ordinary event, of mild interest perhaps, but basically ho-hum. Since my job was the *only* thing in my life that remained relatively constant, their unquestioning acceptance allowed me a breathing space, an oasis of sorts, in my new and uncharted desert. They seemed interested but not prying, helpful but not intrusive, patient with my silences, responsive when I talked, and blind to the colossal stupidity I displayed during some of my darker periods. I count myself extremely fortunate to have fallen in with such a delightful bunch; they were, and still are, essential to my adjustment.

Another set of friends that kept me afloat were the board members of the New York State Division of the American Association of University Women. I was, at the time of all this turmoil, president of the division, and I announced the news to them in one of my regular newsletters. I had visions of a hasty meeting called to drum me out of office. Instead, they called and wrote with messages of support and affection. They also staggered with great good will through one of the worst-run board meetings in the history of the division, a three-day session I chaired (or tried to) about a month after I left my home. They acted as though things were going normally and continued to deal and communicate with me in the accustomed manner. That made me feel loved, and forgiven.

I know that many of my respondents and readers would attribute all this unconcern and disinterest to scorn and rejection. But when I do see some of the people from my "past," they are uniformly cordial and friendly and open, and I have to conclude that far from spending their time and energies contemplating my sins, they are busy getting on with their own lives. It is when we interpret that silence and benign disinterest as condemnation and rejection that we run into trouble. It is easy to imagine ourselves scorned and rejected; but more often than not it *is* imagined. To give an example, when I left, I *imagined* that the mothers of the girls in my 4-H club would, horrified, snatch their daughters from my evil clutches, and I nearly quit before that could happen. But I loved those girls, so I didn't quit, and the club continued in very much the same way that it always had, for another two years. I *imagined* that I would be asked to resign my AAUW position, and in fact I canvassed some of the members as to whether they thought I should resign. They didn't, so I didn't, and no one seemed uneasy during the time I served as president. When I was appointed to a state commission I was "investigated" and asked whether there was anything in my background that would "embarrass the governor." When I left my home, I *imagined* that that would indeed embarrass the governor; instead I was reappointed. I was also asked to move up to the position of Superintendent of Needlework at the Long Island Fair.

These were all very positive experiences. Nevertheless, I still spent a great deal of time wondering what people were *really* thinking of me. When I finally allowed myself to be guided by what they were actually *doing*, which was accepting me, I was able to get past my burdensome, unrealistic assumptions of condemnation. Do not mistake me: my glasses are not completely rose-colored and I do not dismiss all possibility of *real* condemnation, because that does happen, sadly enough. However, in reviewing my responses, talking with my survey participants, and analyzing my own case, it does not happen with nearly the intensity nor the frequency we fear, and thus imagine.

I believe, too, that we must guard against finding veiled criticism and approbation in people's casual remarks and conversation. Let me give an example: I was invited, by a women I know only slightly, to appear on a local radio show to discuss my situation and my book. She listened with interest to my suggestions for the show and the information I wanted to cover, obviously understood and sympathized with my position, and was willing to lend her show as my platform. The night of the show I arrived early. We chatted casually and I asked if she was still teaching at the local university. "Oh, yes," she replied, "but just for this semester. It takes me away from the children two nights a week, and with homework and sports and all, I find I have to spend more time with them, you know. They love to tell me all about their day at school...." She went on in that vein for several minutes. My heart was sinking fast. *I* had opted *not* to do that for *my* children. But it was quite plain that she saw no connection. She was simply answering my question with her own story oblivious to how it compared to mine, and in fact was astonished when I drew the connection myself.

My point is that it is easy to read criticism and chastisement into the most innocent of remarks and to torment ourselves accordingly, to consider ourselves judged and found wanting, and thus to suffer needlessly. For to whom do we give the power to judge us? The *right* to judge us? And what weight do we assign to each of those judges? We, after all, are the only ones with *all* the facts; "outsiders" can only have some of the facts, and so any conclusion they reach must necessarily be flawed. Their reactions, as we have seen in the comments above, also depend in large measure on their own circumstances and are colored by their own needs, desires, secret fantasies, and ideal selves. Thus there are women who see us as heroines, as courageous, pioneering, and "at the cutting edge of social change," as one audience member said to me after a talk. That, I believe, is too lofty an image. We have not set out to be tomorrow's leaders. We have simply done what seemed right. And at the same time, because we have done what seemed right, we cannot (or should not) accept any image of ourselves as selfish or uncaring or cruel, when we know we are not. There will naturally be, as there always is, an entire spectrum of opinion and reaction. It behooves us to focus on the positive responses, which are invariably there, rather than on the negative ones, which just as invariably are there, clamoring for our attention.

So our own attitudes will carry the day. If we are positive about ourselves, others will reflect that acceptance. If we are negative and self-punishing, we are likely to see rejection in the eyes and hearts of those around us, whether or not it is truly there. One must get over the feeling of "poor me, life has treated me so badly." My sister helped me with this immeasurably. I was mooching around, sad sack, sending out thought messages like "I'm not so bad, don't be mad, please feel sorry for me, I feel so sorry for myself"—looking for justification. *She* asked, "are you happier?" I was, infinitely. "So *act* like it," she said. "Let people see that *you* think you did the right thing. Most of them will *see* that you're happier, and be glad for you. If *you* send out signals of doubt and woe, they'll wonder why you did it, and be confused, and find it hard to support you. But if you're obviously glad, how can anyone else judge that you're *not*?" I tried to follow her advice, and it works.

There is, however, another group to be dealt with and that is "the relatives." I do not refer here to husband and children but rather to the extended family—parents, grandparents, sisters and brothers, aunts and uncles, cousins, all those to whom we are close and connected, and who suffer to varying degrees when we disrupt the family configuration. As I have pointed out, friends, neighbors, and co-workers are more often than not unexpectedly supportive and generous. With our family, however, it is sometimes another story.

The reactions of parents—our mothers, particularly—are often the most vehement of all. It is not really hard to understand why this is so; conversely, it is most difficult to *accept* that it is so. We want our mothers to be eternally loving, accepting, loyal, proud, steadfast—all the things the *myth* tells us they should be. The fact that we ourselves are *rebelling* against that myth does not always change our own expectations of our mothers. Of course it is as unrealistic to expect our mothers to live the myth as it is for us to be expected to do so. They wanted us to be good children, to "behave," to do them credit, to make them proud. And the daughter who leaves her children does *not* fill that bill. They also love their grandchildren. The prospect of having those grandchildren in the custody of a son-in-law who may or may not feel a sense of loyalty to them, who may or may not feel any obligation or inclination to keep up a relationship with them, is terrifying.

And parents do not mince words. Not for them the offish glance, the strained silence. There is never much doubt as to where they stand. It was their parents' reactions that caused the most pain to the mothers I surveyed. Apparently our feelings that we had disappointed our parents were just as violent and wounding as any feelings we had in relation to our children.

Nancy Friday has written at length of the relationship of mothers and daughters in her book *My Mother, Myself*. (I have often wondered how that book might have differed if Ms. Friday had had a daughter of her own.) Other authors have approached the subject from other angles, and reached varying conclusions. There are just now beginning to be books on father/daughter relationships. I believe that only the woman who has been a mother, and experienced the mother/daughter relationship in all its fury and pain and surprise and dismay, can truly speak of the relationship between herself and her mother. There is nothing like leaving one's husband *and children* to test the mettle and fiber of one's own mother bond, as those of us who have done so can attest.

There were many responses dealing with harsh and unyielding animosity from mothers and fathers:

- My mother said she would never forgive or understand my leaving. My stepfather said I was a whore.
- My own mother and mother-in-law (and several other relatives on both sides) felt that this move I had instigated was an insult to motherhood, felt I was a disgrace. And I believe they had a lower opinion of me as a woman and a mother.

- My parents and I no longer speak and have no contact whatsoever as a result of my decision of 15 months ago.
- My mother was ferociously upset. She is still not speaking to me after eight months. She has always tried to rule me by guilt and fear—fear that she would withdraw her love, which is what she is doing now. I have always responded to that and toed the mark, but not this time. Even if it never happens.
- Even my mother was reluctant to help me because she though it would be taken as an endorsement of "what I was doing." When I started to cry, she loaned me money for an apartment.
- My mother accused me of "giving up" my daughter. There's been an underlying hostility for four years now, since the divorce.

Sometimes we were so desperate that we went to them anyway, even in the face of that hostility, and found that they *were* there, difficult as it was for them:

Stayed with my mother for a month and got my own apartment after that. Living with her was one of the worst ordeals I went through. I think she resented what I did as far as the children. Families mean well; friends are more objective. Families are too close and can't really help effectively.

That last quote hints at the understanding that begins to develop over time, as we get things into better perspective and emerge from our cocoons of hurt and fear. Sometimes we can even begin to see our roles in the creation of the breach:

- Did not let my parents know until after I moved away. I was ashamed, and fearful of criticism. Looking back, I wish I had confided in them. They would have been supportive and may have suggested alternatives to leaving my child.... I feel I've disappointed or failed them by giving up custody of my child.
- I was never willing or able to tell my parents that my husband beat me, or that he was unfaithful, or that he always spent 10 or 15 percent more than he made, until I left and they didn't know why. My father told me he wouldn't subsidize my poor choice of husbands shortly after I left my husband.... Although he was a wealthy man, I did not want to ask his help ever, after that. Now that he is dead I am sorry about the whole thing, but I'm still not sure what could have been different.
- I told my parents I had gone to live with a female co-worker, not that I had gone to live with my male friend, later my husband, about whom I had never told them. I regret very much now that I have lost a lot of the intimacy I had with my mother because I deceived her in this way. She gives $8,000 to each of my children for their education, so I am "protecting" the grant with my lies.

We begin to understand, as we did with our friends, the part that our parents' personal needs and anxieties played in their acceptance or rejection:

- I was horrified when I saw that my very own parents were practically throwing themselves into my husband's arms—calling him up, asking him to dinner, dropping in on him, spending the night when they were in town—and having nothing at all to do with me. I came to understand that a lot of that was due to their terror about losing track of the grandchildren and really had very little to do with either him *or* me; but it took me years to realize that. When it was happening it damn near killed me.
- I was treated like a child by Mom. She stated, "how can you not see your children grow? What did I do wrong" Now the world is different. I'm an adult and a mother. Let her put herself through these questions. I'll not allow her to continue scolding me.

We realize that they, too, come with a certain set of prejudices, background, and conditioning, and we can accept that:

My mother said, "Don't you know that first comes your husband, then your children, and *then* you?" But I can understand her feelings. She's been married to my father for 35 years and still loves him dearly. She has no basis to understand.... She has just lived her whole life differently than I choose to live mine.

They learned to understand us:

- The remark "when things go wrong you can always go home" has a new meaning for me—a joke! If it hadn't been for my twin sister's support and, most of all, listening, I don't know what I would have done. The greatest source of my unhappiness during my separation from my children was the neglect and open hostility from my mother and father. Thank heaven, they are more understanding now. They know that the reason I left my children with my husband was truly for their own good. At first they thought I didn't love my children, but now after almost three years they know I did what I did because I *do love* my children.
- Telling my parents, especially my father, of my decision to leave my marriage and to leave the children with their father was the most difficult task for me to face. Everyone was shocked (including my husband!) except for a few close friends. But both families were supportive once the initial shock passed.

I have mentioned that my own mother signed her first letter to me after my departure "sickened and shamed." She further stormed that I was weak, easily led, willing to fall for any hare-brained scheme that came down the pike (a reference to my support of the Equal Rights Amendment), that she had known all along I would "do something like this." She claimed that my "poor husband," who had "never objected" to my activities but had "let" me do "whatever I pleased" had done "all the work" while I "lay around complaining about the oppression of women." With the passing of the years I've decided that those words were written in the first heat of shock and dismay and outrage. But at the time that letter came as close to destroying me as anything that has happened before or since. I was paralyzed by its venom, staggered by its intensity, aghast at its injustice, seared by its white-hot fury. When I wrote to tell her about leaving I had asked that she not answer right away. So when she *did* answer promptly, I felt sure she was writing to give me cheer and comfort. Indeed, my former husband had predicted that they would invite me to their Florida home for rest and relaxation and to "think it over." I did not go so far as to imagine that, but I did hope for some indication that they still cared for me and that my entire life had not been a wasted effort to gain their approval and affection. I interpreted that first letter as a sign that my life had, indeed, been spent in vain, that making choices that would please them, denying choices that would hurt them, living as I thought they wanted rather than as I would have preferred, had been to no avail, had bought me no coin; in the end they "always knew" I would be a disappointment to them sooner or later.

All this was difficult business, and for a long time I did not expect to recover from the hammer blows. But time worked its magic for me; time and no small effort on all our parts.

After that first letter I fired off one of my own, which I meant to be reasonable and rational (my brother informed me that it was not). After several weeks my mother wrote to say that she was "unhappy about the estrangement," and that while she would "never understand or accept" what I had done, she would welcome some contact. These terms were not particularly acceptable to me; but after several more weeks I replied, saying in effect that perhaps we each had said more than we intended and had read into each other's letter more than was there. My parents returned north for the summer and stayed with my husband on their way; I did not know they were in town. Two more months passed and my mother's birthday came. I drove out, terrified, to see her. I met my father first and to my astonishment threw myself into his arms, something I am sure I had not done since I was about six years old. He was probably as surprised as I, but he is a taciturn man and said, as usual, something quite noncommittal. It was a strained afternoon, but we got through it; the following month, when my sister was also visiting, it went more smoothly.

My parents then returned to their winter home in Florida. Letters began to arrive, laced with little (and not so little) barbs. Reading them was rather like walking through a mine field; one never knew when, or whether, they might explode. Finally I wrote to say "Enough; let me be or let me go." The letters then became less judgmental, more cordial. While it was three and a half years before they visited my new home, and another two years before they came again, I continued to visit them often when they were nearby in their summer home, and lately they have returned those visits. We have been steadily regaining our former closeness, and the rift is almost completely mended. For me and for many others, then, it has been possible to repair relationships even after horrendous rifts, given a willingness of all parties to make the attempt.

There *are* those lucky ones, however, who find from the start that the bond is firm, the tie holds true. They made these comments:

- My mother didn't say much, but sympathized with the pain I was undergoing and always made me feel that she loved me just the way I was.
- My mother was wonderful and helped me tremendously with physical and mental support. Of course she sent me (or tried to) to every support group she could locate. If I could do it over, I'd have stayed with my parents and kept the children. Hindsight is wonderful, so sayeth my mother.
- My parents told me when I married that I would outgrow him. Unfortunately, that proved accurate. Despite their inner anxiety that I left the children, they backed me *all* the way.

This support, I must add, was not always expected, nor predicted; until you do something you never know for sure what the reactions will be:

My parents and family continue to be very supportive and accepting of my decision to leave. I expected recrimination from them, and there was none. In fact, since the divorce and their response to it, I have felt a new sense of companionship and respect with and for my parents—as though for the first time since becoming an adult I realize how non-judgmental they really are. My relationship to my parents has been one of the best side-effects of the divorce.

And imagine having so supportive and non-judgmental a mother as this woman from Illinois, who says:

Sometimes I feel like my heart is split in two and I'm bleeding and it will never heal. My mother tells me to "lie down and bleed a while and then rise and fight again." That really helps me. She loves me, cares, and understands, and I know it.

In fairness I must add this chilling comment from a New Jersey women for whom no reconciliation is possible:

My father did not speak to me *ever again*. He lived another three years and refused to even answer my letters.

With research of this sort there are always a few "truth is stranger than fiction" stories, like this one from London describing the most unusual mother/daughter relationship I encountered:

My mother lived with my brother, and after my brother died, she moved in with me. This was before I left. Well, my mother and I can get along quite well from a distance, but we can't stand too long in each other's company. So here I had my mother, who was very depressed; she was very close to my brother, she doted on him, and I doubt she will ever get over his death. His widow had bought a house round the corner, so *she* was there with her three children, and I was just swamped. Here I'd got all these people, and I couldn't cope at all. Anyway, we got over all that, and I told my mother I was moving out, and we had this dreadful row. I think she was concerned that I was throwing everything away; but anyway I went and she is still with my husband. This situation was quite unusual, I do admit, but actually he got on with her better than I do. But that, too, has been very difficult because she has been ill, and it is awkward for me to go see her at his home. So we, my mother and I, have just decided to get a flat together. I think I am able to live with her now. I think once we had this row, and I told her exactly how I felt, we've got on much better. In fact she's more supportive now. She's very loyal to my husband, but she said quite calmly the other day that she could quite understand why I'd left him. But it was, as I said, a quite unusual situation, and when I left there was the feeling that I had not only left my husband and children but my own mother as well.

Inquiring about family members other than parents, I learned that, for the most part, brothers and sisters get high marks. Typical are these comments:

- My siblings were also glad that I had left my husband. They had all known there were problems and gave me enormous amounts of emotional and financial support.
- My brothers were wonderful. They helped a lot.
- My two sisters, who may not have agreed with the wisdom of my decision, were always there.
- Most helpful for me was my sister's unmitigated support. I expected her to be judgmental, since she herself had lost her husband to "another woman." I expected her to tell me how much I was hurting everyone. Instead she told everyone that I was "a big girl now," and certainly had good reasons for the decisions I was making. She told me she was "proud" of me for what evidently took "courage." It was hard to believe, hearing it.

That was my experience, too. My sister was unbelievably supportive, and I discovered in her a dear and treasured friend. She called, she wrote, and she constantly encouraged me *not* to feel guilty, to feel free to be happy even if that appeared "unseemly," to be confident that my children *would* still love me, still stick by me, would be all right. She had been through some very rough times herself with an abusive and alcoholic husband, and I felt that her optimism was born of experience and a hard-won ability to accept and affirm and move on. She had always had an absolutely uncanny knack for phoning at exactly the right time and saying exactly the right thing, and she certainly outdid herself in this situation. It is sometimes a bit disconcerting to have her so much wiser and surer than I (she is two years younger) but I can say without reservation that I never would have made it through without her cheerful acceptance and unfailing optimism.

Other family members, *as* family, were not often mentioned in the survey responses. The few exceptions included examples both of support and of condemnation:

- My in-laws attacked me for wanting a divorce, inferred it was because I wanted to "have a career" and was therefore a bad mother and deserved to have my husband take the children. Previously I had "hung the moon." In actuality the separation was precipitated by my husband's adultery and physical abuse—which my mother-in-law knew about, but she thought I should still be grateful to be married to a college professor.... So what if he beats you up once in a while?
- Family members (my side) expressed total disgust that I could do such a thing. Others stopped talking to me. One aunt, who I was very close with, told me over the phone (she didn't want to see me) that I had no right to call myself a mother, and hasn't spoken to me since.
- Your list of people doesn't include aunts and uncles, cousins, etc. They were mostly *horrified*!!!
- Everyone understood and supported me, emotionally. I am still very close with his parents.

With this group, as with all the others, time made the difference:

In the beginning it was "murder" having to run into former relatives and neighbors, and ex-husband. I am not entirely comfortable doing that yet, but the improvement is amazing.

On the subject of former husbands, just these two comments for now:

- I think my husband's opinion of me changed in that he respected me more because he never thought I would actually leave....
- My mother-in-law told my daughter, aged five, that I didn't love her any more. Amazingly my husband stood up for me and gave her hell.

To give due credit, I must say that in my own case what got me through the first, terrible days of living with my parents' reaction were my former husband's horrified assurances that my mother's accusations were indeed cruelly unjust.

"Peripheral" people were also drawn into the picture; this letter from England is an especially interesting example:

- I listened with interest to the Woman's Hour feature today and I felt I would like to share my situation. Since she was seven I have been looking after a young girl whose mother found that she could not manage her two children after the end of her marriage. I was friends with, subsequently lived with, and am now apart from the father. Kay is now 16 and will be leaving school this summer. She is well adjusted to the situation and it was her choice to stay with me after her father left. He pays for her keep, but she is, however, a difficult girl, become more so when she is caught in family crossfire. Her father accepts the situation with ease but Kay's mother and grandparents on both sides cannot accept the situation and upset and hurt Kay deeply by their dislike of me. I think that the feeling of dislike is misplaced guilt for the fact that I am still mothering Kay but have no family connection with her at all.

New partners as step-parents played a very important role, for good or ill:

- I wouldn't have been able to endure the first years if Peter hadn't been so patient, caring, helpful, loving and supportive. He turned out to be far more gorgeous than I'd realized and I'm very grateful and thankful to him. It's because I insisted on staying in this country with my sons that Peter didn't accept a job in America. He knew I wouldn't have accompanied him. Perhaps the best compliment Peter could have paid me came when he told someone that one of the reasons he loved me originally was because I was such a good mother. When most of the world thinks I'm a bad and wicked mother, that was the most valued praise I've ever received.

- It is not easy, when the world stands in judgment of you, to avoid anger and guilt. I have always believed that I made the right decision, but I feel guilty, thus angry. My present husband will not allow me to tell his parents about my children (we live in different states so they are not prominent in my life) because they would think I'm a bad person. This present marriage is ten years old, my children grown. I feel my husband believes, in spite of all he's been told, that my children were taken from me. This is one of the largest problems I have encountered in my marriage. My husband tried but he does not like my children. We meet at my father's every summer and talk day and night. There is little we don't share. We missed a lot when they were young and we make up for it now. I've imagined how it would have turned out if I had stayed in the marriage or if I had custody. And though it is tempting to believe those choices would have worked, I honestly believe I did the right thing.

And there was this wonderful letter from a step-mother to Ann Landers (would that we could all be this lucky!):

Dear Ann:

My husband and I have been married four years. We have one child, six weeks old. Several months ago we received a phone call from my husband's ex-wife. She asked if we would take full custody of their three children. We were thrilled. It was something we were hoping would happen for a long time.

Everyone is happy about this change. The children's grades have gone from Ds to Bs. The presence of these youngsters in our house has strengthened our marriage. The ex-wife looks so much calmer when she comes to see the kids.

The problem: Our friends and relatives insist on making thoughtless and unkind remarks about the arrangement. They say such things as, "No mother of decent character would give her kids away," and "She must be very selfish to have done that— probably wanted to be free so she could run around."

I think it was a marvelously courageous and unselfish thing for that woman to have done. She loves those children very much, but she put their interest first. I admire her a lot and wish the busybodies would keep their mean-spirited comments to themselves.

The reactions, then, can best be summed up as mixed but encouraging. We can generalize about family members' reactions much as we did about those of friends, both as to the role played by our self-perceptions and to what part *their* inner selves contributed to the overall interaction. As was the case with friends, the reactions of family members originate, mainly, out of their own experiences and their own needs. My mother's initial reaction came, I believe, out of her need to see herself as a mother who had brought up, and still enjoyed the attentions and obedience of, a completely normal, conventional and acceptable, modestly but not excessively accomplished daughter. Since I was obviously no longer that daughter, she was no longer that mother. Perhaps her reappraisal of self was as difficult as mine. I know that it required a great many "it's no fault of mine, I agree that she's terrible" conversations with, among others, my former mother-in-law. This was very difficult for me to accept, in part due to my own lingering illusions about the ever-loyal Madonna, a role my mother has said many times she has never been able to live up to, and one against which I was myself rebelling. I needed certain things from her that she was not able to give me because of her *own* coping strategies.

I also believe that the defection of my "best friend" was due to her overwhelming need to cling to the traditional, the known, the expected, and to recreate for herself that sort of relationship however she could, even at the expense of what she once viewed as an important and cherished friendship. Her needs collided with mine, irreconcilably. But they were no less important, nor any less deniable.

If we are part of an integrated whole—part of the jigsaw puzzle, as it were— there is a certain alignment of all parts that is familiar and comfortable. When we drastically disrupt the alignment, we cannot expect the whole configuration to shift effortlessly to accommodate our new stance. Some parts will fit easily and more comfortably. Others will do so only with time and patience. Still other will no longer fit at all. Certainly there will be pain, or at best discomfort, as the parts jostle and adjust. Some women, perhaps most, aware of the disruption that their movement will bring to the structure as a whole, and trained to put everyone else first, choose not to move at all, to remain as before, though their own discomfort is acute. Some choose to drop out altogether and let the remaining parts realign without them.

It seems to me that we who have precipitated, or are perceived as having precipitated, such an upheaval, and who want to remain a part of the new order, have a responsibility to make a great effort to maintain ties with all of the parts as they realign, and to place as little blame as possible on those who simply cannot accommodate us. Most of all, we must not blame ourselves for others' failure to accept our changes. To have remained in spaces that had come to fit us so poorly simply to avoid disturbing the other parts would have been pointless and unproductive. We would *not* have been weightbearing, contributing parts of the whole but simply hangers-on, draining the energies of the group and generating none of our own.

So let us not be too hard on any of the components of that grand and ever-shifting puzzle, especially not ourselves. Let us try to appreciate the efforts of others, minute as they may seem at first, and to forgive the inabilities of others. Let us not give up on those others too soon, but let us *not* waiver, either, in our determination to retain the control of our lives that we have so dearly bought.

How Did You Feel
When You Left?

I began to develop a picture of the non-custodial mother—who we were, why and how we did what we did, and what reactions we encountered from those around us. Next, I sought to discover what our *own* reactions were. How did *we* feel about our situations, and particularly about ourselves?

In some cultures children are purposefully *not* raised by their biological mothers; in fact this insular relationship is considered detrimental to the development of the offspring, and determined efforts are made to reallocate child care and nurturing. Children grow and thrive in those cultures, just as they often do here in adoptive homes, with grandparents or other relatives, in boarding schools, in day care, and in any number of care-providing institutions that are not centered on biological mothers. Unfortunately, this fact is of small comfort to those of us, mothers *and* children, whose culture holds that, barring truly extraordinary circumstances, the child and the mother should be locked into a 24-hour-a-day symbiosis. No psychologist or therapist or even casual observer would, I feel certain, attempt to support this belief with actual cases. In fact, recent studies are beginning to show the opposite. Still, the myth persists; the traditional way is "the way it's supposed to be." Those of us who have decided against the conventional wisdom on childrearing are left with intense negative feelings that must be dealt with before we can begin to function again in positive and productive ways.

A major section of the questionnaire concerned the feelings experienced at the beginning of our separations and then after some time had passed. I devised a numerical scoring system by which women could indicate, on a scale of one to ten, the intensity of various emotions felt during the first three months away from their families, and then at the present. (A score of one was low, while ten was high.) But as the questionnaires arrived I quickly began to realize that my fond desires to quantify my results would not be realized. I had imagined that I would be able to statistically report that, for example, guilt was at first a high ten for 97 percent of the respondents and had dropped to an average 3.5 at the time of their response. I quickly saw that such neat precision was not to be. The words I had used to describe those feelings were interpreted differently. The "scoring" was erratic and often the respondent refused to even attempt it. The time periods were too diverse to compare. Some patterns, however, did emerge. The following pages represent my struggle to understand the intensity of feeling and the diversity of circumstances and experiences among the women who wrote and spoke to me.

Probably the first feeling that one suspects a woman who leaves her children might feel is *guilt*. And guilt there was, in abundance. My dictionary defines guilt as "grave culpability, as for some conscious violation of moral or penal law, either by positive act or neglect of known duty; responsibility for heinous fault."[2] Heavy stuff, that. It is no wonder that guilt weighs so heavily, since we feel we have committed a serious "violation of moral law" by "positive act" *and* "neglect of known duty." Until we are able to confront those feelings, our guilt and sense of shame is a monstrous burden:

- This guilt is *very* hard to shake in social situations, no matter how convinced I feel, intellectually, that it is not right that I should feel it. It still sticks in my throat when I have to relate what I've done.
- I felt a tremendous amount of guilt for leaving my children. Sometimes I felt like I left them at the side of the road instead of with their Dad.
- Lots of guilt. I'm the only one in my family or former circle of friends to get a divorce. In this WASP Bible Belt it is still not a proper thing to do.
- Should I have stayed because of the children? Am I selfish in putting myself before their needs? These are still very real questions for me.
- I felt at first the break-up was my fault—I could have been a "good little wife" and stayed with it. I felt guilty because "only a bad mother" wouldn't have her kids. Now I have guilt because I could have done the whole thing in a better way.
- I think probably I just never *will* get over the guilt. I think the best I can do is to try to live with it.
- I was so *ashamed* of this colossal failure. I had never really failed at anything and here I was dealing with *total* failure, just this great bottomless *pit* of failure. I was sure I would never hold my head up again.
- Oh, guilt. Well, I feel *buried* in guilt sometimes. Worse, it is self-imposed. No one is on at me about what I did, everyone seems perfectly content. So why I continue to torment myself I don't know. Need for punishment, I guess, under the old rules.

Note again the self-inflicted wounds described in that last quote. We were terribly hard on ourselves, harder than we needed to be. We had trouble internalizing our actions; we couldn't believe, or accept, our new identities.

- I repeat, I don't really feel I've left the kids in the usual sense. I sometimes read of other mothers who leave their children and think to myself "but how could they do that?" and then realize, with a shock, "I'm one of those mothers, too."
- This sort of thing is supposed to happen to other people, not to me.
- I believed in the Cinderella myth—I'll get married and live happily ever after. I was shocked to think of myself as divorced.

100

Sometimes our guilt came from an entirely unexpected source; some of us *didn't* feel guilty, or at least not as guilty as we "should" have, and we felt guilty about *that*:

- Other than societal pressures, which are monumental, what bothered me most was just how much I loved being without the children.
- I expected to be weeping and crying all the time, and I was really very revolted by myself when I saw how much I liked being alone.

Custodial mothers engage in constant efforts to "get away from the kids," and we understand that need and sympathize with it. But we don't expect them to *succeed* in any real sense, and when *we* are the ones to do it, we feel confused and dismayed at our own mixed emotions:

My sister used to send her kids away for the summer to camp, and she used to tell me how guilty she felt over the way she could just forget all about them while they were gone. She felt, she said, like a "monster" and now I know what she meant. My kids are OK where they are and I seem abnormally, and awfully, glad. It makes me feel terrible about myself.

There were large doses of pain, and grief, and despair; loneliness, and longing. It was difficult to read and hear the words of sorrow and anguish, but it was important, I felt, to know that this pain and grief were universal; even those women who were the most relieved to be living apart from their children still felt pain at the separation. One of them quoted a line from W.H. Auden's *Age of Anxiety*:

Sob, heavy world, sob as you spin,
Mantled in mist, remote from the happy.[1]

Most of us felt very, very, "remote from the happy":

- I felt like a dog that no one wanted to have around. A stray dog with no home.
- Whenever I see a child her age (four) or when I'm alone, when I try to sleep, see a kid's special on TV, or baking—I miss her laughter, her genuine love, her sensitivity. Her smile.
- I really felt very much alone. I was making a decision that no one agreed with but I believed was a decision of survival. My friend gave me the only support I got. During the divorce my lawyer thought I was out of my mind.
- The loneliness was the *ultimate*. In some ways I enjoy the time alone, but the utter pain of loneliness was incredible. It can be an actual physical pain, you know. Now, I feel loneliness for my kids and wonder how they are getting on. I care so much, but it seems I have to curb that feeling.

I am so detached from them and their lives. That type of loneliness still hurts—a lot.

- I still believe it takes a far greater love to give up a child, or children, than to keep them to oneself out of selfishness, like an object or belonging. But how could anyone understand—truly understand—the pain and grief (near that felt at the death of a loved one). The loneliness. A void so deep and at the same time as close as another child's laughter or tears.
- If I had known what the pain would be like, I would not have done it. I would have stayed and died.

I challenged the tall, elegant, reserved mother of two teen-aged boys who made this last statement. She had left her family nine months earlier and she repeated that she would, indeed, have chosen "death" over the pain she had felt since she had left. "I do not know whether I mean an emotional death, or a physical one, or a spiritual one," she said, "but I know that I would have died had I stayed." I asked her to describe the pain she was now feeling. "It is not a physical pain," she told me. "It is a pain that comes from a symbiosis. When my child hurts, I hurt, and I see he is hurting. And of course it is so much the worse knowing I am the cause of the pain."

Most of us can identify with that kind of pain. Such pain *can* express itself physically, and is described in very physical terms by many non-custodial mothers. A particularly graphic account was written by an English woman for the newsletter of the British organization for absentee mothers, MATCH:

At first when I thought of either of the two children (a boy of six and a girl of three and a half), I felt an enormous painful space or gap in my body around my womb. I would liken this sensation to both a labor contraction and to my gut reaction of rejection by my husband after a really bitter row— only much worse. After this feeling, or maybe at the same time, I would cry, and as the worst of the pain passed the crying was a great relief. I would cry anywhere, on the train or walking down the street, not caring who saw me. The tears were very healing. Each time I could sense I was just a tiny bit nearer to accepting my new self, a single person without husband or children. I listened to a lot of classical music, which also triggered gentle tears but not the agonizing lost feeling in my gut. Sundays were particularly hard to cope with, only to be expected as this day was not structured by essential work, which made more energy available for mourning.

Two months after my decision I went to stay for the weekend with my mother, who lives about a ten minute walk from the sea. I spent most of Saturday getting drunk on Martinis to avoid my pain (I could not communicate it to my mother). However, the feelings must have been pressing for release as I could not get to sleep, and come the early morning I walked towards the sea *howling* my anguish to the empty streets at the loss of my daughter. No one was about, but even if they had been I do not think I could have prevented this massive pain from surfacing and crying out to the elements. As I write this now I can cry in sympathy with the self that bore that searing agony.

Another description came from Kentucky:

> When you first realize that you're going to go, there begins a tearing inside,
> ripping, gouging, deep in the center of yourself. It makes you gasp, takes
> you by surprise, squeezes you, twists and drops you, and you are lost in
> a black desert of hurting.

Another feeling mentioned often, and in many connections, was *fear*—fear
that loomed large and took many forms. Fear of reprisal; fear of the future; fear
of the present; fear for the safety of ourselves and our children, both physical
and emotional; fear in its most unnameable and paralyzing forms:

- The fear was incredible. The first night in my apartment I could not eat,
  I could not cry, I could not sleep—all I could do was lie in the middle of
  the floor in a ball and rock back and forth. I considered suicide, but hadn't
  the strength to get up and do it.
- I was a little (more than a little?) afraid at first. I was so alone. I wasn't
  always sure where my next meal was coming from. I feared I would die
  and no one would know or care and the children would never know
  I existed.
- Anxiety would be a more accurate description of what I felt. It was
  pathologically severe. I was terrified of everything, including the sug-
  gestion that I see a therapist.
- At first I was afraid when Bob came to my apartment because I thought
  he would hit me or take the boys away when it was my time with them.
- For a long time I was sure that someone would come along and make
  me go back, that I would be caught and sent back, like an escaped prisoner.
  That I would be punished for getting above myself somehow, for expecting
  to be free. Trying to be free. Disobeying the rules that said I *couldn't* be
  free. It took at least a year for me to be out of the grip of that feeling, and
  maybe another year to be *really* free of it—to know that only *I* could send
  me back.
- Fear was a big thing, and a big surprise, too. What was I afraid of? This
  was *personal* fear, not fear about what would become of the kids, or me,
  or my husband—personal, physical, fear. I finally decided that I was afraid
  of being spanked. Can you imagine? I misbehaved, and for that you get hit.

Another woman expanded on that childhood fear of reprisal for being "naughty":

> For a long time—two months? three months?—I lived with this certain
> feeling that I was going to be hit, or grabbed, or yanked or something.
> I eventually realized that it was my mother who I was expecting to get me
> back in line, complete with punishment, scorn, anger—these feelings were
> as real as I suppose they were when I was five years old and behaving
> badly. I think I halfway expected to be plunked back into the playpen until
> I could be trusted to know how to act on my own. It was quite a blow to

discover how close to that childhood fear of authority I still was, and how helpless I felt against it, all these years later. It was another several months before I fully accepted the fact that no one could *make* me go back if I didn't want to, that I really was in charge of my life. I still have trouble realizing that.

This actual, bodily fear of some kind of physical attack is fairly common. One woman said she went everywhere for weeks expecting to be hit by a thunderbolt. No religious connection, she felt, no Hand of God, just a striking down, a prevention of action, but the image of the thunderbolt was real. Another woman expected to trip, to have something thrust in her way to prevent further forward movement. Another described a downward-pulling sensation, an incredible heaviness that prevented movement, as though her feet were glued down and a huge effort was required to drag them along. All these sensations were accompanied by fear—terror, some said. They felt mired, exposed, vulnerable and helpless.

I can expand on that feeling of fear and vulnerability out of my own experience. A powerful image in my own case was what I called "the parking lot." In my mind I was faced with the task of crossing, alone, a vast, empty expanse, unrelieved by any marker or landscaping—crossing it completely exposed to stares, sneers or jeers, from whoever it was I saw ringing this parking lot watching me. I was unable to engage in any dialogue, unable to hide myself , explain myself, defend or excuse myself. My task was to cross the parking lot the best way I could without being destroyed in the process. There was a kind of wire-walking involved, too, which prevented haste. The delicacy of movement required was incompatible with my impulse to run wildly, shrieking and flailing and gaining nothing from the experience. The fear was amazing and very, very real.

There was also *anger*, which the women generally identified as anger at being "cheated," deceived, betrayed, not by any one person, but by the whole situation:

- I fell for the whole load— the whole "happily ever after" crap. When I realized it was a lie, I was *consumed* with rage. I hated the whole world and everyone in it.
- I can't believe it turned out this way. Why didn't he help? Why didn't anyone help? Why didn't anyone tell me? I was a bundle of anger.
- Between the courts, and the false promises of my husband, and just life in general, I lost out completely. *That* made me angry, you bet.

A feeling of unreality, of disbelief, disconnectedness, and bewilderment was almost universal. Can this really be me? How *can* this be me? Few if any of us had had the slightest suspicion that life would bring us to this juncture, so it was shocking in its unexpectedness. Sometimes, we can hardly remember how we felt:

- I have large blocks around that time period and what happened when. I opened separate checking and savings accounts at some point around that time (I didn't want to but knew I had to). It's very hard to remember the first three months.
- I remember feeling like a helium balloon with its string cut. Kind of floating, with no security. It wasn't an entirely *bad* feeling, given what I had been cut away from.
- I was quite transient at first. I moved about every three months and I can't remember how many lovers (male and female) I had. Emotionally I was stable enough to keep working and support myself, but I drifted between a lot of temporary jobs, etc.
- I was disconnected from my entire past life, entirely. Everything was new, the experiences, etc. and I felt isolated for the most part.
- At first I felt disoriented. I didn't know what would happen or where I would end up. I ceased to exist to so many people close to me that I didn't know who I was any more.
- People took my identity from me when I ceased to be the "good" wife and mother they thought I was. I knew I was the same person inside but I had to learn all over again who that person was. When people quit talking, etc., I really thought for a time that I had died or something and didn't know it. Now I know who I am.

These sensations had the effect, often, of preventing any sort of meaningful action, sometimes for several weeks or even months. We found that changing course involved no small amount of maneuvering time. I likened it to an ocean liner; there is, perforce, a time of inactivity as it comes to a halt, swings slowly about, and then proceeds. It was like that for most of us:

- It was all sort of calm and collected, but then of course the trauma starts after you go. I spent days when I just sat doing nothing. I'd imagined there was going to be this whole new life, it was going to be so terribly exciting, and I just found that I didn't have the will to do anything. I didn't *want* to go anywhere. I didn't *want* to do anything.
- My esteem was based on being his wife, being a mum, you know, and the actual thought of branching out on my own...I mean moving out was bad enough, feeling very vulnerable and very frightened, and suddenly realizing I had to cope with things like getting the car serviced and sorting out the insurance—the sort of little things I never ever thought about. And all those things overwhelmed me, and I froze for a while, I couldn't do much of anything at all.
- I felt totally disoriented; I couldn't make any decisions at all, not even what to wear in the mornings. I just sat around and did nothing, or cried sort of quietly to myself. But at no time did I ever think, oh, I've done the wrong thing, I want to go back.

No, almost none of us wanted to go back, to undo what we had done. And it appears that part of our sense of disbelief and unreality came from amazement at our own capacity for action. For many of us it was very hard to believe that we had actually strayed out of our passive roles and done something so decisive to change our lives:

- I still have a hard time believing I had the "balls" to do what I did. But I see now that I *am* a capable person, a fairly intelligent person, and a worthwhile human being. So why *couldn't* I have done it? It was the right thing to do.
- Couldn't *believe* I could do it! But I did!

Even such positive feelings contributed to a certain sense of lost identity. We certainly weren't who we had been, so then who were we? We had to begin to find out:

- At first the big question was, without my children, who am I? For I had been a mother for so long and that aspect of my life had been the main focal point. Now I realize that I'm an extension of many things, motherhood being only one of the positive things.
- I would think, "I will never be married, have a white picket fence." I lived that life all my adult life and it has been difficult, somewhat painful, to accept that it will never again be my life. Ignorance is bliss—the more I embrace my new life the easier it is to accept the loss of my old one.
- I used to trust and believe what I "knew," which was nearly everything, because it was revealed in the Scriptures. The Bible covered everything from why there are seashells in the Alps (the Flood, you know) to why God allows man to suffer (because his character needs refinement) to what are UFOs ("lying wonders"). Now I find I have nothing left that I know or believe, yet faith, unreasonably, remains. About my situation, it is all part of the disintegration of what I trusted in. It has been evolutionary, and that seems very real.

The *loss* of an old identity sometimes had the startling effect of clarifying who we were, as this Chicago woman discovered:

I lost my stance as a martyr, and I was horrified to discover how badly I had needed it and how heavily I had depended on it as an excuse. You know the picture: "Sigh, if only I didn't have all these kids I'd go to school, or back to work, or write my novel, or sculpt, or paint".... Then all of a sudden you *don't* have all those kids, so come on, baby, produce. It's a scary thing to have nothing to hide behind. I honestly believe that's why some women hang on so tight and fight so hard for sole custody: if they don't get the kids they'll have to *do* something, something that requires them to be something besides a victim, and that is a daunting prospect.

It has been frequently noted in feminist writings that women are trained to be sacrificers, to be givers, to be second, to be the constant in the constellation. When we married and had children we did expect, at some level, to be "stuck." Imagine us now that we find ourselves "free," most of the time, of the steady burden of childcare. To our shock and surprise, we sometimes found that terribly difficult:

- I felt so rootless. No one was clinging to me and whining and asking and demanding, and I suddenly realized that those clinging children had *anchored* me as well as tied me down, and without them I was adrift. It took quite a while before I developed the balance to deal with that drifting, and to realize that I *was* still connected, but not on such a short string.
- In the beginning I felt like I wasn't whole—missing a big part of me and everyone could see it.
- Initially I always felt there was a mouth I should be feeding, a diaper I should be changing.
- I was unaccustomed to caring only for myself with no need for a rigid schedule, and I felt very unstable as far as utilization of time and sense of direction goes. I acted irresponsibly in the first few months.
- Initially I found it difficult to realize that I was truly on my own, only needing to care for myself. It was difficult to now be responsible for one instead of three people.

Above all else, we were afraid of what we might be doing to our children. We had no one to measure ourselves against, no studies to indicate what effect our leaving might have on our children, no way to know how to reinforce or counteract influences and pressures on them. That confusion added to our pain and guilt, and we felt it in everything we did. I thought that these three school-related stories served to point up the distress we felt, about ourselves and about what we might be doing to the children:

- I went to a Parent Orientation Day not too long after I left. Naturally the approach was to parents, and especially to mothers, and the assumption was that all of them lived in very traditional families. And in fact they all did. My guilt at not being one of them, and of making my children different was overwhelming.
- I just felt so *sorry* that I had had to spoil their nice normal background. I *had* had to—there had been no other way to proceed with my life, or to hang onto my life, but to "break up" the home? All the time I sat there on Open House Day I was thinking, I'm sorry, I'm sorry, I'm so terribly sorry you come from a "broken home." I just wanted everyone to forgive me.
- I went to a Meet-the-Teacher Tea shortly after I left. I was the only "working mother" there (I had taken time off), the only divorced mother there, and of *course* the only non-custodial mother. I was the only one in the whole school, naturally, and I felt so inadequate! The fact that half the mothers of the kids in the class weren't there at all, and

that half of the ones who were were just chatting to each other and not paying very much attention to the presentation, didn't seem to be of much comfort.

Our "famous" women have had their share of anguish, too. For example, after the trial reaffirming her former husband's custody of their children, Mrs. Rockefeller's lawyer reported that she was "deeply grieved." *Time* magazine wrote that a "tangible symbol of that grief, and the optimism that preceded it, was the Rockefeller addition of an entire children's floor—complete with playroom, nurse's quarters, and library—to their Fifth Avenue apartment."[2] Charlotte Gilman remembers how she felt after her daughter left on an Overland train. She wrote:

> There were years, years, when I could never see a mother and child together without crying, or even a picture of them. I used to make friends with any child I could so as to hold it in my arms for a little....[3]

And how did it feel to me, there at the beginning? I agree with those who say that never in their worst nightmares had they imagined how terrible they would feel. I had thought I was fairly well prepared to deal with whatever came along; I had dealt with a great deal already, and had been able to handle it. But the emptiness, the rootlessness, the tearing physical pain, was more intense and more devastating than anything I had come close to in any previous difficulty. I had felt loss before, betrayal by friends, family members' anger, the wrath of my husband, disdain from my children. But I was completely unprepared for what I felt now.

The worst times were before and after school, particularly before, when I knew that my two younger children were on their own to get themselves up, dressed, fed, and out to school. This had probably been my least favorite time of day when I was at home. But now I was desolate, so desolate that after a few weeks I began to get up at 5:30 a.m. and drive the 15 miles to their home in order to be there to get them started. I rarely saw my son other than at this time, and that was a torment to me. But it was also a torment to have my daughter stay with me and then have to drop her off at her father's home. I was perpetually writhing inside; there seemed no peace. The release I had obtained from an impossible situation in the marriage was counteracted by this seething anguish. I wept incessantly and at inappropriate times.

My housemate, who had opened her home to a stable, interested and interesting companion found herself saddled with an ineffectual and inconsolable burden. She was, amazingly, unswerving in her patience and support. She constantly pointed out the good things that were happening, the growth she perceived that I could not, the expressions of affection and forgiveness that my children were showing but that I could not see or feel, and the ways in which I was "hanging in there." She helped me learn to manage my affairs—my car, my finances, my work schedule, even my meals. When, one day, I went completely to pieces over the fact that I did not know how to wash my car (a displacement, no doubt, for all my feelings of ineffectiveness), she carefully got out a bucket and sponge and hose and soap and gently told me that it wasn't really too hard, after all. That incident was only one of hundreds of "turning points," when I saw that I could, however slowly, pull myself together and get going again. I began to recognize these turning points, and to seize them gratefully and count them as markers of my progress.

There were also extraordinary physical signs that I had made the right decision—manifestations quite beyond my conscious control but eminently observable. With no effort and no apparent change in my diet, I lost my extra weight. My skin cleared up. I became, as they say in the commercials, "regular." I watched in astonishment as my signature was transformed, quite without my will. I found I often slept on my back, something I had *never* done. My dreams changed, and instead of the recurring dream of being improperly dressed, unprepared, and unable to find where I was going, I dreamed of getting where I was going quickly and efficiently, with the right clothing, and with whatever supplies I needed close at hand. As I went about my work I realized I had a sense of my whole body, rather than disconnected and awkward parts. I felt stronger. I laughed more. Most importantly, I stopped the drinking that had been becoming a serious and terrifying problem. And I did this not through will or determination or even conscious awareness. There simply seemed to be no need to reach for the bottle. On a conscious level, I was still mired in guilt and doubt and fear, but somewhere below that conscious awareness was a self that was heaving a huge sigh of relief, and making itself known in these strange and marvelous ways.

How Did You Cope?

How did we cope with the pain and the guilt and the disorientation? How did we establish new patterns, discover new identities, find peace and strength and growth? Because, in spite of it all, we did. And it is this confrontation with the demons who dragged us down, held us back, and made us doubt and hesitate and get stuck time and time again that I wanted to share. To identify those demons, to describe them, to engage them fully, to conquer them, and then to move on in joy and wholeness—that is the task that we have faced, each in our own ways, each with our own set of skills and values, and each with our own solutions.

In one section on the questionnaire I asked women to identify those persons or activities that had been "most helpful" and "least helpful," and to explain briefly how they dealt with the unhelpful influences. Interestingly, though probably not surprisingly, many answers cropped up on both the positive and negative sides of the experience. "Family" was one, "friends" another, "church and clergy" still another. Even ex-husbands got some positive comments. One woman, for example, said that the hardest thing for her to bear was "seeing him when he was in a sweet, gentle, caring mood; it made me wish I hadn't left, or could go back and everything would be OK again, even though I *really* knew that was impossible."

There were many more "helpful" items mentioned than "unhelpful"; in the latter category the legal system was mentioned frequently, and very bitterly. We have seen in an earlier chapter some of the experiences that led to this evaluation; certainly our courts, as they deal with family affairs, are in dire need of reform: there is general agreement on this point even within the legal system itself. Far more successful experiences were reported by those who went through a process of mediation; this process is being used more and more by divorcing couples dissatisfied with the built-in adversarial procedures required under our present legal system. Several respondents suggested this approach for readers of this book, and my own research confirms that this is very good advice indeed.

Also frequently mentioned in the negative column was the church and clergy. We have already read some comments on clergy reactions in Chapter Six. It was common to discover that the church's rigid investment in the status quo did not allow it to accept our actions, even when the church was partially responsible for them. One woman wrote:

> My feeling is that the church claims to represent God, yet has refused to take responsibility for the outcome of its idealisms. No matter how things

111

turn out, it is God's doing. This eliminates the need, almost the possibility, of maturing and growing. Yet any minister who truly *cares* for the people *knows* that the idealisms are not functional, and has to begin to transcend them somehow. Self-righteous rigidity, which I accepted as "the Way" and which my husband accepted as "the Way," was the agent of the ruin of our relationship, in my estimation. I feel cheated, but I can find no legitimate human target for the indignation.

Conversely, others listed God, faith, religion, or church as *most* helpful. Most of those who did so had turned to faith, or changed religions, or become churchgoers for the first time after they left their homes. Prayer was specifically listed as a helpful activity by 12 respondents.

Also in the negative column were doctors, mentioned only six times but with fervent emotion. "Uncaring," "cold," "supercilious," "not equipped to help or even respond," and "didn't want to know me any more" were some of the remarks made by those who had turned to family doctors for assistance. None indicated that the doctor had tried to refer them to anyone else.

"So-called friends" were listed, in just those words; my respondents replied that "least helpful" to them were:

- So-called friends, telling me I didn't know what I was doing and would never be happy if I went through with it. Everyone thinks they know you better than you know yourself.
- The so-called friends and acquaintances and people I hardly knew were very cruel. I had an ex-husband that played on my guilt, and used that against me. Having to listen to "how could you desert those kids like that?" "How can you call yourself a mother?" Having to listen to the gossip and stories about me that were absolutely untrue.
- The people who criticized and condemned me and told me I was a freak, etc. The court system which condemned me because I wouldn't follow the whole ownership-patriarchy routine. The silence I met and the isolation I felt.
- So-called "helpful" friends who told me horror stories about children who grow up without the knowledge of their mother's love.
- Married mothers who would not try to understand any part of my decision.

Former in-laws were rarely helpful, though in fairness they were rarely mentioned as unhelpful, either. For the most part, former husbands were also "unhelpful" in the extreme:

- My ex-husband's hatred, revenge, and ultimately successful undermining of my relationship with my children.
- My former husband and his new wife's unrelenting bitterness, self-righteousness, and refusal to communicate. They have been unbearable, obnoxious, unreasonable, rigid ... ad infinitum. It's been *thirteen years* and you'd swear, by their behavior, that it happened yesterday. And

112

they think they're such good *Christians!*

- The gossip that my first husband related regardless of who else it hurt. If I would not live with him then he tried to humiliate me.

We discussed the reactions of parents in an earlier chapter; fully one-third of my respondents mentioned parents as "least helpful." Some comments:

- Everyone I knew said, "What can I do to help?" except my mother. The cup of my bitterness has no bottom.
- My mother and father. Their open hostility damaged my relationship with them; however, it made me rely on my own personal strength and feelings.
- My father. He still hates me for leaving the children. He still does talk to me—but that is only so he doesn't lose track of his grandchildren.

More than one woman mentioned her own ignorance and lack of preparation for such a move as the "least helpful" part of her experience:

- The lack of planning I'd done and the resulting difficulties in dealing with my ex-husband.
- My ignorance of the "legal" profession and matters. My own state of unpreparedness to make a life of my own. Married at 18, I just went from one kind of dependency to another. Although I had lots of ideas, I never had the opportunity to put them into practice. I always had the financial security of a "man" and never really thought of myself as the one who would have to provide that.

I heard of many negative coping strategies, too: heavy drinking, pills (mostly tranquilizers), drugs, several suicide attempts, and general "retreating." I think it would be fair to say that women who continued in this sort of pattern would not have been the ones who replied to my questionnaire, so I cannot say with any certainty what percentage they represent. Among my respondents, however, such destructive behavior took place during the first three months or so of their separations. After that they seemed to get a grip on themselves, their lives, and their futures. They began to get some good help, some good insights and inspiration, and to move ahead, however slowly.

For the overwhelming majority, the most important source of help was therapy. Although in several instances the first, or even the second or third, therapist was not helpful, a supportive counselor was finally found and tremendous strides began to be made. The following two comments indicate the direction most of the therapy took, and show clearly why it was so vital:

- Having a therapist, and gaining the confidence in myself that I was OK, and that what was happening was OK at the time. I had to believe in myself and my convictions to make it through those hard times. I had to learn to turn the other cheek when needed. I developed a tough hide, and a sense of humor. Having someone to talk to that wouldn't judge. Being able to be alone to get to know me, and having a friend when I couldn't stand to be alone.

- My therapist telling me that I did not have to feel guilt for wanting out of a situation that I could not deal with, and that I was not responsible for anyone's happiness but my own. That until I could be happy with myself I couldn't possibly make my children happy, or anyone else happy either.

The support of good friends saw a lot of us through the initial bad times. My own friend who later left me still deserves credit for her support in the early stages of my readjustment; she was vitally important at that time. So were several other good "couple friends" who managed not to "choose" and still make me feel cherished and comforted. The following two remarks sum up the contributions made by the friends who listened, and held us:

- The support of feminist friends who listened without judging and allowed me to voice my feelings and frustrations. It was through that process that I came to realize my own strengths and came to know that it was important to make whatever contribution I could to my children's lives in a positive way.
- My friends and my twin sister. Most of all they listened to me when I needed to talk and held me when I felt lost. They made me feel I wasn't a "monster."

Support was offered by other non-traditional friends and acquaintances. One woman mentioned *men* who had given up custody and with whom she felt much in common. Another referred to a married friend who had decided not to have children at all. Women like her have to bear many of the same "slings and arrows" as do non-custodial mothers; they are deemed selfish, irresponsible, and unheeding of the needs and desires of society and civilization. The non-child-centered philosophies of the group are worth investigating; an organization worth contacting is:

National Organization for Non-Parents
3 North Liberty Street
Baltimore, MD 21201

Talking to other non-custodial mothers was not often listed as helpful, since most of my respondents did not know how to find any. They did, however, think it would be wonderful to do so. Shortly after I began this book I was made aware of an organization called Mothers Without Custody, then based in Boston and headed by its founder, Ellen Kimball. Many of my respondents now belong to this group, which can be reached by writing:

114

Mothers Without Custody
PO Box 56762
Houston, Texas 77256

Another group, based in the Washington, DC area and directed by Jan Koehler, can be reached by writing:

Offspring
PO Box 23074
Washington, DC 20034

An organization in England that has been of great help to me in my project and has provided many of the responses herein related is MATCH, Mothers Apart From their Children. To contact them write:

MATCH
BM Problems
London WC1N3XX, England

Members of these groups have told me that they have been helped enormously not only by the caring intimacy of shared experiences but by the opportunities they have had through their organizations to write, speak, and appear on radio and television. They report that public appearances are often extremely stressful, but serve to renew and strengthen one's resolve, to extend a helping hand to those still unable to reach out, and to provide information and education to the helping professions and the general public.

If none of these organizations is convenient to you there is the:

Family Service Association of America
44 East 23 Street
New York, NY 10010

with 260 affiliates in the U.S. and Canada. The 110 chapters of Parents Without Partners are listed in their respective telephone directories, or you can write their general headquarters at:

Parents Without Partners
7910 Woodmont Avenue
Suite 1000
Bethesda, MD 20814

Additionally, there are literally thousands of local church, government, and private helping organizations that provide support and information to non-custodial parents. The public library or Town Hall in any location can usually direct interested persons to an appropriate organization.

The value of a support group can hardly be overestimated, and my respondents were nearly unanimous in urging that one be located or even, failing that, started. Advertisements in local papers can be a good, and sometimes the only, way of establishing contact, or Mothers Without Custody might be able to give you names of women in your area eager to offer and receive support.

In addition to actual role models and non-custodial colleagues, some of my respondents suggested reading. Chapter One related some stories from life and fiction, and at the end of this book you will find an extensive bibliography of suggested readings for adults and children living in our situation. I hope it will answer the comment of one woman, who wrote:

> To know that fabulously achieving women like Charlotte Perkins Gilman felt guilty, too, or that glaringly visible figures like Joan Kennedy had the nerve to act anyway, was very good for me. I wish I could find more!

If reading was helpful, so was writing. Diaries and journals, articles for publication, and lengthy letters to friends were outlets for emotions and exploration. I was gratified that at least 20 respondents said that filling out my questionnaire had helped them to clarify their feelings, assess their positions, and simply express long-buried emotions. A copy of the questionnaire can be found at the back of this book; I would be grateful to any of you who complete it for me, since my research is on-going. It can be sent to me care of

Mayflower Associates
Box 534
Hicksville, NY 11801

The two other "helpers" most frequently mentioned were "my new husband or lover," and "my children." While only a few respondents said that they had left their marriages for another person, almost half of them, by the time they contacted me, had remarried or were living with another man or woman in a love relationship. These new partners were of paramount importance in helping us to develop good rapport with the children and with the former husband; only three new partners (all new husbands) had proved to be disappointing. Several women had parted from their new lovers on amicable terms, and expressed gratitude for the support they received at a time when they were most needy.

The children, though, were the star performers in this drama of readjustment and reconfiguration. We will hear more about them in Chapter Ten, so suffice it to say here that the steadfastness and loyalty of our own children provided the underpinning for our reconstruction and the fuel for our journey.

Other positive coping strategies were suggested in the responses. Work was one. School was another. Keeping busy, keeping one's mind occupied, feeling productive through a job or a course of study or even a volunteer position, were excellent ways of getting through a bad time:

- Sometimes what you think is the worst thing turns out to be the best thing. I had to go to work! Horrors! I hadn't worked in 18 years! But I *loved* it, grew in it, and found that it has been the thing I needed without knowing it all these years.
- Going to school was an absolute God-send. I of course got prepared for my new career but I also got my mind reawakened, my skills sharpened, and my self-respect back.
- Getting a job, making a rough budget and trying to stick to it was great. Being responsible for the bills. Realizing that I had to rely on myself to get the things I wanted. Happiness is worth working for; it takes a lot of time and sometimes sacrifice but if you want it, then you know what you have to do.

One method for dealing with the negative reactions of certain friends and relatives can be summed up with one piece of advice: ignore it. For example:

- Generally, I ignored it. Counseling beforehand had explored the "guilt trip trap" very thoroughly and given me the strength to put guilt behind me.
- Learning to ignore the cliche remarks of senseless people who have never had to deal with such a dilemma as mine.
- *Ignore, Ignore, Ignore....* At first I would try desperately to explain my actions, but after seeing that this fell on deaf ears I would just say, "It was a situation you know nothing about, it was a mutual agreement between my husband and myself, and we seem to be surviving." Of course we weren't always surviving, but they didn't need to know that.
- Ignoring the comments of ignorant people, fighting for my rights, speaking out to women I met, sharing my experiences, reading about and living alternative lifestyles, continuing my personal growth no matter what happened.
- For too many years I *cooperated* with it, felt I deserved it (guilt). Finally, only psychotherapy could help. They haven't changed, but I have. I just ignore their behavior as best I can.
- Saying "to hell with them."

And, for dealing with the situation as a whole, an unfailing remedy was *time.*

- Learning to take one day at a time. Learning to accept. Most of all, just plain living with it.
- Waiting for time to pass and my actions to speak louder than my words. They saw, eventually, that I truly love my children and honestly feel that I did the best thing for them.

- Wait, wait, wait—time will heal. Believe that. It's hard to do but it's the only thing that works, really, and it's the only thing you get for free!

Holidays and special occasions such as birthdays, graduations, weddings, and the like pose difficult problems for those of us who are establishing new patterns. The old patterns seem to surface particularly at these times and we suffer from nostalgia and sometimes from an overwhelming longing for "what might have been." It is most often the mother, after all, who bakes the birthday cakes and wraps the stocking gifts at Christmas and organizes the family parties and plans and dreams over her daughter's wedding. So to be removed or remote from those tasks can be agonizing. To know that the children at those times are also especially aware of the changes and are perhaps experiencing similar feelings of nostalgia and longing, makes living through them almost unbearably hard. My respondents had varying answers as to how they handle these "family" events, and some of them were quite inventive:

> We *love* celebrating the dog's birthday (now the second dog). We exchange presents, give gag gifts to the dog, which we then distribute to each other with great hilarity. We make cookies in the shape of dog bones, and serve dinner on the floor. Once we even tried to eat without utensils but that was *not* a successful experiment! It's a silly, fun time, and no one told us we *had* to do it. It's our *own* tradition.

Creating "our own traditions" came up quite often, in one way or another. The women who answered me were the ones who, it seems, had discovered that Christmas does not *have* to be celebrated on December 25, that "and-a-half" birthdays can be just as much fun as "real" ones, that Groundhog Day or St. Swithin's Day or just the 12th of August can be turned into delightful and extra-special family events, with the added advantage that they do not create conflicts with others who want to celebrate the same day. Many of the women realized, well before the break, that Mother's Day, with its attendant pressures and expectations and built-in guiltmaking, is really a creation of business interests and can (and probably should) be safely ignored.

We also realize that holiday times are often, perhaps usually, extremely stressful for members of traditional families, too, and that if we are finding them difficult and stressful it is not our situations, necessarily, that make them so. Often those of us in non-traditional roles have managed to eliminate much of the falseness and phoniness that can accompany special occasions, and have gleaned only the gold.

We must also face those "once-in-a-lifetime" occasions— weddings, graduations, bar mitzvahs, christenings. Those of my respondents who, like myself, have passed some of those milestones, say that how these events are dealt with tends to reflect the status of the relationship in general. Where there is still bitterness and hostility, the event is often difficult and painful; if some degree

118

of cordiality and communication has been reached then the event is pleasant and even enjoyable. To predict the success one will have in rising to these occasions one must assess how well one is relating with the parties involved. Quite possibly, all to the good, the prospect of the coming event will spur improvements in the relationship. Possibly, too, each subsequent event will be an improvement as those that preceded are assessed and analyzed.

Communication was the key, we found, to success in these instances. Clear understandings about responsibilities, schedules, financial arrangements, and the like are vital. So, too, are discussions about fears, feelings, and expectations. If you can break through whatever barriers you have to this latter kind of communication you will find that these family events can be happy and rewarding. It will be worth the effort.

We have no way of knowing whether these celebrations would have been easier or more comfortable had our families remained intact, or if the stresses would simply have been different. Certainly, some illusions would have been preserved, and that would have afforded some measure of stability and comfort. But perhaps there are better ways of providing stability and comfort, ways *not* based on illusions, where honesty can provide the basis for a firmer foundation.

To close this chapter I want to share with you, at random, some of the briefer responses to a questionnaire items on how women have coped with being a non-custodial mother. I think they are meaningful and valuable and reflect the actual experiences of the women who wrote and spoke to me. They wrote, "I dealt with it by...":

- being loving and understanding with the boys; by acknowledging my pain and hurt at the lies that were said; by including them in my life via phone calls, letters, visits, intimacy, so that they *knew* I was still their *mom*.
- keeping a weekly journal about my feelings. Writing an article about it.
- physical activity—took up bike riding and prepared for a long bicycle trip to another state.
- reading self-help books like *How to be Your Own Best Friend*, etc. Keeping up communication and trying to be positive and accepting about my son.
- explaining, explaining, explaining to myself, my children, and everyone else. Always remembering that it was the best choice for the children.
- talking to myself. Telling myself I'm still a mother and my children will always love me. Maybe more.
- the worst way, with pills and alcohol. I also punished myself in more ways than one.
- realizing that it is out of my hands unless I have a great deal of money and nothing else to do with my life.
- educating myself and demanding certain changes in the agreement which the lawyers put into "legalese."
- taking support where it was offered. Being demanding and selfish. Crying when I had to, dancing when I needed to. Letting myself be free, go with the mood, and get through one day at a time!

- therapy, crying, trying new ways, and continuing to be *very* honest with my children, so they see a *real* picture of what's what.
- surrounding myself with people, mostly women, whom I knew understood and accepted me, and avoiding other people. Reading a lot of feminist theory and books about strong foremothers (Charlotte Perkins Gilman did a lot for me!). In periods of real sadness, absorbing myself in novels, working hard in school and in feminist and political activities, and making love with congenial people.
- keeping very busy. I even became involved in theater production to fill up many late evening hours.
- making a list of the 20 things I loved to do. Then every day I did at least one of them. I meditated twice a day. I maintained amazingly good spirits during that tough time.
- learning, conceding, arguing, retreating, attacking, going to therapists, ultimately accepting my priority of my well-being and seeing that over time the kids are not damaged, are still warm and close to me, and share their feelings and concerns with me, maybe even more than before.

Many women, many ways of coping. We tried; sometimes we failed. We tried again. For some of us, several years have gone by since we left. It is to these women that we can put the question, "How did it turn out?"

How Did It Turn Out?

After the dust settled, after the reality of the situation was accepted and internalized, after the new ways of relating had been established (or at least outlined), when we had a chance to do some appraisal and reflection, what did we see? How did we feel then, about ourselves, our children, our friends and relatives, our neighbors and co-workers? And how did they feel about us?

In gathering material for this chapter I dealt only with women who had lived apart from their children for five years or more; this gave me a sample of about 35. I felt, and in general my respondents agreed, that a year or two is not enough to establish a truly workable new pattern, and that it had taken at least a year for us to know which end was up, so to speak. It takes an enormous amount of time and energy to turn one's life around and proceed in another direction: there must be a seemingly stagnant "turning around" period before we can set off again. That time is *not* stagnant, of course, but the movement is less perceptible and may seem unproductive, and so we fear we're going nowhere. Once we do get started again, however, we are able to see how very far we have come; this viewpoint comes only after time. So while this sample is smaller, it has great value.

As I observed in my introduction, many of the answers I received did not fit my carefully delineated categories. The next two narratives are from women whose original arrangements worked pretty well, but who now fear that life changes have complicated their situations considerably. I include them here as a reminder that things never completely "turn out," but only shift and change constantly:

> After I separated I had custody of the children for several months. At that time I was having a great deal of trouble coping with being a mother and a single parent. I didn't know where I was going myself and felt I couldn't be a good mother at that point. My husband suggested taking custody and after much thought and discussion he moved back into the family home and I moved out. Regardless of what the problems were between us, he was always a good father and I felt I didn't have a right to say that I could be a better parent than he could. At that time I was unemployed and emotionally he was a much more stable person than I was. These arrangements were by an oral agreement, and when it seemed to be working the legal papers were drawn up and incorporated into the final divorce decree.
>
> This custody arrangement worked fine for some time. I was working

so I saw the children when I could, called them every day, and occasionally took them overnight or on weekends. I worked days and also worked nights as a waitress, so this was not always possible, and the visits were not as frequent as I or the children would have liked.

Then I met and married a divorced man. Due to the economic situation in Wisconsin, we moved to Texas, where he is now employed. The main problem was the fact that I would be so far from my children as to make it nearly impossible to see them more than once a year. There were a number of ways to look at the situation, but they all boiled down to the fact that if we stayed in Wisconsin, there were no jobs. I felt I had to make a choice between a life with him and being close to my children. The one thought I held on to was that someday my children would grow up and have lives of their own, but if I gave up my life with my husband, who would I have when the children no longer needed me? My children were happy and secure with their father....

We have been in Texas for three months and I'm afraid that I have not yet learned to cope with the situation. Not having custody and being only nine miles away from my children was one thing, but being 1,000 miles from them is a totally different thing. I call them once a week, write them letters, send small gifts, etc., but it just doesn't seem like it is enough. I still feel guilty and wonder what effect my not being with them will have on them later on in life, when they are old enough to fully understand the situation. I live in fear that they will say that I wasn't there when they needed me, so now they don't need me. In summation, the adjustment to living without my children is still very much up in the air and difficult to live with. There is still a great deal of uncertainty and questions to be answered. I don't feel that I will ever fully know whether my decision was right or wrong, until I've proven it one way or another. I do have the support of a very loving and understanding new husband who, having been through the same type of situation, can comprehend what I am going through and the doubt and guilt I still feel. I do not know if the custody arrangements will ever be changed or, if they are, what the end result will be. I only know that a divorce decree by no means is the end. It may end the obligations of a husband and wife, but once a parent, always a parent. I want what is best for the children, myself, my new husband, and my ex-husband. I don't think there is anyone or anyway in the world to know what the right answer is or even if there *is* a right answer. Regardless of what decision is made, there will always be some doubt in one's mind as to whether it was the right decision or not.... The only thing I know for sure is that I love the man I am now married to and I love my children, but the hurt, loneliness and guilt don't go away with time.

My children have visited me each summer since I moved, although for less time that I would have chosen. One year my older son had to attend summer school; the same was true of the younger boy another year. Last summer their father and stepmother wanted them home when their baby was born. This year will be the first time they have been able to spend the entire summer vacation with me. I recently learned that my ex and his wife are in the process of divorcing. As a result of this information, and the apparent problems the boys are having, I have decided that, when they come for their summer visit, I will not return them to their father—assuming, of course, that they want to stay. This decision has not been an easy one to make. I have now been virtually childless for five years, and my life is orderly, satisfying, and busy; I cannot anticipate what havoc the resumption of my maternal role will wreak on my existence. For one thing, it will be impossible for my man friend to continue to live with me if the boys are going to stay; he is a 41-year-old bachelor and has little tolerance for the normal behavior of teenagers. Nevertheless, I can't believe that it wouldn't be better for the children to be with me under the circumstances, and will make whatever adjustments are necessary (hard as that will undoubtedly be) to fit them back into my life.

The following account is another story of change, interesting for its twofold view of non-custodianship. I had not included women who have given children up for adoption in my survey, because I wanted to place emphasis on non-traditional, continuing relationships with children. This woman, however, can speak to both options:

I have a 17-year-old daughter Debbie who was placed for adoption when she was born because I was 18 and unmarried and definitely unable to provide the kind of home she should have. Since I have always been Debbie's non-custodial parent, although not through divorce, it was from that point of view that I answered your ad....

I also have a daughter Amy, 15 years old, from my first marriage, which was a disaster right from the start. I married someone who loved me but whom I barely liked, just so I could escape my parents after they forced me into surrendering Debbie. Amy was born two years later and I had tried desperately all that time to conceive a baby to replace my first. Shortly after Amy came along I realized I could never replace Debbie and that I really wasn't ready to be a parent, but I was in it up to my ears and had no choice but to be the best Mom I could. We've had our ups and downs, believe me, and I know it is because of my ambivalent feelings toward Amy. I love her for herself and because she is my daughter, but I resented her terribly for a while when she was small because I had plunged into something I wasn't ready for. It took a long time to work through my feelings and we're OK now, for the most part.

When Amy was three and a half I remarried and now have two more children who are the apple of my husband's eye and Amy has gone right to the bottom of the list. Consequently she tried very hard to make life miserable for her sister and brother and it's a vicious unending circle: my husband aggravates and needles Amy, she verbally attacks the younger two, and then I am in the middle trying to mediate this mess. He and I used to have a good relationship but now we are barely speaking and I am anxious to put this dying beast out of its misery.... A divorce is definite in the near future and he has told me, in no uncertain terms, that he will never give up the younger children... The younger ones want to stay here because they don't want to leave their school and friends, but they don't want me to go either. Also, I know I couldn't live with having them only during the summer, so I am in a real quandary right now.

As for Debbie, I became involved with Concerned United Birthparents and through their support I decided to search for her and last October we were reunited! She came to live with my family and me for three months and it was one of the greatest experiences of my life. Unfortunately she told me that she never felt like she "belonged" in her adoptive family and has spent most of her life rebelling and getting into trouble.... My heart breaks for her because there is no way to know if she'll ever be able to straighten out. I honestly feel, given the circumstances at the time of her birth, that I did the best for her, but I am living with a lot of guilt because I wasn't strong enough to stand up to my parents and tell them that they were *not* going to make me give up my child. All that is behind me now, though, and I can only hope and pray that Debbie will survive all of this and come out of it OK.

I wrote to thank this mother for her response, which was far lengthier than is quoted here, and in a letter written three months later she said:

Thank you for your letter.... I feel that if there is anything I have been through or thought about that can help others I am only too willing to do what I can. Surrendering a child for adoption is supposed to "set everyone free" (in essence that is what "friends," family, and social workers tell us) but what it does is sentence everyone involved to a lifetime of pain, tears, frustration over the unanswered questions on the part of both child and mother, and rage at the system that finds it easier to destroy a family than to invest the time to find ways to keep it together. As for becoming a non-custodial mother through divorce, I think I am going to find that a lot easier to handle just for the simple reason that I can see my children whenever I want to and most important, *I know where they are, who is raising them, and that they are loved.* When I gave up Debbie I knew none of these things. I didn't know for sure if she was even alive, and trying to live a life around such a huge missing piece of yourself is truly swimming upstream! And as for the upcoming divorce—my bags are packed, the children have been talked to and are as prepared as possible, household affairs are in order, and *I am ready....* Amy and I will be on our way. Wish us luck in our search for a better life. I feel that wherever we go it will be a 100 percent improvement over the mess we are in now.

Two other essays were especially interesting. The first is a continuation of the story we started in Chapter Two, from the woman who as a child had fantasized about finding an abandoned baby in a meadow. She has been apart from her children for five years, and is now 28 years old:

After I signed the papers I was depressed for days and my friend (female) with whom I was staying urged me to seek counseling. I started going to a counselor and he was supportive and understanding toward me. I began to wear make-up, go out and have fun (something I never did once while married). I began to date men who were interested in me as a person and that made me feel great! My husband was never interested in *me*, what I said, my ideas, etc.... These men were. They were not lovers, although my ex-husband believed so. I was visiting my children once or twice a week and I noticed they were enjoying me—and I was enjoying them even more! They would squeal and laugh when they saw me on visits. I was comfortable with them and they with me. I enjoyed them! I was beginning to really think I had made the best decision. I was working as a waitress at a job I enjoyed. I was relaxed and I felt free!

Sure, many people had criticisms, mostly my family. I was stunned that so many people view the role of a man differently from that of a woman. A woman is supposed to accept her fate without question, normally the role of wife and mother. Whereas a man is free to choose between a race car and a wife. If a woman asserts her personality she is viewed as a whore or a wild permissive creature, egotistical. Strange how men of this nature, who assert their destinies, are considered *daring* and *macho*, a mind of their own. But let a woman stray from the norm and she is branded as *unscrupulous, immoral, selfish*.... My occasional use of drugs/alcohol was no longer needed. I was too busy experiencing life! I remarried and had another child, a daughter....

My story is not unique. I know that. However, I have learned a great deal. I have learned to really reach out to my fellow human beings. I have learned that it really isn't what you are but *who* you are! My heart has been broken, but in the shattered pieces I have found a diamond—myself. I will never relinquish custody of my other daughter because the answers I sought have been found. And the questions I have yet may not be answered, if they are you'd better believe they'll be right—if not right, then at least I will be able to accept it. I have grown into a deeply compassionate person! And I'm proud of me, regardless of whether or not the "Moral Majority" considers me undesirable. I've learned there is a lot of grit inside of me and a strong will to go on.

The section of the questionnaire on feelings after some time had passed elicited, for the most part, very positive descriptions of the current situations of the women writing. Strength, joy, growth, awakening, excitement were some of the words used there and in interviews. It was exciting to read and hear these responses, because it was so clear that the positive was increasing for them every day. They wrote of the relief they felt at being out of impossible situations, the joy they felt at the realization of their own power and capability, the surprise and admiration they felt for themselves as they coped with new and difficult problems, found solutions, and at the same time maintained their relationships with the important people in their lives. Most often, they spoke of growth and strength:

- I find this is the only point I'm positive of. I have seen lots of times when it would have been easier to give up. I am an entirely different person than I was five years ago—or two years ago. I was a child then. I've matured.

- I'm now able to live like *I want*, and I know I can handle almost any situation. I've gotten somewhat stronger mentally in the last year. I've gone from timidity and doubt to self-confidence and achievement.
- Sometimes I amaze even myself. Moving furniture, fixing things, signing contracts, opening bank accounts, sawing firewood—not just physically capable but mentally confident. When I think of all those years when every check I wrote I was worried he would blow up and denigrate the decisions I had made,... I just shake my head.
- Strength I never knew I had. It is neat to find it. I enjoy challenging myself now. I *seek* new ways to improve competencies and to test myself.
- With every decision I get stronger, tougher, lean and mean! I am a far stronger person now than I've ever been. And it's that strength that has alienated my family (parents); they want me to stay a little girl.
- I feel stronger, because I have some individual achievements and my own identity. There is less demand on my strength now that I don't have to carry around a touchy husband, who was a "dependent autocrat."
- My strength comes from realizing finally that I *did* do the best I could, given the obstacles. It comes from seeing that the children are strong, stronger than I could have hoped, that they really do like me, that *they* did the best they could.
- The divorce and subsequent separation from my daughter forced me to grow. As I didn't fit the old mold I had to create one to fit me. In the process, I discovered me, that I like who I was and where I was going and what I was doing. This person is genuine and without pretenses or prejudices. My daughter and I grow closer every year. We're growing up together. It's not unpleasant to be changing.
- I am growing all the time. I am beginning to really like myself.
- It's hard to imagine myself in my past life because I was such an amazingly different person. That seed (of the person I am now) was a very determined life force that is helping me fulfill that vision of myself as a strong, competent, equal and important woman in my own right.
- It's good to go over it every now and then because you tend to think that you were then as you are now, and of course that's terribly untrue. It's good to realize how far you've come.

That positive attitude toward ourselves and our decision began to form and grow and soon became second nature, so to speak, and a touchstone to be counted upon:

- I feel it is very important to be positive about oneself. Although I do have my down periods, more and more I can see them as passing and can get on with doing things that will make me happy and ultimately make my children and everyone I come in contact with happier too.
- I wasn't sure at first. Now I know I did the right thing. My children are happy and have advantages I never could have provided. I believe they

have the best of their father and of me, and that through me they see that people can be different from the "norm" they see around them and still be good, loving people.

- I think everyone involved now knows that I made the right decision. Their father is happily married, etc. My sister recently told me that she knows she was wrong to desert me during that time. She said she can't imagine how I made it alone and is sorry she wasn't there for me when I must have needed her most. My mother also told me that she could see she had judged me wrongly, and that I had courage she never had when I left a situation that was not happy. She said she admired my courage. My children have told me that they know I make special efforts to visit them and spend a lot of money on gas for the car, etc. They have phoned me with news of special awards at school and seem to know that I am here for them. They know I love them. I think that's all that matters.

My own experience led me to realize that the process of pain, acceptance, and recovery led to a new self-knowledge and a positive philosophy of living that I cannot imagine having developed in any other way. This experience of personal growth was shared by many others, who wrote of the ways they had improved their approaches to life and living and attained a serenity that carries them through difficulties that previously would have laid them low:

- I think one of the main things my experience did was to turn me into a radical feminist/humanist or whatever you want to call it. Society's institutions have to change before people will be free to choose the lifestyle that suits them best. I feel I was channeled by the expectations of society into the whole marriage/children/housewife thing. There weren't any alternative role models available for me when I was growing up. "Old maid" teachers, maybe, but nothing positive. I still haven't reached what I would term my ideal lifestyle, but I'm not afraid to try, and I'm not afraid of changes like I used to be. I think that whatever additional options are open to women today (and those still seem few enough) are there only because women like me have cleared the trail. I hope those who come after us can widen it.
- Life is far poorer now financially but so much richer in other ways. I have made friends with people who would never have been approved of by my spouse and I am no longer governed by his thinking. I love my children but see that I was involved so much in their lives at the expense of my own. I feel I can cope now with my mother but I see her as a woman now and our relationship is better.

There were, as we know, many women who were enormously relieved to be released from full-time mothering, who believe their children are better for the separation, and who are at peace with their new lives:

- I love my children and like to see them, but I find I'm not involved in their lives as I once was, and I've developed my own interests now;

so their life, or a lot of it, is unknown to me. And I find after a weekend that quite honestly, I think, well, it's nice to see you but I am enjoying life as it is now. Which is not to say that if they wanted to come back with me I would say "no," but it would take a lot of adjusting. You sort of get out of the habit.

- The first Christmas I went back and cooked the Christmas lunch, and by the afternoon I found I felt slightly bored, and I felt really constricted and tied down, and felt afraid I was going to get sucked back into the "family," which I didn't want.
- They are always happy to be with me (boys 11 and 16). I know they would be happier if I came back. Sometimes I wonder if it wouldn't be for the maid service.... I'm happy and can tolerate their personalities better. I can overlook little things that used to drive me up the wall. It's also easier to relate to them as people, and not just another chore to be taken care of.

These women realize that their current lives suit them far better than their old:

I became, through no doing of my own, a non-custodial mother. My then 14-year-old son elected to go and live with his father in California. After a great deal of initial anger, grief, and hurt, I discovered that not only did the world continue to turn, but in many ways it got better! Today I am back in school working on a degree in speech pathology, quite a bit sooner than I had anticipated; I have more time to pursue other interests; and best of all, my new marriage is relatively hassle-free and greatly improved. My relationship with my son is different in many ways (most of them good) and continues to change and grow. In many ways I would be truly upset if he decided he wanted to return to live with us and I would not encourage it; I could not have said that even a year ago.

When this choice is *not* open to them, some women resent it bitterly:

From the outset of answering this questionnaire I want you to know that I was a non-custodial mother for only the first three months of my divorce and I have been divorced seven years. But I feel my input is valuable because I *wanted* to be a non-custodial mother and my life did change dramatically when I left my family. But at the end of the first three months (of my freedom) my husband said he could not handle the children and I must take them or put them up for adoption. For me that was no choice at all, and my world ended for a long time.

Four more, longer, reflections seem important to share:

- Living on my own for these eight years was essential to my building strength. In combination with therapy and starting college I finally became an adult who is not fearful of independence and who is able to pursue creative fulfillment.

It was a rare woman in the fifties and sixties who was in touch with herself. As a Catholic woman, especially, I believed the highest spiritual attainment was to put the self out of existence altogether. My purpose as a young, Catholic wife and mother was to give all my strength and ability to those around me, to devote myself to God through self-sacrifice and attain reward through eternal bliss in the afterlife. It felt as if I had no purpose at all that meant anything—only drudgery which no one appreciated in the least. I had no idea of who I was at the time of marrying and becoming a mother. I wasn't allowed to have a self by the social system and by my religion. But I have come to know exactly who I am, what I want, what I can do. I feel better now than I ever have in my life. Now, I want to learn, study, travel, write, to soothe other non-custodial mothers. Emotionally, my growth has been good and has meant that I could stay alive. It continues still, of course. I am learning in my second marriage that I value commitment and am adapting to accommodate it. Another satisfaction has been the development of forgiveness. I have forgiven everyone who reacted badly to me, and that is a marvelous relief.

I miss not only my children but my sisters. Living far from family is an unwise development, it seems to me, of our mobile society. Being able to interact with the people you know love you, which becomes more keenly felt by me every year, is a very important part of leading a high-quality life. I was upset when I left by the paradoxes involved—having to inflict pain on others to save myself—but I have never felt what I did to be a mistake, in spite of all the pain it created.

• Filling out this questionnaire was very revealing and very helpful to me. For the first time since I became a non-custodial mother I had the chance to sit down and contemplate what led me to the place where I am now.

One of the things not covered in the questionnaire and which was of enormous interest to me was the issue of family background of non-custodial mothers. I had a very unhappy childhood and found myself ill-equipped for being the kind of parent I had always envisioned myself as being. I have always felt like a house without a foundation. I look good from the outside (I learned early on in the game of life to present myself very well; it was a marvelous tactic. My home life was a horror show—so at least I could make every effort to have a normal life outside of my home). Inside I still feel like a little girl at times. I never felt terribly successful as a mother. I did not really appreciate just how good and loving a mother I was until I was no longer living at home with my husband and kids.

Reading over what I have written in the several months that it has taken me to answer all the questions, I realize more than ever that I am basically a negative person. I learned when I was very young to prepare myself for disappointment because that kept me from getting hurt over and over again. Maybe I did not fight for custody as long as I should have. Perhaps I expected to lose, so I gave in too easily; I am really not sure to this day. I know now pretty clearly who I am, why I act in certain ways, and how I got to this place. It certainly has not been easy. You need courage and guts to be a mother without custody. Not one day goes by that I don't think about my children and miss them. I know that some people think I do not care about my sons, or that I must have been a bad person to leave them, but I do not believe that about myself. If I was wrong or bad, it was in not believing in my own goodness more, in not demanding more of my marriage without feeling that I had no right to make demands; but as a human being I have tried to be the best person and the best mother I know how to be. Because I did not function well in my own marriage, I did not feel it was necessary to blame my ex-husband or take away his home and children. I made the ultimate sacrifice. In order to gain my freedom, I gave up being a full-time mother. I never, not for one particle of time, ever gave up loving my sons or being their mother!

- In my marriage we never argued. I was subservient, and accommodating— "women don't make waves." Somewhere along the line this became intolerable because in leaving I certainly made waves. I often wonder, if I had known how to negotiate, felt free to express needs and emotions, could this marriage have been saved? Probably not. To the best of my knowledge my husband *still* doesn't respond to this kind of confrontation. I know one thing. I *never* should have married (him, or another) then, I was not at all sure of "me," had no skills to rely on on an interpersonal level. I looked for a Prince Charming who would know what I needed, wanted, what was best for me. He expected the same thing! Parenting? I knew so little; I have regrets there. I'd love to have another chance to parent a child. Maybe that is why I have several women friends 15-20 years younger. We support each other, learn from each other. My older sons and I don't have that. I know I could give a lot, experientially and through example, but it hasn't worked for us. It is not a big regret, that I haven't been able to parent, but a sense of disappointment that it went that way. A lot of skills are diffused in other directions, like my job, my volunteer and community work, and with friends. I worked then on instinct. Now I work on informed instinct—aware of repercussions of my performance but accepting of my instincts. Any anger I have is directed toward whatever it was (parents? society?) that never challenged my feelings of inadequacy; somewhere around the age of 12 I felt I was lacking beside my peers. Only well after the age of 35 did I begin to feel good about myself.

My mother died four months ago and I have been thinking a lot about mother-daughter relationships, about my situation now of being at the top of the line, as it were, with four sons who see me as a person rather than as a mother. And not having a mother to check it all out with. I think about that with a sense of irony, because even if my mother were still here she wouldn't know what to tell me, any more than I can tell my children. There's an awful mystique about being a mother. Somehow you are supposed to know all the answers or at least most of them; if we are honest we admit that conception, pregnancy, and delivery do not make us omnipotent. And at the same time many of us reach towards our own mothers for answers we couldn't possibly be expected to know! So how could our mothers? But we all want to know someone who has all the answers even if, being realistic, we know that no one does. Do most of us expect to remarry? I suspect we do! I firmly expected *another* Prince Charming to come along! One of the hardest things I had to face was that I was responsible for me—for my values, needs, etc. that no one would provide them or, at least, no *one* person! Maybe some wives are turned off men completely, but I suspect the needs that channel us into marriage set us up for expecting another someone to come along to fill them even if the first try doesn't work. The big crunch comes, I think, when we have to realize that we ourselves have to resolve those needs.

- It has been several years since I have been living apart from my children. Yet I feel as much their mother and as close to them as I did the day we were first separated. Because of my husband's seeming inability to separate his needs from the children's needs, I feel I have carried the heavier burden. I have to determine what life situation would be most "life-giving" for the children, taking into account physical and emotional needs as well as financial needs. I had to sort out my values and priorities regarding the children. For example, I concluded that the strong emotional support that I could give the children would be useless if we had to live in the fear that they could be taken away again at any time (and that is the reality). So I decided I would find alternate ways of providing that kind of love and support. As my mother said to me, "We all have to let go of our children at some point in our lives. Perhaps you are having to do it sooner than others." I am still not sure I have been able to "let go," but this statement from her has been a consolation to me many times.

There have been times I look at my life over the past five years and painfully wonder what I have gained when it appears I have lost so much. I have asked myself, "was it all worth the price?" Then when I get in touch with the inner peace that is beneath all the pain, I realize that I have gained my own freedom, the freedom to be myself. And that has no price tag.

My thoughts often return to my children. Mothering is hugging and kissing and caring and guiding. It is providing space for children to be free to discover themselves. And my fondest hope now is that through my life and my actions I can give them this freedom, so that they may reach their own destinies.

From another part of the world comes this wonderfully positive testimony, reprinted from the monthly newsletter of the British organization MATCH:

But for me, the personal struggle has ended. My resolution stood firm. I started by building with my children a "positively cheerful future" rather than bemoaning what we had lost. We went out and about at weekends, saw people, did things and generally enjoyed everything. Mid-week we missed each other like mad, phoned and wrote (we're five miles apart!) and have built an ever firmer relationship on the foundations already laid. I realized then that curtailed access couldn't spoil the love we have for each other—it's open and warm and real. I find notes in my bed at night when the children are staying, saying "I love you, Mum. You're nice." and "To Mum. Thanks. Thanks. Thanks."

I know that I've won through and I'm on the home straight. Meanwhile I looked at my own life and decided it lacked purpose. At 37 I'm a teacher in a technical college working with disadvantaged adults. I love my job but I'm in the seventh year there and feel very much on top of the work. Promotion chances are slim since I don't have a degree, so I decided to apply for a part-time B.Ed course. I have been accepted and start in September. I know it will be hard and time-consuming (three years) but it is purposeful. It was then that I realized I hadn't many months before September to get going on a few projects of my own—redecorating the house, planting the garden, etc.! Somehow, with that decision made, everything else followed. On the work front, since then I've joined a couple of committees, learned how to use a computer and consequently speeded up my two-finger typing, started writing learning packs relevant to the course I run, going on courses and conferences myself, joined a working party and generally livened up my day to day work.

All of these things had repercussions at home. I felt more alive, perkier, more confident and able to cope with everyday decisions—budgeting, council repair grants, crumbling garden walls, etc. without panicking. I selected, checked over and bought a car on my own and it hasn't fallen apart yet. I could never have done that before. I also felt the need to be active again, to blow away the cobwebs, and have taken up jogging, swimming, and a weekly session in the multi-gym. Consequently, I've shed weight, changed shape, and look disgustingly healthy! I've talked the editor of a local music magazine into giving me a regular column where I review local groups. It keeps my brain and pen happy and me on my toes as I have to meet his deadlines. I have to go out and about to different clubs in four counties and meet people and interview them. I love doing this and I now have the confidence to do it and the chat to go with it; six months ago I had neither. I have dropped organizing an arithmetic evening class in favor of doing a lady driver's maintenance course. I have taken up pebble painting again, an old hobby which I dropped when I lost the confidence and the creativity. Friends have commissioned me and my ego knows no bounds!....

My bad times are over for now. I've come through older, wiser, more mature in every respect, more hopeful, more confident and having a degree of closeness with the children which I never thought possible. And best of all, I'm happy, really happy, for the first time in my life. Gone is the former depression; I smile a lot now. I even catch myself singing the good old children's hymn "Glad That I Live Am I!" It must show on my face—people are so complimentary of late, again a marvelous ego boost. I must be giving out all the right "vibes," I think. Please don't think I'm boasting. It could all go wrong tomorrow, although I'm sure I'd be better equipped to cope now. I just wanted to say to MATCH mums who haven't made it through yet that the pain *does* ease, things *do* improve and as long as you work towards that "positively cheerful future" you'll be OK.

A friend used to call me "The Dormouse." He said I lived life as though inside a teapot, only coming out for quick looks around. My retort at the time was that every time I took a longer look, someone banged the lid down on my nose, i.e., I got hurt. It doesn't happen like that any more. I don't live in a teapot now and my friend has stopped calling me Dormouse. He calls me by my name instead and this is the highest accolade I could wish for—to be known as me.

Let us not forget our "famous women" in our discussion of "how it turned out"' and listen to Joan Kennedy as she rejoices in her emergence as the woman she wanted to be:

> I have a wonderful life of my own now; I mean an inner life. It gives me incredible serenity that I never thought I could have. I have this incredible energy. I have so much zest for life and living, and maybe another 40 years to live. I think we have to think about what we're going to do for the second half of our lives...I think about that.[1]

And Margaret Trudeau writes:

> My relationship with the children and with Pierre was growing more healthy by the week. My independence and my attempts to work were giving me a far more balanced attitude to motherhood. I longed for my spells at home, and when I got there, threw myself into loving the children properly, caring for them and actually listening to what they had to say in a way that I never had before. I was a real mother to them at last. When after five days at home, I set off back to New York, leaving them with the two wonderful "care-mothers" I had employed, I left them good tempered and serene. I missed them and was always ready to come home.[2]
>
> I see my children for five days every two weeks when I go back home to Ottawa to share with Pierre a life we never had before. I take them to the dentist and buy their shoes. Only now can I love them as they should be loved.
>
> Pierre and I like each other very much as parents. We have compromised on schools and pets and he has helped them understand that I need to work, "to explore my freedom," if I'm to be a good mother to them.[3]

How did it "turn out" for me? Much has happened in these ten years, and I have experienced the same growth and strength and joy as that of my respondents. My friend and I still enjoy a warm, interesting, and comfortable life. My part-time library job has grown into the assistant directorship of one of the largest and busiest libraries on Long Island, and I love my work. I have good and supportive friends and colleagues, some new and some of more than 30 years' standing. I have time for my volunteer work, though not as much, and for hobbies, family and new interests (like writing).

My "children," now grown, are thriving. My youngest daughter came to live with us after almost two years with her father. She graduated from the local high school and is now spending her junior college year in Florence and London as an Art History major. Her army of friends whirls through the house whenever she is here, and seem perfectly comfortable and at home. My son, after he graduated from college, became a New York City policeman. He married a lovely and lively woman, and has two darling little girls. My older daughter has also married, and after moving six times in three years has settled outside of Washington, D.C., where she and her very successful husband delight in their baby son. My relationship with all of them feels warm and supportive and close. The older ones include us in nearly every major event and share their babies fully and freely; one of the joys of my life is seeing what marvelously caring, competent, and enthusiastic parents they are. The youngest trusts me with confidences that not in my wildest dreams would I have shared with my mother and this, too, gladdens my heart. There has always been an element of amazement in my view of my children; I never thought I deserved very much credit for their looks, or their brains, or their successes; nor, may I add, much blame for whatever shortcomings they may have. I have always had the feeling that they aren't "mine" in the sense that they belong to me. I was often struck by the *temerity* I showed in actually *creating* three whole human beings— causing them to *be*— and then expecting them to do and believe and act as I thought they should. So as they go about their adult lives I simply watch and applaud and rejoice and exult. Rarely, however, do I tell them so. There is so much I want them to know without, apparently, my having to say so. I despair of ever really communicating the depth of my caring or the faith and trust and sheer delight I take in them. I sound fatuous to my own ears when I try. Nor do I ever ask them how they feel about my behavior, then or now. I find them happy, productive, and interesting people, and I seem to leave it at that.

There is, in short, very little missing in my life except, I suppose, that comfortable sense of being "normal," of having followed the rules, and done what was expected. And maybe I don't really want that anyway.

I can say with complete assurance that a positive and optimistic attitude, developed over time, was absolutely typical of over 90 percent of the women in my survey, including myself. We were, and are, growing and changing and becoming what we hoped to be. We have found new friends, new interests, new careers, new partners. We can report that we are happy—but not, interestingly, content; this word seemed too stagnant for my respondents. "Content? That's for cows!" scoffed one. "Content means finished, to me," said another, "and I am far from finished!") We feel in charge of our lives, and have accepted that which is unchangeable. We seem to have a much clearer perception of who we are, what we want, and where we are going. And we are eager to keep going. As one woman wrote, in large letters:

I don't know what the future holds, but I look forward to finding out!

I think this is true of all of us. But we were not the only players in the drama; our children were vitally important, also. They have figured largely in the stories we have read so far. But there is other material on the subject that I want to include, in order to help answer another important question: what about the children?

134

What About the Children?

As I indicated from the start, this book is *not* about the children and how they fare in an arrangement with a non-custodial mother, though this is certainly an area worth exploring. We can, however, get some insight into the question from the observations of those non-custodial mothers.

In my questionnaire I went back to the "beginning" on this subject, and asked how fully the children had been prepared for the change. Naturally this depended on the ages of the children and how much they could really understand, but in most cases (82 percent) the mother's departure was abrupt; the children had "no warning." The reason for this seeming callousness can be seen in the following replies:

- Left abruptly. I had contemplated leaving about two months before I actually made the decision. I never told anyone what I was thinking about because I was horrified that I could.... Once I made the decision I couldn't bear the thought of deceiving the kids.... I did realize that it was a chicken way out but came up with no alternative.
- I really left in a rotten way—I just left. I told my ten-year-old in the morning that I couldn't stand the fighting. She just shut her eyes, clenched her fists, and asked where I was going. I said to my friend, and she seemed to have expected that answer. So I got dressed, went to work, and never came back. My son was still sleeping when I left and I never said anything to him at all, his father told him I was gone, I don't know how. My oldest was away at college and I just wrote a letter, and I have no idea now what I said. After about two years I told the two oldest the whole story, but I was completely unable to do that when I left. I think I was too shocked at myself to talk about it.
- I was gone overnight with no warning. I found an apartment but it took another day to move. I told my husband and children about two hours before I left. It was the best I could do.

Only four women felt that their children had been "fully prepared." I doubt whether it is possible to "fully prepare" anyone for so drastic a change, but those who replied in the affirmative said they had shown their children where the new home was to be, worked out visiting schedules ahead of time, discussed fully the reasons for the move, had the children assist with the actual move, etc. Most of us were not that well organized, or so able to conduct rational discussions with the children we felt we were wounding so deeply. We were afraid we would waver in our decision if we left ourselves open to the pleadings of others beforehand. And we suspected that we would never quite get over the sadness we were feeling. That proved to be true rather consistently; even women who were happiest with their new lives expressed moments of doubt or sadness. We can see this kind of mixed reaction in the following:

- I have two children, now nine and eleven, living with my ex-husband. I see them regularly but find the hardest thing is saying goodbye after a happy weekend or holiday. I have been without them for eight years but seem to feel worse now than I did then. I thought the pain would have gone by now. I have remarried and have a son of 16 months, a great joy, and perhaps it will be better when he is older and able to communicate with me more.

- She is very happy, better educated, definitely more "privileged" than I can afford.... That makes the pain of not having her with me worth it.

- I wish their father would take them to the store and help them purchase Mother's Day or birthday cards for me. I have done this to help them buy gifts for their half-siblings and father, but he doesn't help them in that way. Now that they are older, they do sometimes make gifts for me or make cards for me and give them to me late (when they see me). My daughter, especially, makes gifts for me. I also wish they would write more often. Their step-mother makes an effort to show me their report cards, etc. My ex-husband did phone me a couple of years ago when our daughter was in the hospital with pneumonia, to tell me, and I did make a special trip to see her. All in all, I think we work things out fairly well. I try to be as flexible and reasonable as I can and it seems as though their father is following my example.

  I do make a special effort to take them to visit my mother when they visit in the summer or at holidays. They say they are lucky because they have two mothers and two fathers and eight sets of grandparents, double what most kids have. I'm glad they feel this way. They seem extremely well adjusted and do excellent school work and are involved in many extracurricular activities. When they visit me we go on with the regular household schedule for the most part. They help with the housework, etc. During the summer we try to do something special and I arrange my vacation to be with them as much as possible. I have always tried to have a space for them in my home, their own bed, etc. At their father's home my son does a lot of outdoor work, farming, etc., and my daughter does housework and babysitting, so I try to switch when they visit me, and have my son watch my youngest daughter and do the dishes and have my daughter mow the lawn, and things like that. I want them to learn a little of non-sexist lifestyles....

- Peter and I now have a baby son. When he was born I found myself crying for the lost babyhood of my two elder children, for all those years, when we were so close as a family, that can never be recaptured. Happily, our new family has settled into place. The baby thinks his big brothers are gods and they have been pretty wonderful with him so far. I was scared they might feel displaced and I never, ever, want them to feel that they are. I know nothing could ever replace them. I just wish I could spend more time with them before they grow up and leave both their homes. We've simmered down a lot in the six years, though. The children's stepmother (who moved in three years ago) is fair and kind to them, for which I thank her. I've been forced to do without them for certain weekends but I've grown to value the uncluttered time I've been given. The children themselves are emotionally well adapted to our timetable. And now that they are older they are happier spending time with their father, making models and having their friends in to run around their big house. On the other hand, at my place they have the advantage of a huge garden and a couple of school friends living close by. The other day I heard my eldest boasting to a friend that he was lucky because he gets two lots of pocket money! I know that as the boys get older they will want to spend less time with either of their parents and more time with friends. I don't think I'll like that very much but I am very thankful we've been able to live these early years flexibly because I'm sure they've made the children feel OK about themselves.

- When my kids were in a good place I would think I had the best of both worlds. I enjoyed the richness of being a mom and also enjoyed being an independent, self-sufficient, vibrant *woman*! When my children are in trouble, which happens periodically, I am incapacitated. I have often felt helpless at such times because I cannot remove them from their home and I would like to; so I would be their friend, support, therapist, mom. I'd be there for them and help them understand what was going on and what they could do about it.

For a few women, the decision to leave has led to a deterioration of their relationship with their children. The percentage of women in this category was remarkably low; some of their responses are as follows:

- My ex has been vindictive, has turned the children against me and makes it almost impossible to visit. I knew he was angry with me but I never thought he would use the children to hurt me.... It breaks my heart to hear the bitterness in my daughter's voice (she is 11) when she is speaking her father's words, "You don't care," when I do, so much.
- My son chooses not to see me so we have stopped the weekly arrangements. He is going to be 19 so I haven't pushed...
- Ex-spouse and children have put me out of their lives successfully. I hope I can do the same regarding them. Mental cruelty is far worse than physical abuse. My husband knows the trauma and shock I went through— doesn't do anything, as far as the kids, to ease my pain. Between hospitalizations, divorce, degradations, and humiliations I have permanent scars.
- The court said "reasonable visitation." Children were too young to talk on the phone. I would call and ask how they were doing. I went to visit but could only visit in *his* home, with *him* present. He said *he* would

decide what was "reasonable." Every time I went, about every two weeks, he would sit there and watch, like he thought I would steal them. I always cried all the way home after a visit.... After a while I didn't visit at all. It was too painful, I went for a whole year without seeing them at all.

- I sent for your questionnaire on the advice of my counselor at the mental health center. You see, I tried to O.D. two years ago this coming August. To me it was because of an almost complete break with my two oldest children.... I am not allowed to have them come to my house any time, day or night. My son was calling me collect three or four times a week and sometimes more than twice a day, but his father put a stop to that. The pitiful part is that I am not the only one who suffers from all this.... There are four children from this marriage and I have custody of the two youngest, twin girls. My four children have not been able to spend a night together since Christmas of 1979. He does not want and won't have anything to do with the twins. The twins write their brother and sister, and their father will not let them answer.

  It is one hell of a world when a person takes out his problems on his children. The only thing I can say to women who are thinking about leaving without their children is, you had better not have one second of spare time to think about your children, or if you do you better get a good counselor to help you get through life. For those who have already left, I only hope that somewhere out there we will all find peace of mind for what we have done to our children and ourselves. Maybe we will all get lucky and our children will not hate us too much when they grow up. How many times have I said "if only I had known," or "why did I do it this way?" How many times have you said it?

The writer of that letter, and many of the rest of us, may be comforted by the reports of what I came to call "long-lost" children. These were cases where, after many years of estrangement, contact was reestablished. We have often read of the struggles of adopted children searching for their birth mothers; this same phenomenon occurs with mothers who have relinquished custody and have lost touch with their children. Consider the following brief reports:

- My latest news is that after ten years of hearing nothing from my children I received a birthday card this year. I had always written to them on birthdays and at Christmas but no contact was allowed by their father. Now they are becoming older and apparently beginning to take their own initiative. Imagine, I have no idea what they are like and there were only the two names on the card; but the first step has been made.

- I felt unwelcome when I visited, and he made little attempt to send the children to me (I had to pay their transportation costs). After about three years I stopped going, though I tried to keep in touch with letters. The emotional strain on me was too much; to pay for car rental, to go to their (previously *our*) home, and have no privacy with them or to find he had other plans for them—it was really too much. He told the children that my absence was because I didn't care. I didn't see them for years. In later years, good relationships have been established with three of the four. The fourth still believes he was abandoned.

- I didn't see the children again or talk to them for four years, even though I worked in an office three blocks from where they lived and lived only five miles away. He had influenced the children. They hated me and told me so. Even though I had visiting rights, I did not see them. But I always sent Christmas and birthday cards and gifts, and let them know where I was just in case they ever did want to see me. After four years my youngest, who was then 14, came into my office. After a slow start to get to know each other (about two years infrequently) we now see each other every week.

In a similar vein I heard about changes in the custody status, precipitated by the children themselves. As they grew older and better able to take some control over their lives they returned to the mothers who had been living apart from them, sometimes for many years. This was accomplished with varying degrees of difficulty:

- The boys all came here in 1979—Don arrived on my doorstep and six months later Mark came too. However, family pressure was enormous and Don literally ran away and Mark was forced to confront his father and grandmother and reject them, simply because he had chosen to come and live with me. I'm very angry that the boys have been forced into a position where choosing to live with Mom *equals* rejecting Dad.
- We had separated before, and gotten back together. And I worked *very* hard and we set up all sorts of guidelines—trips away, dinners out, etc. But it didn't work. It lasted about a year, and then we told the children I was leaving. My daughter said, "I don't see how you lasted this long." My son said, "But you solved all your problems!" Completely different reactions. My daughter came with me and my son stayed with his father and for about a year we had almost no contact. Then his father remarried and my son went to live with a friend, and then came to live with me. He said he had hated me for breaking up his family, ruining his life, but after a year with his father he had begun to see a lot of the behaviors that had bothered me all those years, and he understood a lot more. He would never let me explain. I guess he had to have the experience. Now he is very understanding of me.... My daughter and I have become pretty good friends.

Every once in a while the courts changed the custody arrangements, but it was a rare woman who tried this route. This news article goes a long way toward explaining the bias of the courts towards a non-custodial mother, as you will see when you reach the last line:

LIKE IN THE MOVIES, MOM WINS SON, KRAMER-STYLE
Lansing, MI (UPI)—The Michigan Court of Appeals, in a case resembling

the plot of the movie "Kramer vs. Kramer," said yesterday that a woman who leaves home in a bid to "pull herself together" should not be punished with the loss of her child.

In fact, the court said, Kim Stein's actions were "Laudable, not damnable."

The ruling upheld a Wayne County Circuit Court decision transferring custody of six-year-old Ian Stein from his father, William, to Mrs. Stein.

According to the court, Mrs. Stein left home in March, 1978, about one year after the child was born.

She later testified that her husband agreed she could send for the boy as soon as she found a job and a suitable home. He denied it.

Stein sued for divorce, which was granted through default, and he received custody of Ian. Two years later, Mrs. Stein successfully sued to have custody changed.

The Appeals Court acknowledged that both the mother and the father have "a genuine love for their child." But, it said, Stein's interference with Mrs. Stein's visitation rights and his alleged propensity for violence, alcohol, and bad language tip the balance in favor of his ex-wife.[1]

One might hope that a "propensity for violence, alcohol, and bad language" would do more than just "tip" the scales of justice. But the actions of the woman who leaves her children however temporary she may intend that separation to be, weigh very heavily against her, and most of us had to wait until the children sought us out of their own accord if we wanted to actually reverse the custody situation.

Feelings of powerlessness assailed many of us. The following story illustrates our frustration, often, at the helplessness we seemed unable to combat:

My son was three and my daughter seven when I left their father. My daughter was old enough and verbal enough to ask questions and understand answers, a process she continues to use. As she has grown, the questions have become much more sophisticated, and I have had to frame my answers accordingly. If she does not ask for a long time I make a point of asking her if she has any more questions. She also talks to me about her relationship with her father, and I sense that she is using those conversations to expand her understanding of what happened. My son is a different matter. He was three when I left and would not even stay in the same room the day we told him I was moving. He seemed to be fine and to adjust well, but he would *never* talk about the divorce, nor would he ask any questions.... About six months ago a colleague of mine, a guidance counselor, was giving him an intelligence test. When my son asked her what a guidance counselor does, she listed a number of things, including helping youngsters whose parents were divorced. When she commented on how well he seemed to have adjusted, he broke down and cried and said he was miserable. When she asked him why he didn't tell me, he told her he didn't want to hurt me. I passed this information on to his father along with the counselor's recommendation for immediate further help. His father has done nothing despite my repeated requests, and legally there is nothing I can do myself. This is a real problem for a parent without custody. In many respects I am powerless, and that I resent. I can protect myself, but not my children (at least legally). I have, however, decided that I am willing to risk legal repercussions by obtaining counseling for my son. It is interesting to me that this particular episode, despite its pain, is still another example of how far I have come personally and as a parent.

Ambivalence is common, even in those women who are satisfied with their new status:

- I do continue to feel very close to my children (who are both top students and outstanding athletes, by the way!), talk to them frequently on the telephone, visit them occasionally. To be honest, I do enjoy the freedom I have now to prepare for my career and enjoy my new marriage. To be honest, I do sometimes ache for them and the parts of their lives I am missing. They enjoy visiting us, get along well with my husband, and even pretty well now with his kids. Fortunately we can offer them a wonderful, though somewhat cramped, place to stay on the beach and interesting things to do. We have seen enough of the sad "Disneyland Daddy" syndrome that we try not to plan expensive, event-filled amusements when they are with us, but attempt just to be with them companionably.

    However, the temptation is great to be excessively concerned with whether they are having a good time, to worry about whether we are organizing visits to everyone's benefit.... I am bothered when I find myself waiting on them hand and food when they're here—cooking every meal and snack, cleaning up after them, washing their clothes for them, satisfying almost all their whims (something I never did when they lived with me full time or even half-time). I so want them to be happy, and I've always had a tendency toward overprotection anyway. And I do worry that in my search for personal happiness I may have damaged them somehow. They don't seem angry with me (though I know it is there somewhere) and they appear to love me, and it's so very important to me that they continue to do so and that they know I love them.
- My children are with me Saturday night and Sunday. This fits into my work schedule. I can call them any time I wish. They would like more time with me, but I am finding I like my time alone. The guilt feelings associated with this left me a mess until I faced the fact that this was the way I feel and accepted it as OK. I still have my moments.

Yes, we all do, most assuredly, "have our moments," even those of us who have made a success of the new arrangements. Some of those "moments" come from our relationships with the new women in the lives of our children. I did not delve much into the women's reactions to and relationships with their children's step-mothers, though this, too, would be rich terrain to explore.

The following accounts cover the spectrum of feelings about this new family member:

- My ex-husband married a woman with three kids. They have formed an aggregate family. I see my role as kind of an "Auntie Mame" to all five kids. I've taken all five to musical events and on picnics. They all call me by my first name, including my sons (they also call their father by his first name).

- I remarried and had a third child. My first two children (who live with their father) have a good relationship with my present husband. He has two sons by his previous marriage; the oldest (17) lives with us and the younger (15) with his mother. I never know whether to say I have three children or five children or two children when asked. My former husband remarried and has four more children with his present wife. Whew. He and his present wife and I get along agreeably and seem to be able to resolve things in the best interests of the children without too much problem.

- I also suffer the pain and jealousy inevitable when one's son is taken over by "the other woman." My ex-husband was granted custody of our children with my consent. Had I known this "other woman" was to take over my son as well I would never have granted custody to him. I honestly believed that our children, then aged nine and ten, would be better off with two happy people rather than with one miserable person, as I was then.... I went into hospital with severe depression and our children went to live with their father. I have to listen to remarks like "I like her better than you, Mum," and "Daddy does, too, so it must be all right." I never speak to her, it's really best not to if you feel hatred for another person. I only spoke to her to pass my very low opinion of her. It only made matters worse, really. The fact that she is the "other woman" in my husband's life I have come to terms with. I feel murderous that she is the other woman in my son's life.

- I think the most difficult part of dealing with the situation, from the children's point of view, has been to balance their feelings of anger (at their perceived desertion) and love/loyalty to me. They have further been stressed by the demand that they transfer at least some of their allegiance to a stepmother whom they were bound to resent. In the more than three years since she has been their stepmother, they have never gotten past the attitude that "she's not our mother, and we don't have to do what she says," for which I blame their father.

- I am grateful to her, both for being the sort of "other woman" and stepmother she has been for the past six years and for gracefully finding her own little niche during my daughter's wedding and allowing me to play the mother-of-the-bride role to the hilt. She even made no fuss when Laura's father and I, having accompanied her up the aisle, sat together during the ceremony. I feel affection and gratitude toward the woman who has taken on the role of mother toward my children in my absence. I know that even though she is very different from me in her approach to motherhood, her intentions are as generous as I like to think mine would be in a similar situation.... I know my children will always feel great affection for her and that pleases me.

Finally, let's hear again from Shirley Glubka, whose son has lived with a foster-mother selected by Shirley for nine years:

As far as I can tell, Kevin is not now a particularly angry person; and he does not seem to have any resentment (at least at this point in his life) about having been required to leave me and adopt a new mother.

I can say this with some confidence because this spring I found the precise mixture of relaxation, courage, and support from other people in my life that allowed me, finally, to ask The Question. The setting was an A&W restaurant on a busy road along with K-Mart, G.I. Joe's, and quite a number of auto dealers. Kevin and I were having hamburgers and root beer and waiting for the theater to open so we could watch a science fiction movie called "Hangar 18." In the middle of my hamburger, I asked him: "So, Kevin, what do you think about the fact that I am your real mom and we don't live together?"

He was quite ready with an answer and considerably calmer than I was. He had a theory: he supposed that I had not been able to afford having a child and so had given him to Gretchen. (Other children in Kevin's situation have expressed similar theories. It seems that children who do not live with their parents are likely to come up with an explanation of their situation that absolves both them and their parents of responsibility for the separation. In Kevin's case it was lack of money; in another child's it was immigration laws that required the parent to leave. In neither case did the external force actually have anything to do with the separation.) I told Kevin that money had not been a problem and talked a little about the real reasons for my decision. Then I held my breath.

His response was calm and thoughtful. He said it was a good thing I had given him to Gretchen. He was sure the job of being a mother would have gotten harder and harder for me, and Gretchen was a good mom. He added, clearly not ready to abandon a well-thought-out theory, that he supposed I would have had financial problems if I had kept him.

Before that day in the A&W I had a recurring fantasy that Kevin would, somewhere around the age of 30, go to a psychotherapist and, hour by expensive hour, unearth his anger at me for "giving him away." Perhaps he will do just that, I cannot know. But the fantasy does not come to me now. I have asked the crucial question, which is really many questions; is it all right? do you hate me? were you damaged? And I have received the gift of a calm answer from a child who seems to believe his life is just fine.

Dealing with children during and after a divorce is the subject of innumerable books and articles on divorce, remarriage, step-parenting, and the like. Non-custodial mothers face additional problems in our relationships with our children because of the unusual nature of our arrangements. Children can easily find other children living with their mothers as single parents, but those who live apart from their mothers are more apt to feel different and vulnerable. Still, much of the "usual" advice found in the books and articles mentioned above applies, and can be adopted to good effect. I did ask my respondents for specific discussion on how to deal with the children, and got a few answers:

- Go ahead and make the decision that you know is best for yourself and the children, don't let guilt choke you to death. Know that *nothing* will change your mother-child relationship. Also remember that generally children are much more adaptable to changes in lifestyle than we are as adults. Why should we feel guilty about doing something which will ultimately be to the benefit of ourselves and our children? I am confident that my children will grow into responsible adults who will recognize the love that it took for me to let them go.
- I try to treat my children and step-children the same way I treat other people, with respect. I listen when they talk and don't interrupt them. I don't guilt trip them. I hug them a lot. They teach me more than I probably teach them, but if they ask my opinion I give it to them from my experience, also telling them that not everyone has the same experiences in the same situations. I try to help them to develop their own sense of good judgment by letting them do things and see if it works or not. If not, I help them clean up the mess if they want me to. I've been trying to teach them the skills of everyday living that they will need, like cooking and cleaning and laundry, boys and girls both. I try to teach them to be tolerant by being tolerant of them. I hope it works.
- Consider all your options, devise legal arguments that allow for flexibility later on. Don't use the kids as pawns. If they are old enough to understand then they are old enough to be involved in your thought processes and in their own fates. Give them credit for being the products of your loving mothering. Don't badmouth their father; they have loyalty to both. They're smart enough to make their own judgments. Just try to be the kind of human being you'd like them to be able to use as a positive role model. They will respect you for being true to yourself.

I, like many others, believe that honesty is the bottom line when dealing with our children in this situation. Opinions do vary as to how *much* honesty is healthy and wise. Some people feel that children should know exactly what the situation is, no matter how scary and painful, because it is reality and they will have to deal with it sooner or later. Others feel that children can be hurried into adult situations and decision-making long before they are ready to cope, causing them undue stress and hardship.

There is, no doubt, much to be said for both points of view, but I and most of my respondents have come down on the side of total honesty. Certainly I would have had an easier time of it if I had not preserved an illusion about my marriage quite so carefully. "You sure know how to shock the shit out of a person!" said a friend when she heard the news. My parents, I imagine, would not have been hit so hard if I had been more candid about my struggles. And certainly that applies to my children as well; they heard the fighting, and the stony silences, and saw me crying, and more than once found me sleeping in the den. But there was never any discussion of what was wrong and how we might *all* work to fix it. Such honesty is harder and more dangerous, but the foundation is firmer than one built on a false security. It is better, I feel, to allow your children into your humanity, however frail; it is, after all, their reality, too. That honesty also allows children to see how essential they are to the operation of the unit in which they find themselves, how valuable and needed, and this is a powerful motivation for positive action. I believe this is why the children of divorce (and, I might add, the children of working parents) are so often mature, independent, and able to make their own decisions. They know that they are needed, as confidantes and chore-doers and even money-earners, that their ideas and feelings *are* important, that they are trusted and relied upon. If there is no longer a Mommy hovering 24 hours a day, no Daddy dishing out the cash, no more invented chores aimed at "character building," children are much more apt to see themselves as important, contributing members of the group, and will almost always act accordingly. In the new configuration we have established, whatever it may be, everyone *is* needed; there is a great deal of security in that knowledge, no matter how difficult the actual living of it may be.

Non-custodial mothers do face one major difficulty, however, in their efforts to be honest; trying to walk that fine line between explaining that while they could not stand to live with their husbands any longer, their children will like it just fine. If the answers to "Why did you leave?" involve tales that might be better left untold, then sticking to the line, "We just think this is best for all of us" is probably wise. This is perhaps a cop-out of sorts, but is generally true enough to be acceptable. I once sat down with my younger daughter to explain something and began by saying, "Now, I don't want to say anything bad about Daddy...." She interrupted, teeth clenched, saying fiercely, "Then, *don't*." This is really very good advice, albeit sometimes requiring superhuman restraint. Children will, whatever their family set-up, come to their own conclusions about the strengths and weaknesses, and successes and failures, of their parents, based on what they see and experience, regardless of how anyone tries to color their thinking. Recall how several respondents said that their husbands "poisoned the children's minds" against them. That may have been possible in the short run. In the long run, however, those same children will make their own investigations and come to their own conclusions. I believe that if you have built a foundation of honesty that they can trust, then you can continue to build on that foundation even after a gap of many years.

While we are on the subject of honesty with children let me offer some advice that is contrary to almost everything you will read in the books on divorce and "how to tell the children." Those books will advise you to repeat, over and over, that while you have stopped loving Mommy/Daddy you will *never* stop loving him/her, that Mommies and Daddies *never* stop loving their children and will *always* be right there. To my way of thinking it is a pretty dim child who is going to swallow that whole. If you can stop loving one person you can stop loving another, the children will reason, with justification. In their eyes you have proven that you are not very good at long-term promises; they hold this view even when you explain that you meant your promises at the time you made them (at the wedding). And any child who can read can see that Mommies and Daddies certainly *do* stop loving their children, that some parents never even start, that some are capable of wounding and even killing them. So sweeping statements about *always* and *never* are not going to create much initial solid ground. Short-term, well-kept plans and promises, reasonably thought out and agreed upon, will go much further in building the kind of confidence you want to give your child.

Children will test your commitment, of course, and I think in the beginning it is wise to go overboard in proving you will do as much as you can to be responsive. I remember that I stopped off after work one day to see my son, then 16, and he had a pair of overalls that needed alteration. I asked if he wanted me to do it and he said no. Shortly after I got home he called, and said he had changed his mind and yes, he did want me to fix them. So I drove the 20 miles back and did the sewing. I wouldn't have made a practice of answering such demands if they had continued (which they didn't), but I felt at the time that it was a test of my commitment and was worth going out of my way to meet. On the other hand, this same son often suggested that he would like a little extra cash. I genuinely did not have enough to give him, and said so; he seemed to accept that this was true, and not a rejection of his needs.

Full explanation, all along the line, about the difficulties you are having in establishing new patterns and your firm intentions to continue to try, is essential (if, of course, you *do* have such intentions; if not, you'd better tell them that, too).

Worry, guilt, fear, and concern about the the impact of our decisions on the welfare of our children is perhaps our thorniest problem. So perhaps the very *best* advice came from this woman in New York:

> Be prepared for the awesome truth that your children can, will, and do grow up quite well without (or in spite of) you.

My mother used to ask me, "Don't you hate to see them grow up?" The answer is, no. I loved that; it is what children are meant to do. And as children grow, they change, and our relationships with them change. A charming and lovable toddler becomes an intractable teenager; an impossible 14-year-old becomes a helpful and interesting young adult. They change, and change again, and our relationships must change, and the dynamics of those relationships must change, too. My older daughter is married with a family of her own. My son is now a husband and father himself. My elfin younger daughter has become a stunning and mature college student. How could my relationships with them *not* change, no matter what our life style? The children become no longer children, and we have to then ask ourselves, how long *did* we intend to hang onto them? As one woman quoted her mother as saying, "we all have to let go of our children some time." How, in the last analysis, does one define "custody"? It is, when you think of it, a terrible word, implying helplessness, incompetence, stagnation—an institutional word, one applied to mental patients and criminals. Should it also be applied to the bright, alert, thoughtful, able persons our children are becoming? We resist mightily, and fight wars, over the possibility that we will be in someone's "custody," that is to say, under someone's control. Surely the true goal for our children *is* non-custody.

I was discussing, with a young man of 22, his mother's participation in a television show where she spoke about her experience as a non-custodial mother. "She was *fine*," he told me. "Articulate, clear, not at all nervous. But she was, well, shall we say, miscast. I think there is a big confusion here between non-custody and empty nest. Children *do* leave home, after all. My mother called me not too long ago and wanted me to come for dinner for some occasion or other and I told her I had other plans, and she said, 'well, I *do* have custody.' 'Well! Right! I'll be right over, you have custody.' I mean, she thought she had custody while I was away at college. I mean, when does it *end*?" His aunt, who was listening, laughed. "My mother thought she had custody of me until the day she died— and I was 47!"

A mother I interviewed came to the realization that "custody" was "over" when she had a conversation with her boss:

> I was discussing research on non-custodial mothers with my boss and he seemed somewhat puzzled. I reminded him that I was a non-custodial mother myself. "Well, yes," he said. "But somehow I don't think of you in those terms. Your children are grown." And suddenly it hit me—*they were grown!* I had made it! I didn't have to hurt for them any more.

As she related this story she fairly jumped up and down; she seemed not only to be telling the story for me but to be re-experiencing the exuberance she felt in knowing that they *have* come through it, that her children *have* "grown up" successfully, and that she can relieve herself of the burdens of guilt and pain she carried for so long. She *had*, as she came to see, "made it."

And that is true, at base, for most of us. We have made, or are making, it work. Some more successfully than others, but then that is true of *all* parents and children, regardless of family structures. If love is the key (and most studies, and our own common sense tells us that it is) and we have been able to continue to give it, and our children have been able to receive it, and to return it, how can we not succeed?

We do, however, all need help and guidance. It was for this reason that the final page of the questionnaire asked: What advice can you share with others?

What Advice Do You Have For Others?

There are literally hundreds of books and thousands of articles offering advice on the divorce process: on deciding to divorce, recovering from divorce, on child custody, on single parenting, on finding a new mate, on living in step-families and on all sorts of related topics. I was not particularly interested in rewriting them. I did want to discover some of the unique ways this particular sample of divorced women had identified and faced its problems and how these women would advise others, from their unique points of view. This sample group had much to offer that is not found elsewhere. So little of the existing material deals with this aspect of divorce, custody, and remarriage, though it deserves careful and increased attention. I was glad to discover, then, that my respondents were so generous with their guidance and opinions. We can certainly extrapolate implied advice from the chapters that have gone before, but there is much more to be gleaned from their direct answers to the question: What would you advise other women? Some were reluctant to characterize their words as "advice," though their answers were among the best:

- I wouldn't propose to advise anyone. Advice is usually something the person giving it feels you want to hear. It is not their true feelings—those come out later. Just do your own thing; don't feel guilty if you change your mind. People change and so do their minds. You can be sure today and unsure tomorrow. It's all just a chance. It's never black or white, good or bad. We wish it could be; we convince ourselves it is; but life is not that way. And overall, I'm glad it isn't.
- *No*! I might share my pain, hassles, fears, hurts, and all of the positive—loving, smiles. But Advice? No. Only they know for *themselves*, *their* husband, *their* children. It isn't easy for either parent to be the absentee—nor is it easy for either to be the only one at home. And it is *never* easy for the kids. The only thing I can tell anyone is that any way you go it will hurt *everyone* involved. There is no good, or right, or easy, or honorable solution. There is only the initial pain, the inevitable numbness, and, hopefully, the conquering power of love. It is a hard, tearful way to live, but it can be done. And if you try, desperately hard, to keep viable relationships alive with your husband *and* your kids, it might hurt a lot more, but it will make it all possible.
- This is awfully tough to answer because I believe no single piece of

149

advice can be appropriate for every woman. Maybe the best broad piece of advice is to "know thyself" before making a decision. For a woman like myself, who had not been nurtured well enough in childhood and who should never have become a mother, relinquishing custody is probably most often the best for her and her children. For other women, it may not be best, but only *they* can truly know after examining their feelings, abilities and disabilities, and needs. And I am a firm believer that a person must and ought to do what he or she knows to be essential to their well-being. Maintaining custody out of a sense of duty only is just plain destructive to all involved, just like maintaining a marriage "for the sake of the children."

She's right, of course; it is "awfully tough" to find advice to apply to every case, or even most cases. It was very difficult to summarize and categorize many of the answers, and impossible to capture their flavor and intensity when I tried. Let me start, then, by sharing some of the replies just as they came to me, written and spoken. They range from the strictly practical to the spiritually enabling, and they all came, obviously, from the heart.

There was, first, the sort of advice I came to think of as a definite "call to arms":

- Don't be afraid of a fight. Don't count on things being friendly and so be accommodating, as women always have. Better a fight now than living for years with a lousy arrangement. Don't think you can count on your spouse for anything. Don't trust him! Even if you have known him for 20 years, don't trust him. People are unpredictable.
- Demand your rights, keep calm, and pursue the system. Continue to write letters, make phone calls, etc. Don't give up for anything less than you believe is right.
- Worry about yourself and your kids, not about your mother or the neighbors! Fight for what you want—you won't always win, but you'll never get anything if you don't fight. Don't be scared and if you are, fight that too!
- Don't be afraid to make demands. Insist on your right to personhood. Be selfish, love yourself, go for it!
- Know, and be prepared emotionally, intellectually, legally, for the battles that lie ahead. So many think that "it couldn't happen to me, we're on such mature terms." That's great, but often it doesn't last. As situations change (marriages by either spouse, moves, even personality changes of those involved), the children become a battling ground.
- *Fight* all the way. I didn't take my children originally because of taking them from school, not having a job, and taking them from their father. However, now, I would have waited, saved more, and taken all the children and never backed down. I'd never give up custody if I had it to do over.

Then there was the more practical and yet encompassing, reflective kind of advice:

150

- Contact a women's center, get the name of a feminist therapist and feminist lawyer. Don't feel ashamed of being indecisive; talk it out with as many people as you can. You'll then know what feels right to you! Get a job, no matter what it is, and talk to people. Do volunteer work. It doesn't cost money, you meet people, and you are needed. Don't feel uncomfortable or conspicuous; you are *not* the only woman in this situation and there are other things going on in the world besides your re-entry! Watch out for non-productive evenings with alcohol, drugs, vegetating. Reach out for people, but don't feel disappointed if you meet some "losers." Keep trying and learn to be alone with yourself. Remember your marriage break-up is only one part of your life. You have other parts to you; do something about those. The public library is cheap and can provide magazines, bulletin boards, records, entertainment, public contact *and* books.
- *See a counselor* (preferably a women who has some experience, or a man who is not a woman-hater). Talk to other women who have been through this. Don't try to defend yourself; it's not worth it and it won't work. They have already made up their minds in most cases. Let your kids know you love them, and you care a great deal about them. But *know* that they will stick by the custodial parent in the end. Let them know you are and always will be their *only* mother. Try not to play games with the kids and the ex. Everyone loses. Be aware that the kids are not dumb and will play on your guilt very handily. You must be tough and not get caught in the game of one-upmanship. And don't let them play the game of "if you're not nice to me, I won't come over here again" or "Dad is taking us skiing in Aspen next weekend, where will you take us?" And basically realize that you have a life, too. The kids will be on their own one day, and you will still have to carry on your life. Bear that in mind. You are deserving of a good life, too. And they are, too, and your ex is, too. We have not done anything so bad that we need to carry a cross for the duration of our life. If that were the case, we might as well give up now. Motherhood doesn't mean a lifetime of self-sacrifice anymore. We are people first and mothers second.
- Take advantage of every outlet. Check out and *hear* suggestions from agencies available. If you feel you are not a "mother-person" and did not have this in perspective before birthing, convey this information to a professional who will help you deal with it before a rash decision is made. *Never, never* feel like nature's oddity! My major comfort has been gotten from studying nature. The animal kingdom, humans' cousins, offers many examples of alternative lifestyles and the fact that not every female is adept at reproduction and mothering. Parenting involves a whole lot of maturity. Children cannot successfully raise other children.
- Achieve financial independence as much as possible (that's a hard one); trust to your own strengths; struggle to achieve whatever it is you may desire, no matter how different it seems; don't be afraid; find supportive women friends; ignore the comments of most of the people you know and follow your own heart. Fly like an eagle!
- Consider all options. Stay with positive people and avoid non-supportive

others. Provide children with quality, caring love. Avoid custody battles whenever possible, as the children will always see through the superficial and come back to you if you are the honest parent. Admit your needs and shortcomings.

- Don't let anyone—ex-husband, parents, anyone—deny you the right to be close to the children. Some people want to punish you, but you're never bad for your children as long as you love them. Forget other adults' crap and concentrate on those growing people who have *not* lost their mother.
- Try to be prepared for the loneliness; it's great. Also try to have a best friend to rely on. Realize that whatever you do you're thinking of yourself now. If you don't no one else will! Be strong and selfish. It's your life! Do with it as you wish.
- Mother your children as you would love to have been mothered. Trust the deep wisdom within yourself. Learn to play freely, spontaneously, outrageously. Get yourself together; commit to health and growth. Laugh!
- Make a path where there is none, and become your own best friend. Lean on other people, but not too much. Most of all, tap those inner strengths because they are *there*!
- Follow your own deep, inner knowing, despite what "society" says you "should" do. We each, as women, must make new definitions for ourselves of what being a mother means. Give up the guilt, because that means you are stumbling over the past and using up your "now" moments. Live each day as though it were the last you had with yourself and with your child. Mothering means (to me) to be the most perfect Me I can be— not the most perfect mother! But to be real, honest, and the best model I can be for my child. That means feeling OK with myself and my decisions and living in ways that make me feel productive and happy.
- Always look ahead in your life. Dwelling in the past, trying to make up for things past, rehashing the same stories over and over really doesn't do any good. There is, of course, something to be said for learning from your mistakes, but there is also a time to move on. Admit it, accept it, but always remember that it can't be changed now. Our possibilities lie in the future; that is where our energies need to be concentrated. Many a night I would play or remember the song by Joan Baez, "I'll Live One Day at a Time." Yesterday's dead and tomorrow is blind, so ... the future holds our vision. Like playing cards, sometimes you get dealt a rotten hand, but that doesn't mean the whole game is over. There are always going to be people in this world who are not going to like you. There are those who can hate you just because your skin color doesn't match theirs, or your religion doesn't, or your lifestyle doesn't. Some need to feel superior and can only do it at the expense of a convenient target. These types of comments need not be taken seriously. You *must* believe in yourself and it gets much easier to see through the game that you know you are not playing. People cannot hurt you, cannot "win" if you are in different ball parks.

I like these broad, encompassing answers. I found them positive, encouraging, hopeful, helpful, and inspiring. But I also tried, in dealing with the advice, to discover specific suggestions for specific concerns: How do I start? What should I do? How can I handle this or that?

I found that *take your time* was probably the advice most often offered. You will recall that many of us acted in extreme haste, and most of us regret it. Therefore, carefully consider these comments:

- Do not make any hasty decisions; remember that your life might not be the same six months later. Once a decision on custody is made it will be difficult if not impossible to change; you may someday have to make the choice between the children and a new man in your life. Realize that whatever decision you make, right or wrong, you will have to live with it for a long time and you can't let it affect your everyday life.
- Do not rush into divorce; do not assume that the grass is greener on the other side.
- Think things through carefully; make a plan. Don't trust the father, no matter how honest he seems.
- Before you do it, think about it a lot, and then think about it some more.
- Think very long and hard before leaving your children, because after you have done it, if you regret it sorely, you may not be able to correct your mistake.
- Don't allow anyone to force you into a decision you are not ready to make. Consider all aspects carefully, and have in-depth family counseling. This is not a decision to make alone. It affects many lives for a lifetime.
- Make sure you are doing the right thing, because the mental horrors will tear you apart. It isn't like a weekend or a week away from your children. You had better be ready for the many years of guilt, loneliness, hate you will feel for yourself, and of trying to remember what they look like when they sleep, or kissing them before they go to bed or to school.
- *Do not be in a hurry!*

The hastiness with which many of us acted meant we were unprepared; a large number of the suggestions referred to that need for preparation in areas of finances, law, and general decision-making:

- Have independent credit, checking, and savings established.
- Think of the practical aspects of moving; have somewhere to move to, build up a network of people for support and have money, however little, of your own.
- Be financially prepared.
- Be sure you can pay for what you want. Don't depend on anything else.
- Shop around for a lawyer until you find one *you* want.
- Get visitation rights nailed down in detail. Document and record any discussion of financial arrangements and provide for the rate of inflation, etc. beforehand.
- Get all the legal data you can. See several attorneys before selecting one.
- First, get a lawyer and discuss all your options. Second, don't let anyone make you feel inferior or wrong. Third, think the situation through and *do*

153

not hurry. Fourth, make sure everything you want is specifically stated in the divorce and custody papers. *Do not* take someone's word for it! Have it in writing and make sure it is iron-clad! Most of all, be sure it is what you really want. Then, stand tall and be proud.

Stand tall and be proud; know thyself; love yourself. This was the underlying message we wanted to share. There are many roads to that goal, and many were touched on, but perhaps the path most often cited was counseling and therapy. The growing body of feminist therapists who are willing and able to explore non-custody as a viable option for women will make good therapy easier to find. A reply from Ohio sums up:

> Get competent, thorough counseling. If at all possible, counseling should begin before the separation decision, to clarify the issue and expose the alternatives, and should continue through the whole divorce process.

Probably it should continue even beyond that. I thought the following was a particularly clear description of how counseling and therapy, and support systems in general, can further the process of growth and adjustment:

> You develop certain opinions of people who do certain things—build a description, as it were. You have a certain mental picture of what a person who does a certain thing is like. So, you have a mental image of a person who "walks out" on a family: irresponsible, shallow, a failure, uncommitted, uncaring. So when *you* do it, you find yourself with two definitions of yourself, old and new, neither of which fits. Here is a king-sized identity crisis. And you begin to measure yourself against that mental description. *Am* I irresponsible? *Am* I shallow?
>
> Here is where one's support system comes in; they help you to redefine yourself, to blend those two descriptions, because of course the first one is now incorrect. Traditional wife, Mommy, obedient daughter, community activist, pillar of the church—a lot of those descriptions no longer apply. And if you have people around you saying you certainly *are* irresponsible and shallow and unfeeling, your 'recovery' will be terribly slowed. And conversely, if your companions assure you that you are just who you've always been, only now you are having to use all those sterling qualities in new ways, you can accomplish the process of redefining yourself more easily and more effectively. You can begin to say, "well, I used to be a parent *in* a home, and now I am a parent *outside* that home, but I am *still a parent*. And I used to show caring in *these* several ways, from *inside* the home. Now I will show caring in *other* ways from *outside* the home. But my *goal* is still the same—to show caring." When you *do* have to redefine yourself, as you must when you leave your children, you have to do an enormous amount of introspection and that is why it is so often so valuable to have professional help with it. Because you *do* have to examine each facet of your character to see whether it is really true. Now, when you are living traditionally you don't have to bother (maybe) because you *know* what the definition is, and

154

because you're doing it, it must be so. "I must be loving and caring because I am here every day cooking and washing the socks." The fact that you don't always *feel* loving and caring doesn't matter, because the myth protects you and your image, and you and the world know you must be real in the role because you are living the role.

But when you are *not* in the role, you *do* have to find a true definition of yourself and that is something that very few people have a chance to do. Once having done it, however, ever after your decisions will be easier and your actions clearer because you will *know* who you are and what you want and where you are going and how you will get there. And your children will see that you are a *real person*, not just a stereotyped role, and that's the grandest thing a child *can* know. That's providing a real role model, not a label. And your counselor or therapist and all those people around you *do* see a real person and can tell you about her and help you to grow to love her, too. I like this definition of a friend that I read in a pamphlet from the Christophers: "A friend hears the song in my heart and sings it to me when my memory fails." One way or another, once you figure out who you are and share it, there will be someone singing all the time.

Obviously, the best information comes from the voices of experience. I hope that books like this one will help. There is also an excellent book, authored by Dr. Geoffrey Greif and Mary Pabst, entitled *Mothers Without Custody*, which has recently appeared. Based on interviews and questionnaires from over 500 non-custodial mothers, it is altogether supportive, accepting, and informative; I recommend it highly.

Personal contact may be even more helpful. Some of the groups mentioned in the last chapter can help one to follow this oft-offered advice:

- Talk to someone who has done it before.
- Before you surrender custody, *talk* to other non-custodial mothers.
- Talk to other women who have coped with the same decision. If you don't know any, track them down before you make a final decision. Find a support group.

Support groups, it should be remembered, come in many forms. The formal gathering of people with similar problems and goals is only one sort of framework that can buoy one up. Family, as we saw earlier, may be another; friends, yet another. Friends, perhaps, in situations that seem at first glance to be the very opposite of yours. Do not overlook this group, and consider this observation:

The very best thing that any non-custodial parent can do is to be sure to maintain friendships with parents in "intact" families, with children around the same ages as yours. I can't tell you how heartening it is to hear that teenage boys in intact families *also* smoke pot and drive too fast and forget what

155

time Grandma's birthday party was and never write home from college. And that 14-year-old girls with both parents in the home *also* hole up in their rooms for hours and never have anything to wear and "forget" their gym suits regularly. Or that many five-year-olds wet the bed, that not all two-year-olds are toilet trained, that other nine-year-olds do flunk math....No, your children are not perfect and do doubt your leaving them had a major effect, but it is almost surely not the cause of all that goes awry. *No one's* children are perfect, and there are thousands of examples of children who "go wrong" despite what appears to be an ideal family set-up—and their brothers and sisters turn out fine. And there are thousands more who succeed and flourish despite terrible home lives, much worse than your children are in, situations that ought to produce hopeless psychopaths and instead produce leaders and winners. Do not believe for a *minute* that there is one right way to produce a happy, successful, well-adjusted kid; there are dozens of ways. The ingredients are the same—love, honesty, appreciation—but you can offer those things in many ways. And if *your* way is from outside the original marriage, and even from a very non-traditional lifestyle of your own, like lesbian mothers, then do it your way. You'll get through to them— maybe not the first week, or month, or ever year, but they'll hear you eventually. And admire your courage. Guaranteed!

Knowing what can reasonably be expected of children of various ages is indeed important and can save a lot of grief and worry. I had a woman come to me very distressed over what she saw as her deteriorating relationship with her son. "He won't talk to me!" she mourned. "Oh, he calls me and we talk on the phone every day but he hardly says anything—maybe he tells me one thing about school and sports or something, but that's all. He used to talk a lot. Now he won't!" I asked her how old this boy was. "Sixteen." she answered. I think it would have helped this woman considerably to know that many 16-year-olds talk in monosyllables to their mothers, when they talk at all. "Good Heavens!" exclaimed another friend at this story. "Mine can go for days without saying anything to any of us!" To get a daily phone call is probably much more than would be expected from the average boy, as she would have known if she had had friends with boys that age. I know that if I had not had a friend with whom to compare teenage sons, and getting-married daughters and the general effects of growing up in the fifties, I would have had a much harder time of it. Knowing that, despite her traditional family and intact marriage, my friend experienced some of the same anguish, doubts, and chagrin I was experiencing helped to keep that anguish and doubt in better perspective. Keeping, or forming, friendships with traditional women whose similarities to you may exceed the differences is advice worth heeding.

And here is another bonus that might accrue: in the process of seeking supportive friends and companions, you will also discover that this is a good time to reassess your *existing* social and familial ties. With whom do you *want* to maintain a bond? This might be a good time *not* to call Lucille, or Marge, or Aunt Amy. Contacts that could not possibly be ignored before often fade painlessly away. And bonds that *are* renewed, without illusions and false expectations, are forged firmer and truer. I repeat a comment from the woman who wrote:

> A situation like mine reduced things to skeletal simplicity.... In the end there were a few people standing by my side. The chaff blew away in the wind and truly my life is better now.

Maybe the ladies of the PTA aren't calling you any more for cookies, but then, do you *want* them to? Perhaps you do! Perhaps baking a fancy cake for the Parent's Day raffle was really your thing. In that case, keep baking, maybe for another school in another town, but so what? On the other hand if going door to door collecting for the high school band made your skin crawl, now is the perfect time to say "No, I no longer can volunteer in this way." Then, what you do you can do because you *choose* to, not because you have been "guiltied" into it. Do you *really* miss those weekend parties where everyone drank too much and the men made sexist jokes and the women collected in the kitchen to complain? Be *glad* you are no longer included. And maybe try something new, like this woman did:

> Most of the people we socialized with bored me, they really did. But there were a couple here and there who seemed really interesting, and I thought I would like to keep up some kind of contact with them. But I couldn't imagine inviting a couple over on Saturday night, which is the only kind of entertaining we ever did. So I didn't do anything, and I was really lonesome and hungry for some contact and conversation. One day I saw a sign at a restaurant advertising a brunch and I thought hey. Saturdays and Sundays were tough days to get through when I didn't have the kids, so I invited three couples for brunch, just a plain thing with coffee and brioche and Bloody Marys and cheese. It was great! Now that's how I entertain. If I want to have more than eight to ten, I call it an open house and no one thinks it's strange that it's not "couples only" the way a weekend party is. Now that the kids are older they come, too. I really like having them meet my friends, and this is a perfect way to do it. I think we get stuck in the old social patterns and just never think that when we *leave* the old social pattern there might be a new and better way of doing things.

Dealing with negative or "cool" reactions from family and colleagues is extremely difficult, as we have seen. I believe that the best advice in this regard is to remember that they, too, are having to change, adjust, and reorient themselves. It is unreasonable to expect to be treated in exactly the same way as before, because we are not the same as we were before. Other people have to incorporate the change that we have made in our lives into their understanding and perception of us, and this is is not always done easily, or quickly, especially for those closest to us. Think of the people you know who have undergone major changes, of a different sort—death of a spouse or child, traumatic illness or surgery, economic reversals (or great advances). It is difficult to know what to say or how to behave, and so we sometimes wait to see how they react. Our friends and family will also wait, and take their cues from us. Perhaps our married friends will fear that in rejecting *our* coupled state we are rejecting theirs. Perhaps the mothers who have been our companions fear that we reject their roles along with our own. They do not know, at first, where they stand with us, and we need to let them know. Many of my respondents wrote that "no one called me," but when I asked them about calls *they* initiated, most of them replied that they hadn't made any, or only a few, fearing that they would be rejected.

Being open to the outreach of others, recognizing it in even the most tentative of gestures, is also good advice. As I have said, the people in your life need time to adapt. To expect instant acceptance and understanding is perhaps unrealistic; to turn from a person who has not been entirely supportive, initially, is to invite a loss that might not be necessary were one more patient and understanding. I felt sad for the woman who told me:

> My mother wouldn't have anything to do with me for over a year—wouldn't even speak to me, returned my letters unopened, all that. And then, would you believe, last month for my birthday she sent me a sweater she had knitted for me! Can you *believe* it? I sent it right back. Who needs it now?

This woman was very bitter toward her mother and in fact had good reason to be, so perhaps it would not be wise for her to open herself to the possibility of more rejection and hurt. However, perhaps the hand-knit sweater might have been a message of acceptance and need that her mother could not express in any other way; I would wish these two women, who had been essential to each other for 35 years, could re-establish contact. As others have said, wait and see. The first reaction may not be, and in fact seldom is, the final one.

Many women mentioned having to face the hollowness of the myth of "happily ever after." "Don't throw good money after bad," said one, and I think these comments reflect that same advice:

- Do not remain in an unhappy, no-win situation just because it is "safe." Life is too short for that. If a marriage can be saved by outside assistance, by all means take the chance and stay with it. If not....
- Do what you have to do. If a marriage is not good, then it is not good for the children, either. Too bad that every marriage isn't made in heaven. If they were, then love could prevail. Children suffer and this is so heartbreaking. But sometimes we must take the lesser of two evils.... A woman owes something to herself. I believe a good woman should follow her own

inner voice. She should have much say over her life and her destiny. Every marriage is not right.

- Accept the fact that being a good wife and mother is not instinctive and not the right thing for all women. I've seen children destroyed by women who couldn't walk away even though they wanted to. Men can be good parents and many are anxious to take on the task. If we can't quit judging ourselves and each other by existing stereotypes, we can't expect to move forward. I wish I had easy answers for other women but the only thing I found helpful was my belief in myself.

Several women also suggested trying to look on the bright, or lighter side, of non-custodial custodial parenting, to consider the trials and tribulations of the custodial parent and, in effect, count one's blessings. It is not easy to come to grips with the realization that there *is* a bright side; we saw that earlier when we heard from women who felt guilty about *not* feeling guilty. A few women offer these reflections on the positive aspects of their non-custodial status.

- It is important to face up to the realities of difficulties for both the custodial and the non-custodial parent. Each tends to think the other got the best of it, but of course that is far from true. I have lost and can never regain the joy of day-to-day life with the children I gave birth to. But I also don't have the day-to-day responsibility and there's something to be said for that. It took me many years to realize that and admit it.
- Being a single parent is a hard, isolating job, make no mistake about that, whether you are a clock-watching working parent or struggling on social security as I was for six years. The single parent has to establish a pattern to suit all concerned and it is natural to resent outside interference which all too often rocks the boat. The situation is further exacerbated by maintenance payment breakdowns, disruptive behavior of the children after access visits, resentments and guilt of the other partner and the ever-present fear that the children might wish one day to live with the other parent, not to mention the personal feelings of failure, diminished confidence and loss of divided friends. Yes, it's all too terrible being a MATCH mum away from her children, but at least we do not have the aggravation of single parenthood. Having been on both sides of the fence, I feel that those MATCH mothers, who, in particular, left their families for their own (let's face it) selfish reasons, surely must expect to pay the price of their freedom and would do well to occasionally dwell on the many obstacles dad is daily having to contend with.

And then there was my British friend who refused to feel guilty about her former husband's plight:

People tend to feel sorry for the man. I've had people say things like, "how does he cope with the wash?" And I say, "well, he does what I did, puts it in the washing machine." Or they say, "but he can't cook!" And I say, "well, he should learn like I did."

Another valuable piece of advice that I gleaned from conversations with women over the years is that we must *accept our own growth*, and not try to beat ourselves back into places where we no longer fit. You will remember that in Chapter Three on why we left, several women spoke of feeling too capable, too skilled, too "big" for the job of full-time mothering. You might also remember that those quotes contained either outright or tacit apologies for that feeling— a sort of "please don't think less of me because I am more." Many women suffer terribly from guilt about their own strengths, from what Matina Horner and others have called the "fear of success." And not without cause. Consider these "compliments": "Oh, I *hate* people who are so talented!" "I can't *stand* people who are so well organized!" "Oh you're so clever you make me *sick!*"

You've heard these remarks; maybe you have even made them. Perhaps these remarks are well-meant, but I wonder. I have a friend (a full-time wife and mother) who is superorganized, superefficient, witty, articulate, compassionate, and impeccably dressed at all times (I once dropped in on her when she was in her laundry room ironing, and found her doing so in heels and hose). "Oh!" mourned a mutual acquaintance, "if only her slip would ever show!" I wonder why we do that to each other. But we do, often, and it is small wonder that if what you are and what you do makes people say, even in jest, that they "hate you" or that you make them "sick," you'll be inclined to try to do less of it. And to do what you *do* do apologetically, guiltily ("Oh, it's nothing Oh, anyone could do that!"). But what kind of blasphemy is that? Too many lights are being hidden under too many bushels in the efforts of too many women to conform to the "norm." When we do shine, we do so with diffidence and reluctance.

When we leave our children we also do so with apologies and guilt. We have let our figurative slips show, and there will always be some people who take gleeful delight in what they view as our grievous lapses. When people can construe our actions as making us less, they can imagine themselves to be more. This is the basis of all prejudice and, as with all bigotry, this smug self-righteousness is unfounded and false. These are the people we can and must ignore. We must keep our eyes and hearts firmly fixed on what *we* know to be true and let those lesser folk preen themselves in their narrow and constricted molds, knowing that it is only their limited vision and understanding that makes them view us negatively. I am reminded of a puzzle often used in workshops on self-realization. It asks that, without lifting the pencil, one connect the nine dots with four straight lines, touching each dot only once:

·   ·   ·

·   ·   ·

·   ·   ·

The solution lies in one's ability to realize that there are simply *nine dots*, and not a box, that the parameters we tend to see *are not really there*, and it is only when we can train our eye to see *outside* that imaginary box that we can solve the puzzle:

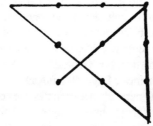

Talents, skills, energies, abilities, creativity, all parts of what constitutes our larger selves. These are not to be apologized for. They are to be nurtured, explored, shared. *Not* to do so is perhaps a greater crime against nature and society than is acceptance, out of guilt and fear of external pressures, of a role to which we are not suited and to which our finest selves are not drawn. So, too, is refusing personal growth, even when accepting that it means radical changes in actions, perceptions, and lifestyle.

I used to like that slogan one sees on posters, plaques, and buttons: "Bloom where you are planted." Ah, yes, I would think I really should try to bloom here where I am planted. But not long ago I set out a dozen impatiens plants in a sunny garden. They did pretty well for a time, but then they began to droop and fade and shed their leaves and blossoms. So I took them up and replanted them in a shadier spot, and as the gardeners among you will know, they began to thrive—a riot of color along the driveway, three times the size they had been, and delightful to the eye and heart. There was no reason to expect them to bloom where I had first planted them. They needed to be in a place that suited them, and when they were, they became what they were meant to be. Perhaps it is too obvious a parallel to draw, but surely no flower, nor woman, should wilt and die when in another place fulfillment can be reached, where full flowering can bring rewards to all who come into the garden.

Another example of how our own perceptions affect our lives and adjustment is that when I was well into the writing of this book, another book on the same subject was published: *Absentee Mothers*, by Pat Paskowicz, a non-custodial mother with whom I had had some rewarding correspondence. I had awaited this book eagerly, I rushed to buy it, and I read it avidly in one sitting. I came away stunned at its negativism and defensiveness. Her approach was amazingly similar to mine: advertisements, questionnaires, interviews. Her outline, too, parallels my own: an introduction, a discussion of women in fiction, and then the results of her investigation. But her treatment of the information could not have been more opposite. She, too, mentions Joanna Kramer, a character in the book *Kramer vs. Kramer*, but she puts her in the section she calls "The Absentee Mother as Self-Centered Bitch," and describes her as a "vicious caricature,...A Franken-

161

steinian concoction." Her retelling of the story is fair; her perception of the portrait of Joanna is, to my mind, astoundingly *unfair*. How could Paskowicz be so completely unsympathetic toward a character who opted out of motherhood because she "just couldn't do it" when, in fact, that had been her own reason? Next, she dismisses that most complex of fictional heroines, Anna Karenina, as having been simply "ruled by sexual passion." Charlotte, in *Autumn Sonata*, is a "cold-hearted career woman." So, Paskowicz remarks, is the real-life Shirley MacLaine, and the renowned author George Sand. And, in a blazingly insulting throw-away line, she describes Margaret Trudeau as "the most visible of those self-centered bitches." The parallels between the lives of these women, and those of herself and her sample, seem to have escaped her completely; for some reason she does not accord them the same understanding she later asks for herself and her respondents. The book left me with a sense of anger and defensiveness that still puzzles me.

I do not mean to set myself up as a better reporter than Ms. Paskowicz, and undoubtedly some will think her interpretations are more realistic than mine. I recommend her book highly, as it is replete with quotes from her respondents and charts and tables and tabulations of her data that I have not provided with mine but with which I basically agree. I most emphatically do *not* agree, however, with her conclusions and observations. Reading her book will, I believe, show how much our perception of another's situation is colored by our feelings about our own. Perhaps if you cannot empathize with a Margaret Trudeau or a Shirley MacLaine or a Joanna Kramer, then you cannot in fairness expect others' sympathy for yourself. I hope my book will also point out that acceptance from others depends largely on whether you accept yourself and how you accept the needs and constraints of those around you, who react as they must, according to those needs.

For that is, as should be clear by now, the thrust of my advice, which I hope has permeated this book and reached at least a corner of your consciousness, however disheartened and wounded you may feel at the time of reading it. Simply put, it is this: our realities are shaped by our own perceptions of ourselves, and the degree to which we view ourselves positively will determine, in large part, the degree to which we are able to perceive our situations positively. If we are not confident of our decision and our actions then we will perceive that others are equally negative. If we can believe in ourselves and the rightness of our paths, then we will be able to find the acceptance and support that is all around us.

I contend that the same energy that is wasted when you "expect trouble" can be much better expended in expecting acceptance. The experience I related about my conversation with the radio show hostess is a good example: I had a choice, and I chose to see the positive. We almost always have that choice.

I have a friend who invariably answers the question "how are you?" by saying "better and better, thanks!" I think that is a response we could all use to good effect. We might also take to heart the advice offered by a woman from Kansas:

I (secretly, naturally) used to use the line suggested by, I think, Emile Coue many years ago. I would say to myself as often as I thought of it, "Every day in every way I am getting better and better." Sometimes I would try to look in the mirror while I said it, and look at myself and say, "You are a Good Person." After a while I began to think that it might actually be true! And now I do believe it. It doesn't really matter whether everyone I know agrees; enough of them do that I don't change my mind. Norman Vincent Peale really has something, I think, with his Power of Positive Thinking theory. Anyway, it worked pretty well for me.

And there you have it; advice freely given, freely shared, based on personal experiences, hard-won growth and triumphant emergence into a new and better life. These are the words of the women who have been there, lived through it, emerged whole, and are becoming the women, and mothers, they were meant to be. Surely there are lessons to be learned from these experiences, lessons not only for other women but for today's society and for the planners of the future.

What About the Future?

We all know the words to that grand old song about mothers that begins "'M' is for the million things she gave me...." 'T' is for Tears, it says, 'H' for Heart of purest gold, 'E' for Eyes shining with love. Abraham Lincoln said he owed everything to his "angel mother," as did John Quincy Adams; Edgar Allan Poe said the angels could find no more devotional word than "Mother." Oliver Wendell Holmes wrote that while "youth fades, love droops, leaves of friendship fall," a mother's love endures. The love of Kipling's Mother-o-mine would persist "though he be hanged from the highest hill." Samuel Tayler Coleridge tells us that a mother is "the holiest thing alive." "The sweetest sounds to mortals given," writes William Goldsmith Brown, "are heard in Mother, Home, and Heaven." "Is not a young mother," asks Thackeray, "one of the sweetest sights life shows us?" And we've all been told that "God couldn't be everywhere, so He made mothers."[1]

It seems to me that these, and the many other rhapsodies to Mother, are not so much attempts to actually define the word as to describe that Someone we all *want* to have in our lives. That nurturing, caring, loving, ever-present, ever-patient giver of unconditional love and support that we all yearn for. We want to believe there is such a person. We want to believe that we deserve such riches of love and support and that we can have that person.

It is time to begin to structure our lives and relationships based on the realization that no one person can ever be that "mother" and, as a corollary, understand that when we do not have such a person it is not because we are bad and unlovable. We and our children can learn to see that our needs for love and affirmation and acceptance can be answered in many ways, from many sources. It is unfair, and unrealistic, and doomed to failure to put that kind of responsibility on one "mother."

Accomplishing this goal involves huge changes in attitudes and perceptions about the very structure of society, the make-up of human beings, even the nature of reality itself. But we should try to begin, monumental task or not. We have the scientific knowledge, the surveys and research. We have the truth of what we observe to be so, and we have our own instincts. We can begin to make these changes.

First, perhaps foremost, we must know as fact that not all women, married or unmarried, want to be mothers, and as a society we must work toward presenting childlessness as a viable and acceptable choice. Next, we must understand that not all mothers want to *continue* as mothers in the ordinary sense. These mothers want to fade out of their children's lives permanently. This, too, must be accepted as a viable and usually very sensible and correct choice for these women, and we must help the children involved to understand that the "fault" did not lie in them, and that the choice was a loving and supportive one based on self-knowledge and a desire for that best course for everyone.

Third, we must understand that "mothering" comes in many guises, from many sources. We need to begin to look to many sources to fulfill all the needs that are ostensibly met by the stereotypical mother.

Perhaps modern science can give us some help with this task of changing descriptions and expectations. The technology of fertility and gestation has caused us to add to the language such terms as birthmother, genetic mother, biological mother, adoptive mother, caregiver. It is becoming increasingly difficult to decide just who the "mother" really is. Is it Woman A, who provides the egg for the petri dish, which will be fertilized there? Is it Woman B, who hosts that fertilized egg after it is implanted in her womb, and carries the fetus to term? Or is it Woman C, who takes this genetic child of Woman A, gestated child of woman B, and brings it home to care for? And, must Woman C stay home full time with the child in order to qualify for the title Mother? Can Grandmother D and DayCare provider E and, yes, even Daddy F, qualify?

In vitro fertilization is becoming almost commonplace, and the embryos thus created can be implanted successfully in the egg-donor mother or in a surrogate mother. It is also possible to flush an embryo from the womb where it was conceived and transfer it to the womb of the woman who will carry the fetus to term. We have even seen an instance where the mother of a woman who could not conceive carried that child for her daughter, therefore becoming, in some way, both mother and grandmother to the same child.

We are able to keep fertilized eggs alive in the laboratory for longer and longer periods of time. (We can even freeze them, a fact which led to an extraordinarily bizarre custody case, where the multi-millionaire parents of two frozen embryos were killed in a plane crash, raising questions as to whether the embryos were heirs; who, if anyone, was responsible for them; and whether, if they survived thawing, they should be implanted and borne, and by whom.) At the other end of the gestation period we are able to rescue fetuses born at less than one pound and bring them to viability in special incubators. Thus, the time required for a fetus to actually be in the uterus of a human woman is becoming shorter. It is not unreasonable, then, to expect that it will eventually be possible to "grow" a baby entirely outside the human body.

Clearly, we are going to have to reexamine our definitions and our assumptions.

And, while we are rethinking our concepts of mother, we might also give some thought to redefining our images of family. Divorce and remarriage, sometimes more than once, have created extended, blended, step-family configurations. Further, unmarried couples live together and have children and behave in every way like "legalized" families. An increasing

166

number of gay and lesbian couples are raising children.

I once attended an all-day conference aimed at giving some preliminary guidelines to a White House conference on families, but we never got off the ground. We spent all day thinking of the myriad kinds of family structures we all knew or lived in, and failed totally to agree on a definition of what we were discussing.

We know that the single-parent family is becoming commonplace, the single parent being the mother in 90 percent of the cases. In ten percent of single-parent families (more if one uses other statistics) we find single-parent fathers and the non-custodial mothers to whom this book is devoted.

At this point I would like to discuss the women we may not see in quite the same light but who can be called part-time non-custodial mothers; that is, the women who have what is called "joint custody." It is important to say briefly that this trend may help to bring the full-time non-custodial mother into respectability, so to speak. Under a joint custody arrangement the mother who relinquishes custody of her child for varying periods of time can be considered not only a good mother, but positively heroic in her willingness to share the child with the father, allow the father exclusive time with the child, and set aside her needs so that the child can maintain contact with each parent. She is obviously up-to-date and fully versed in child psychology. Consider the very positive tone of the following letter from a woman with joint custody, who described herself as a half-time mother:

> This fall I became a working mother and a single parent at the same time....I always planned to go back to work when my youngest was in first grade and, coincidentally or intentionally, this is when my husband and I decided to separate....We decided on having the children remain in the house all year, with my husband and I alternating living there for six months each, the other six months in a nearby apartment....I have now been living alone in the apartment for about six weeks, and my life has eased greatly. Cooking, cleaning, and laundry are out, for the most part, and time has increased. I do still "go home" to take care of the children after work each day, until my husband gets there. I also am with them one evening a week plus half of each weekend.... It does feel strange to be a "visiting" mother, but I'm trying to enjoy this unique time in my life...I do feel lucky that my husband and I have been able to come up with this arrangement, as inconvenient as it is sometimes, or hard to adjust to emotionally. It seems like uncharted territory, forging a new way to still meet parental responsibilities as well as to express and receive the love one feels as a parent.

Joint custody, no matter what the physical set-up, can make it possible for each party—mother, father, and child—to retain a sense of connection. The child has not been "given " to one or the other parent; one parent has not "won" and the other "lost," and the child knows there are still two parents in the picture, however remote one or the other might be. The mother who agrees to this kind of plan can see herself not only as unselfish, but generous; not abrogating her responsibility but sharing it, not depriving a child of a mother but making way for another fully involved parent, which fathers are not always thought to be. And she can feel that she has the best of both worlds. "It really got me off the hook," said one mother of her joint custody arrangement. "I was scared stiff I would get sole custody and then what would I do? I could *never* take on two kids and a job. I must say I feel guilty about being so happy about not having them all the time, but it is easy to live with that guilt when in the eyes of the world I have been very open-handed with my parenting time...letting him have some of it, that is."

Semantically it has a lot to recommend it, also. One of my respondents was completely satisfied with her joint custody arrangement, even though the actual plan was for her son to join her and her new husband in England every summer and a week at Easter, and the rest of the time to be in New York with his father. Another was desolate over having "lost custody" even though she lived across the street from her children and saw them daily. The actual words seemed vitally important.

Not all my respondents agreed that joint custody is a good idea:

- I refuse to yo-yo the children. Mad at Dad, move in with Mom. *No way!* They are always welcome to come back with me, but forever. No bouncing back and forth...
- She became very confused with the co-parenting thing, would wake up not knowing whose house she was in.
- I do not think shared custody is an emotionally stable situation and I will have no part of it. I feel that one place to call "home" is needed for any child, any adult for that matter.

The point made in that last comment is well taken. I read Isabelle Ricci's book *Mom's House, Dad's House* with a great deal of enthusiasm, as she has many excellent suggestions about sharing a child with someone you are not particularly enthusiastic about, and also some wonderful new vocabulary to use in these situations. Throughout the book, though, I felt there was something missing and at the end I decided that the clue was in the title—if there is Mom's House and Dad's House; then, sooner or later, the perceptive and even not-so-perceptive child will ask, "Then where is *my* house?" Even with a room of his/her own in each house, and even with a whole established social life, toys, games, new families, etc. there still remains the question of *where is Home?* When I have to fill out a form, what do I write? Both? Choose one? Alternate? My daughter gave me a rather stunning insight into the perceptions of a child about home and space. During the two years she lived with her father she would refer to visits to my home as going "out there," as in "I'll be out there this weekend, right?" Or, "I left my green shirt out there." Geographically and coloquially speaking, when one is on Long Island the further east one goes the further "out" one is, and since I lived east of her father the term made sense and I never gave it a thought—until she moved to my home permanently. And then she began to use the *same* term, in the very same way, to refer to her father's house, saying she would be "out there" for Christmas Day or she had a color TV "out there." And it struck me that "out there" did not mean a geographical location to her at all; it was anywhere away from what she understood as home base, and when the home base changed, so did her perception of what was "out there." I think this is a valuable lesson to bear in mind when making decisions about living space; joint custody might be a soothing and guilt-relieving term for the divorcing parents and a good indication for the child that he/she is still connected to both parents. But for the basic question "where do I live?" I think there had better be a definite answer.

I bring all this up as a way of suggesting that the woman without custody might try to think of herself in some of the same ways as we have described above. There might be a lesson here about attitudes, and about one's view of oneself. If one can see oneself in a non-custody situation not as an unloving, mean-spirited, selfish woman who wants to get rid of her children but as a generous, open-hearted, loving woman who shares the child with the father, who unselfishly relinquishes part of the pleasures and fulfillments of mothering that are "rightfully" hers so that another can share in the rewards, then the healing process is helped along and the bonds that are formed are strengthened. In an "intact" family it is considered quite dear and charming for the father to play a major role in child care; why should it be different in a restructured family?

We might also console ourselves by remembering that we will have an easier transition as the child grows older; we are unlikely to suffer the famous "empty nest" syndrome, since our nest has been partially empty for years. It can also help in the very important "letting go" process, so difficult for women who have spent their whole lives in the service of their children and find themselves out of a job mid-life. A mother is, after all, constantly enjoined to "give up" her child—to the teacher, to the team, to the coach, to the gang, to the spouse, to the grandchildren. And if she fails in any of those she is considered a bad mother—greedy, grasping, demanding, clutching. Why, then, if she gives up the child to its father, who by all sensible standards has equal claim, should there be condemnation?

As to what custody arrangement is best, I leave you with two quotes, one a caution and one a study report. The first appeared in a *New York Times* news summary in 1982:

The only California condor egg known to have been laid this breeding season was knocked off a cliff by the parents, who were quarreling over the care of the egg, according to specialists who were looking on half a mile away. The experts, who were trying to save the huge, endangered birds, said that the four-inch egg broke on the rocks below

169

the condors' cave and the embryo was eaten by ravens.[2]

The next appeared in the *Psychological Bulletin*, the bi-monthly publication of the American Psychological Association, at the end of a 25-page article entitled "Joint Custody After Divorce; Major Issues and Goals for Research." The article is replete with citations, statistics, and pronouncements of various sorts under headings like Interdependence of Relationships, Mechanics of Alteration, and Social and Demographic Variables. After all that the authors wrote:

> In conclusion, we can offer no generalizations about the effects of joint custody or its advantages and disadvantages vis-a-vis sole custody arrangements. The available studies are egregiously inadequate, and for the most part the debates have been nourished solely by opposing ideologies.[3]

All of this brings me back to my original premise: we must begin to see and accept the great variety of family structures, not labeling any of them abnormal or unfortunate or potentially damaging, but as interesting, workable, and exciting alternatives to that Mom-at-home, Dad-at-work, big brother, little sister, puppy dog and picket fence stereotype, in which only about seven to ten percent of us actually live.

I think there are many ways to accomplish this goal.

Schools can help. Teachers can learn to view each child's family as acceptable, and avoid quick judgments about "children from broken homes," "children of divorce," "abandoned children," and the like, instead basing their opinions and their methods of teaching and counseling on the child as he or she actually performs. They can avoid emphasizing occasions like Mother's Day and Father's Day and plan more universally applicable projects and crafts. They can spend time discussing various family configurations, giving each equal status.

Clergy of all faiths can help, by ministering to their congregations according to actual needs and realities; they can avoid condemnation in the name of some higher power and bring the message of hope, forgiveness, love, and individual goodness and godliness that is common to all religions.

Social workers, psychotherapists, doctors, and other professionals can help, by stressing the importance of choice, of self-esteem, of individual differences and needs, and can offer support and encouragement to women making unusual choices.

Government and the legal system can help, by offering equal protection and support to all families, whatever their make-up, and by ensuring equitable and non-punitive divorce and separation agreements, in the courts and in mediation hearings.

The rest of us can help, by seeing to it that these changes are being made by all these segments of our society, by insisting that attitudes can and should change and that support is offered to everyone, whatever their situations. Those of us who have followed the path of non-custody can help most of all, by accepting ourselves and our choices, by demonstrating the viability of our lifestyles, by being frank and open with family, colleagues, and our children, and, to repeat the words of one of my respondents, by standing tall and being proud.

I hope in some way this book will help all of us reach these goals. I have tried to include a lot of information, descriptions, facts, reactions, and outcomes. Mostly, I have tried to show that there are many different currents that can carry us to the same safe harbor, that life offers many options, many paths, many vistas; I have tried to convey the truth that I see: that all these ways can be right.

So this is really a book about choices. It is a book not only about the choice to parent from outside a traditional (and in many ways outmoded) family structure, but about choosing to see that choice as possible, positive, energizing, brave, freeing, and right. It is about choosing to rise above guilt, and fear, and the largely self-imposed feelings of isolation, shame, and rejection. It is a book about self-knowledge, self-acceptance, and the joy of self-affirmation. It is, I hope, a book to offer you the peace of knowing that you are not alone, that you are not the only one, that you are not doomed to a lifetime of despair, loneliness, and condemnation; that many thousands of women have lived and are living this lifestyle and making it work for themselves and their children, and that you can, too. That "happily ever after" happens in many different ways, and your way can be one of them. It is my hope that those of you who have made this choice, or who work with those who have made this choice, or who live with and love those who have made this choice, will find something in this book to help all of us reach the universal goals of happiness, freedom, and love.

And so we come at last to the initial question, to the question posed in the title of this book. How Could You? And we answer:

- I could, because I value myself as highly as I value others, and I do not feel that a choice has to be made among us.
- I could, because I examined all the options and found this to be the best, and perhaps the only, one open to me at the time I made it.
- I could, because I have faith in the love and strength that lie in my children, and that they know and believe the truth of my love for them.
- I could, because I have faith in the love I feel for my children, and know it will overcome any burden of guilt or blame.
- I could, because I have learned to have faith in myself, and in my goodness, and in the future we will all share.

Notes

CHAPTER 1: WHO EVER HEARD OF SUCH A THING?

1. "The vulnerable soul of Joansie." *Time*, November 5, 1979, p. 19.
2. MacPherson, Myra. "Joan Kennedy: 'Win or lose, I win'."
McCall's, June, 1980, p.30.
3. Brothers, Joyce. "Joan Kennedy's road back from alcoholism." *Good Housekeeping*, April, 1979, p. 114.
4. Markfield, Alan. "A flower child in the jet set, Margaret Trudeau bids farewell to martyrdom." *People*, September 4, 1977, p. 18.
5. Markfield, p. 18.
6. Markfield, p. 22.
7. Trudeau, Margaret. *Beyond Reason*. London: Paddington Press, 1979, pp. 235-236.
8. Trudeau, p. 248.
9. Grutzner, Charles. "Mrs. Rockefeller loses suit over four children." *New York Times*, October 2, 1964, p. 1.
10. Raske, Richard. *The Killing of Karen Silkwood*. Boston: Houghton Mifflin, 1981, pp. 8-9.
11. Durkin, Mary Brian. *Dorothy L. Sayers*. Boston: Twayne, 1980, p. 10.
12. Brabazor, James. *Dorothy L. Sayers: A Biography*. New York: Scribners, 1981, pp. 103-104.
13. Gilman, Charlotte Perkins. *The Living of Charlotte Perkins Gilman: An Autobiography*. New York: Arno Press, 1972, reprint of 1935 edition, p. 83.
14. Gilman, pp. 96-97.
15. Gilman, pp. 163-165.
16. Hickok, Martha Jane Cannary. *Calamity Jane's Letters to her Daughter*. Shameless Hussy Press, 1976, (unpaged).
17. Hickok, unpaged.
18. Sheff, David. "John Lennon and Yoko Ono." *Playboy*, January 1981, pp. 99-101.
19. Gelmis, Joseph. "From fame to scorn—and back." *Newsday*, August 31, 1982, Pt. II, p. 5.

CHAPTER 3: WHY DID YOU LEAVE?

1. Bernard, Jessie. *The Future of Marriage*. New York: Dial Press, 1974, p. 39.
2. Firstman, Richard C. "Still struggling toward recovery." *Newsday*, March 12, 1983, p. 3.
3. Trudeau, p. 229.
4. MacPherson, p. 30.
5. Trudeau, p. 214.
6. Russell, Diana. *Rape in Marriage*. New York: Macmillan, 1982, p. 351.
7. Russell, p. 18.
8. Russell, p. 344.
9. Russell, p. 27.
10. MacPherson, p. 30.
11. Gilman, pp. 87-89.

CHAPTER 4: WHY DIDN'T YOU TAKE THE CHILDREN?

1. "Jobs: Women at work." *Newsday*, May 10, 1988, p. 47.

2. "Half of matriarchs poor." *Newsday*, April 30, 1982, p. 11.

3. Baker, Russell. *Growing Up*. New York: Congdon and Weed, 1982, pp. 64-65.

4. "Lesbians Madeline Issacson and Sandy Schuster find 'marriage' happy but hardly untroubled." *People*, July 9, 1979, p. 53.

5. Van Gelder, Lindsy. "A tragic day in court." *Ms.*, September, 1976, p. 72.

6. Weldon, Fay. *And the Wife Ran Away*. New York: David McKay, 1967, p. 4.

7. "The fitter parent." *New York Times*, February 19, 1982, p. A30.

8. Brooks, Andree. "Mothers defending rights of custody."
New York Times, February 26, 1983, p. 48.

9. Brooks, p. 48.

10. Walker, Alice. "The Abortion." in *You Can't Keep a Good Woman Down*. New York: Harcourt Brace Jovanovich, p. 67.

11. Bernard, p. 51.

CHAPTER 6: WHAT DID PEOPLE SAY?

1. Gold, Herbert. "What a friend in need needs is friends." *Newsday*, December 3, 1982, p. 79.

CHAPTER 7: HOW DID YOU FEEL WHEN YOU LEFT?

1. Auden, W.H. "Age of Anxiety." *Collected Longer Poems*. New York: Random House, 1969, p. 330.

2. "Modern Living: the family: A question of custody." *Time*, October 9, 1964, p. 88.

3. Gilman, pp. 163-165.

CHAPTER 9: HOW DID IT TURN OUT?

1. "Joan Kennedy: Life without Ted." *Ladies' Home Journal*, April, 1981, p. 64.

2. Trudeau, p. 251.

3. Trudeau, p. 255.

CHAPTER 10: WHAT ABOUT THE CHILDREN?

1. "Like in the movies: Mom wins son, kramer-style." UPI Lansing, MI, March 8, 1983.

CHAPTER 12: WHAT ABOUT THE FUTURE?

1. Stevenson, Burton. *Home Book of Quotations*, 10th edition. New York: Dodd, Mead, 1967, pp. 1351-1353.

2. *New York Times*, March 6, 1982, p. 3.

3. Clingempeel, W. Glenn and Rewpucci, N. Diclon. "Joint custody after divorce: major issues and goals for research." *Psychological Bulletin*, January, 1982, p. 124.

Bibliography

Periodical Articles On Non-custodial Mothering*

Berke, Jill and Goldstein, Marilyn. "Weekend mothers." *Newsday*, LI Magazine, March 16, 1979, p. 14+.

Billotte, Louise. "Mothers don't have to lie." *Mother Jones*, May 1976, p. 22-25.

Blinkhorn, Lois. "Mothers find they're not alone." *Milwaukee Journal*, November 18, 1981, Lifestyle.

Campbell, Bebe Moore. "Mothering long-distance." *Essence*, October 1981, p. 92+.

Carter, Sharon. "Running away; When it is better to split than to stay with insolvable problems." *Glamour*, March 1979, p. 128.

Casady, Margie. "Runaway wives." *Psychology Today*, May 1975, p. 42.

Cottle, Thomas J. "Goodbye, kids, Mother's leaving home." *Atlantic*, March 1980, p. 43-48.

Deckert, Robert A. "Mothers minus their children." *Working Woman*, October 1983, p. 180-184.

Doudna, Christine. "The weekend mother." *New York Times Magazine*, October 3, 1982, p. 72+.

Dougherty, Ruth. "When a mother gives up her child." *Parents' Magazine*, May 1978, p. 46+.

Evans, Irene L. "Even without children's custody, they're still mothers." *Denver Post*, May 28, 1980, p. D32-33.

Fischer, Judith and Cardea, Jane M. "Mother-child relationships of mothers living apart from their children." *Alternative Lifestyles*, Fall 1982, p. 42-53. 17 refs.

Fischer, Judith and Cardea, Jane M. "Mothers living apart from their children: A study in stress and coping." *Alternative Lifestyles*, May 1981, p. 218-227. 4 refs.

Fischer, Judith L. "Mothers living apart from their children." *Family Relations*, 1983, vol. 32, p. 351-357. 10 refs.

Fitzgibbons, Ruth Miller. "Fighting for their lives." *D*, June 1984, p. 78+.

Foreman, Judy. "Motherhood begins a new chapter." *Boston Globe*, May 10, 1981, p. A1.

Fulks, Nikki. "Social perceptions of divorced parents: The effects of gender and custodial status." *Dissertation Abstracts International*, Vol. 46 (3B) September 1985. p. 946.

Gladstone, Valerie. "The Bad Mother." *New York Woman*, February 1989, p. 87-89.

Glubka, Shirley. "Out of the stream; An essay on unconventional motherhood." *Feminist Studies*, Summer 1983. p. 223-234.

Goldstein, Marilyn. "What it's like to leave the family behind and become a weekend Mom." *Glamour*, November 1980, p. 82+.

Greenberg, Diane. "When mothers give up custody." *New York Times*, May 1, 1983, Sec. LI, p. 12.

Greif, Geoffrey L. "Mothers without custody." *Social Work*, Vol. 32, #1, 1987. p. 11-16.

Herrerias, Catalina. "Non-custodial mothers: a study of self-concept and social inter-actions." *Dissertation Abstracts International*, Vol. 46 (4A), December 1984, page 1089.

Hirshey, Gerri. "When Mommy leaves home." *Family Circle*, August 23, 1977, p. 70+.

Hoover, B. "When mothers give up custody." *Detroit News*, April 21, 1982, p. 1.

Isenhart, Mary-Alice. "Divorced women: A comparison of two groups who have retained or relinquished custody of their children." *Dissertation Abstracts International*, Vol. 40 (10A), p. 5628A, April 1980.

James, Adrienne. "What happens to mother when father takes custody of the child?" *Vogue*, September 1978, p. 122+.

Kadonaga, C. "Therapists seek to erase the stigma of mothers who leave children." *Los Angeles Times*, 1974, Sec.R, p. 18, 22.

Kircheimer, Anne. "Mothers separated from their children." *Boston Globe*, December 22, 1981.

Klepfisz, Irena. "Women without children/women without families/women alone." *Conditions: Two*, October 1977, p. 72-84.

Koehler, Janice. "Mothers without custody." *Children Today*, March-April 1982, p. 12+

Konracke, Millicent and Konracke, Morton. "Runaway wives—what makes them run?" *Parade*, March 26, 1978, pp. 8-10.

Lantin, Barbara. "Would you ever walk out on your children?" *Woman's World*, August 1982, p. 53+ (British publication).

McIntosh, B. "Mothers without custody." *Houston Post*, April 27, 1982, p. 1F+.

Mall, J. "Support for women without custody." *Los Angeles Times*, September 20, 1981.

Manuel, Diane Casselberry. "Mothers without custody: A painful decision." *Christian Science Monitor*, September 13, 1982, p. 18. also in *Newsday*, October 19, 1982, Pt. II, p. 7. and *Los Angeles Times*, September 30, 1982, Pt.V, p. 10.

Markey, Judy. "When *he* gets custody." *Cosmopolitan*, April 1984, p. 164+.

Marks, Jane. "We gave up our baby for adoption." *Woman's Day*, April 2, 1985, pp. 52-60.

Melcher, V. "Why some women have to leave home." *Boston Globe*, June 8, 1981, pp. 33-35.

Mungen, Donna. "Forgotten women: Noncustodial mothers." *Ms.*, February 1986, p. 70.

Murray, Linda. "The Runaway Wife Phenomenon." *Practical Psychology for Physicians*, June, 1975. pp. 40-45.

Olivo, Darlene Hingle. "A family parting." *Distaff*, October 1973, p. 17.

Preston, Patricia. "Parenting in absentia." *Branching Out*, May/June 1977, pp. 8-10.

Remington, Judy. "Particles of silence." *Hurricane Alice*, Spring 1983. p. 1+.

Reichers, M. "Mothers without custody: Reversing society's old stereotypes." *Single Parent*, October 1981, pp. 13-15.

Rogak, Lisa. "When Mommy moves out." *New York*, January 5, 1987, pp. 36-41.

Rooney, R. "When Dad is given custody." *Parade*, February 24, 1980, pp. 4-6.

Rosenblum, Karen. "The route to voluntary non-custody; How mothers decide to relinquish custody." *Journal of Alternative Lifestyles*, Spring 1984. pp. 175-185.

Rosenblum, Karen. "Leaving as a wife, leaving as a Mother." *Journal of Family Issues*, June 1986, pp. 197-213.

Schlesinger, Benjamin. "Motherless families: A review." In Benjamin Schlesinger. *The One Parent Family, Perspectives and Annotated Bibliography*, 4th ed. Toronto, University of Toronto Press, 1978. 224p. bibliography.

Scott, Gail. "Singles: The mother's case for non-custody." *Washington Post*, May 6, 1981. Section E, p. 5.

177

Scott, N. "Divorced mothers giving up custody are judged unfairly." *Houston Chronicle*, November 10, 1983, sec.5, p. 8.

Shepherd, Rose. "Could *you* walk out on your kids?" *Honey*, September 1982, p. 45+ (British publication).

Span, Pauline. "What is it like for the mothers who give up custody of their children?" *Glamour*, June 1985, p. 242+.

Todres, Rubin. "Runaway wives: An increasing North-American phenomenon." *Family Coordinator*, January 1978, pp. 17-21.

Valeska, Lucia. "If all else fails, I'm still a mother." *Quest*, Winter 1975, pp. 52-63.

Westhoefer, Janet. "Mothers under stress: the psychological correlates of relinquishing custody." *Dissertation Abstracts International*, Vol. 45 (8B), February 1985, p. 2675.

* Copies of articles can be ordered from Mayflower Associates, Box 534, Hicksville, NY 11801, for $3.50 per article.

Transcripts: Phil Donahue Show

#11200 Mothers Losing Custody
#02051 Divorce: A Man's View
#02121 Mothers Resigning Their Families
#04281 Mothers Without Custody

Books: Non-Fiction

Mother As Non-Custodian

Greif, Geoffrey L. and Pabst, Mary S. *Mothers Without Custody*. Lexington, MA: Lexington Books, 1988. 292p. index, notes, references.
    After my very negative reaction to the only other book on this subject (see Paskowicz), I approached this one with great trepidation. I knew that Dr. Greif had begun his work in this area by studying custodial fathers, and I thought he might be less than kind to their ex-partners. That fear was laid to rest within the first few pages. The tone is supportive, interested, gentle, and thorough. The questionnaire sample of 517, and the interview sample of over 100, is reported on carefully, using many quotes. Recommended reading.

Paskowicz, Patricia. *Absentee Mothers*. New York: Universe Books, 1982. 248p. index, notes, tables, charts.
    This is the first book to be written on the "explosive" (publisher's word) subject of mothers without custody. It is based, as mine is, on questionnaires and case interviews. It was staggering to discover how differently she treated much of the same information, and her radically different conclusions. The *Library Journal*

178

review decided that "the ingredients don't quite jell, the text—though often moving—is difficult to follow and sometimes colored by special pleading." It was this "special pleading" that I found particularly offensive. It should definitely be on your reading list, but don't be frightened off by her dire warnings about a vicious and vindictive society; that is not your fate.

Mother As Non-Custodian: Biography

Brenton, Myron. *The Runaways: Children, Husbands, Wives, and Parents*. Boston: Little Brown, 1978. 239p.
There is some useful information on motivation in this book, and considerable discussion of the feelings and actions of those left behind.

David, Lester. *Joan: The Reluctant Kennedy*. New York: Funk and Wagnalls, 1974. 264p. index. illus.
A biography, prophetically titled, which ends long before Ms. Kennedy's alcoholism and marital breakup, but which outlines the stresses and constraints that led up to those events.

Gilman, Charlotte Perkins. *The Living of Charlotte Perkins Gilman: An Autobiography*. reprint, 1972, Arno Press, New York. 341p. index, portraits.
It is difficult to obtain this book, I found, but it is worth the trouble. It is not very personal but it does give a good flavor of her life and the times in which she lived it.

Hickok, Martha Jane Cannary. *Calamity Jane's Letters to Her Daughter*. Berkeley, CA: Shameless Hussy Press, 1976. 48p.
Rumor has it that "Calamity Jane," deserted by Wild Bill Hickok after the birth of their daughter, gave the child to Helen and Jim O'Neil to raise. She saw the child only a few times, but wrote a diary-type correspondence to be shared with Janey. Somewhat disjointed and contradictory, but a splendid glimpse into a fascinating time and life.

Sklar, Anna. *Runaway Wives*. New York: Coward McCann and Geoghegan, 1976. 219p.
Interviews with "drop-out" women make up most of this book. The tone is vaguely angry; the women seem somewhat irresponsible. The author left her son behind and took her daughter.

Sullivan, Judy. *Mama Doesn't Live Here Anymore*. New York: Arthur Fields Book, 1974. 243p.
This "Southern belle" left her husband and 11-year-old daughter and went to New York. Most of the book is background, relating details of her life at home. There is much good material about masks, pretenses, a dense husband, etc. It ends with her departure.

Trudeau, Margaret. *Beyond Reason*. London: Paddington Press, 1979. 256p. illus.
The autobiography of the former wife of Canadian prime minister Pierre Trudeau, lightly, carefully, and honestly told, with plenty of clues along the way to explain her final decision to leave after six years of marriage and the birth of three sons.

Trudeau, Margaret. *Consequences*. Toronto: Seal Books, McClelland and Stewart-Bantam Ltd., 1982. 192p.

Ms. Trudeau outlines the two years following her first book, in terms of her personal growth and her increasingly stable relationship as the unofficial joint custodian of her three sons. This one is disturbingly unclear and often contradictory, and her use of the word "horror" and its derivatives becomes irritating after a while. However, her observations are sound, her growth unmistakeable, and her optimism refreshing.

Father As Custodian

Greif, Geoffrey. *Single Fathers*. Lexington, MA: D.C. Heath, 1985. 194p. index.

The results of a survey of fathers with custody form the basis of this book. It deals with the fathers' adjustments to cooking, cleaning, etc. (things we'd rarely ask mothers about) and includes interviews with the children involved. A most interesting book but a curiously shallow discussion of this side of the story.

George, Victor and Wilding, Paul. *Motherless Families*. London: Routledge and Kegan Paul, 1972. 232p. index, bibliography.

Six hundred families in the Midlands of England were investigated to provide data for this rather lengthy and statistically oriented book. It concentrates on the father and the family and how they manage, but there is lots of interesting information on how the children feel and react. Chapter One, its study of motherlessness, and Chapter Three, on the children, are particularly interesting.

McFadden, Michael. *Bachelor Fatherhood*. New York: Walker, 1974. 158p.

A superior, upbeat account by a man who has had sole custody of three small children for (then) three years. He makes the situation sound so patently normal that I wondered why I was bothering to write about the subject at all. You will enjoy his attitude of full acceptance.

Father as Non-Custodian

Atkin, Edith and Rubin, Estelle. *Part-time Father*. New York: Vanguard, 1976. 191p.

As the title implies, this book deals with the issues and strategies involved with continuing a relationship with children after divorce. Much of it can be applied to mothers. A chapter called "Full-Time Fathers" deals, a little more harshly than we might wish, with the departing mother.

Gatley, Richard H. and David Koulack. *Single Father's Handbook*. Garden City, NY: Anchor Press/Doubleday, 1979. 196p. index.

A guide for separated and divorced fathers who live away from the family home. The authors are psychologists and divorced fathers themselves. It is full of practical advice; much of it also applies to mothers, especially sections on handling anger, on reactions of parents, and on relating to the former spouse.

Newman, George. *101 Ways to be a Long-Distance Super-Dad*. Mountain View, CA: Blossom Valley Press, 1981. 107p.

This is a list of ways to keep in contact with a child. Some of the suggestions are wildly simplistic ("an attractive location to place stickers is on the back of the envelope just where the V-flap adheres to the envelope."), and some are not too wise ("ask your child what he or she learned in school that day." In my experience the answer is almost invariably "nothing.") Some are quite imaginative, and helpful for any parent, live-in or not, who wants to establish a good caring relationship.

Rosenthal, Kristine and Keshet, Harry. *Fathers Without Partners*. Totowa, NJ: Rowman and Littlefield, 1981. 187p. index, bibliographies.

The book's subtitle is "A study of fathers and the family after marital separation." One hundred twenty-nine men were interviewed; you will recognize yourself in lots of their stories. There is a great deal of description and discussion of various styles of "co-parenting," relating to the former spouse, and building a new family. If for nothing else, check this book for its excellent bibliography.

Rowlands, Peter. *Saturday Parent*. New York: Continuum, 1980. 142p.

While this is an attempt to reach the non-custodial parent, it is not very good. The tone seems tentative, apologetic, and vaguely guilty. It is full of pop psychology, not too sound, some astonishing advice (do not allow a child under ten to make his/her own selection in a candy store), some fairly dull ideas for activities, and some pompous and incorrect pronouncements. There is a chapter for "absent" mothers, wherein he covers the parent who "dislikes" the child, and the one who is concerned with the child's health, neither of which apply solely to mothers.

Joint Custody

Galper, Miriam. *Co-parenting; A Source Book for the Separated or Divorced Family*. Philadelphia, PA: Running Press, 1978. 158p. index, bibliography.

This is not really a "source" book, as it depends very heavily on the author's four years of experience, which come across as near idyllic. It might have been more useful to cover the bad times; I think it is rare to reach the level of the Galpers. However, there are some useful and interesting quotes from other parents and some very positive observations about a parenting style that in fact *requires* that the mother relinquish custody for at least part of the time. It is also extremely reassuring about the fate of the children involved, and includes many of their cheerful comments as well.

Luepnitz, Deborah Anna. *Child Custody: A Study of Families After Divorce*. Lexington, MA: D.C. Heath, 1982. 191p. index, bibliography.

With a heavy emphasis on direct quotes from the mothers, fathers, and children involved, the author explores the vast territory of custodial arrangements, including day care, finances, discipline, support systems. Her comments are thoughtful and encouraging, and the children's responses are particularly interesting.

Ricci, Isolina. *Mom's House, Dad's House*. New York: Macmillan, 1980. 270p. index, bibliography, notes.

This marvelously positive book is a must for those trying to disentangle from old relationships and establish good, solid, "up-time" with their children. It is matter-of-fact, sympathetic, practical, understanding, and full of valuable advice. The author's background in family therapy, divorce counseling, and teaching courses and seminars on the single parent has given her an extensive expertise that is well-demonstrated in this grand handbook. There is also an excellent bibliography on divorce and co-parenting.

Roman, Mel and Haddad, William. *The Disposable Parent: The Case for Joint Custody*. New York: Holt, Rinehart, & Winston, 1978. 215p. index, bibliography.

This is indeed a case (one might say an impassioned plea) for joint custody—a rather rose-colored one that glosses over some very real obstacles to successful co-parenting. But in philosophy and acceptance it is sound, encouraging, and sensible. The authors make some Utopian suggestions for reform, but setting goals high is not a bad idea.

Wallerstein, Judith and Kelly, Joan Berlin. *Surviving the Breakup: How Children and Parents Cope With Divorce*. New York: Basic Books, 1980. 341p. index, bibliography.

Considered the leading experts on the topic, these authors write extensively of findings and case studies. I find them unnecessarily and possibly erroneously negative (even the title of this book is bleak).

Ware, Ciji. *Sharing Parenthood After Divorce*. New York: Viking Press, 1982. 349p. index, bibliography, appendices.

Here is a book replete with suggestions, anecdotes, actual cases and candid expressions of feeings and emotions from people involved in shared parenting. Like all these books it presupposes equal commitment from both parents, which may or may not be the case. Recommended for its excellent information and positive tone.

Wheeler, Michael. *Divided Children: A Guide for Divorcing Parents*. New York: Norton, 1980. index, bibligraphy.

Probably the most sensible book on custody I have come across, because it emphasizes, on nearly every page, the near-impossibility of making totally satisfactory arrangements, and the almost certainty that they will change anyway. The author makes clear the extraordinary difficulty involved, and stresses the lack of finality in divorce-related decisions, due not only to court reversals but the refusal of the parties (parents and children) to comply fully. He makes recommendations for reform and suggests ways in which divorcing parents can at least attempt to minimize later disasters. A must.

Mothering

Alpert, Harriet, ed. *We Are Everywhere: Writings By and About Lesbian Parents*. Freedom, CA: Crossing Press, 1987. 260p.

In essay, poem, and narrative, lesbian mothers, their children, their lovers, and their ex-lovers relate their stories and points of view. Some are new or even prospective parents, some have been parenting for many years. Most are custodial, though several are not. Interesting reading.

Badinter, Elizabeth. *Mother Love; Myth and Reality: Motherhood in Modern History.* New York: Macmillan, 1980. 360p. index, notes.

If you have any lingering doubts about whether the maternal instinct is indeed a myth, this book should dispel them. Covering four decades of French history, Dr. Badinter recounts harrowing tales of maternal neglect and indifference, carefully builds a case for the impossibility of anyone meeting the standards of "mother" (and in fact makes it sound absurd to even try). She concludes that mother love is certainly real but not inborn, and ends with a description of the "ideal" family where (surprise) men and women share equally in the problems and joys of parenting.

Bernard, Jessie. *The Future of Motherhood.* New York: Dial Press, 1974. 426p. index, notes.

"This book," says the foreword, "is concerned with both the way our society institutionalizes one of its most important functions, namely the bearing and rearing of its children, and the forces—technological, political, economic, and ethical—that shape its operation." It is scholarly, thorough, relentless, informative, thought-provoking, very readable, and will shore up your belief that you haven't failed at something that to everyone else comes easily and naturally.

Blaine, Graham B., Jr. *Are Parents Bad for Children?* New York: Coward, McCann and Geoghegan, 1973. 157p. refs.

Answers the title question affirmatively; suggests full-day day-care centers from three months on to relieve the burden of child care on the parent, and to give the bulk of child care to people (male and female) trained to do it and enthusiastic in their work.

Dally, Ann. *Inventing Motherhod: The Consequences of an Ideal.* New York: Schocken Books, 1983. 360p. index, notes, bibliography.

Dr. Dally, in the preface to her book, notes that "When large numbers of mothers have never before the mid-twentieth century been shut up alone with their small children for most of their working hours, suddenly it appeared that this was the ideal, the norm, essential for the healthy psychological development of the child and a demonstration of feminine normality in the mother.... The era of unbroken and exclusive maternal care has produced the most neurotic, disjointed, alienated and drug-addicted generation ever known." A British psychiatrist and mother of six, Dr. Dally then proceeds to review attitudes toward children and motherhood historically and, in Part II, discusses the current situation and makes suggestions for reform. Also includes an excellent bibliography.

Faber, Adele and Mazlish, Elaine. *Liberated Parents/Liberated Children.* New York: Grossett and Dunlap, 1974. 238p. index.

A fictionalized account of the five-year progress of several families under the tutelage of Haim Ginott. Somehow more humanized than Dr. Ginott taken straight; these mothers have frequent lapses (as when, despite years of learning "techniques," one shrieks, "Shut up! Shut up! Shut up! Shut up! Your voice makes me crazy!") His suggestions are certainly valid, and useful for non-custodial mothers as well.

Friedan, Betty. *The Feminine Mystique.* New York: Norton, 1963.

The classic that must be included on every list dealing with wifehood and motherhood. It won't hurt to read it again.

Friedland, Ronnie and Kort, Carol. *The Mothers' Book: Shared Experiences.* Boston: Houghton Mifflin, 1981. 363p.

Sixty-four women, many anonymous, share, in brief individual essays, their experiences of motherhood at various stages, and discuss their husbands, work, parents, friends, etc. Sections on stepmothering, single parenting, parenting the special child, and the death of a child are included; there is one essay on absentee mothering. An interesting overview.

Genevie, Louis and Margolies, Eva. *The Motherhood Report: How Women Feel About Being Mothers.* New York: Macmillan, 1987. 482p. index.

Based on a survey of 1,100 mothers aged 18 to 80, this extensive report chronicles, mostly, the ambivalence of the experience. The authors note that only four percent of the respondents said they would not do it again, but only one in four reported feeling "positive" about motherhood. A copy of their questionnaire is appended. Interesting reading.

Kitzinger, Sheila. *Women As Mothers.* New York: Random House, 1978. 239p. index.

Ms. Kitzinger describes her book as being "about birth and motherhood in different cultures and historical periods so that the reader can get some idea of what it was like to have been a mother in these different societies." I found it fascinating to go through this very readable book and realize again that there is no one right way to be a mother.

Lazarre, Jane. *The Mother Knot.* New York: McGraw Hill, 1976. 188p.

Retells the experience of a first pregnancy, and the first four years of life with Benjamin. Good analysis of ambivalence and honest discussion of real resistance to reponsibilities of motherhood.

Pollack, Sandra and Vaughn, Jeanne, eds. *Politics of the Heart: A Lesbian Parenting Anthology.* Ithaca, NY: Firebrand Books, 1987. 358p. bibliography.

Sixty essays, poems, articles, and journal entries are divided into eight sections, many dealing with non-custody and *all* of them dealing with non-traditional parenting. There is much of value for mothers of all persuasions in this moving and eloquent anthology, and the 156-item bibliography is excellent. A list of 22 support organizations for lesbian mothers is included.

Radl, Shirley L. *Mother's Day is Over.* New York: Charterhouse, 1973. 232p.

Some valid observations are made here, but the point is overstated, I thought; children are not all this bad and gloom-producing.

Rich, Adrienne. *Of Woman Born: Motherhood as Experience and Institution.* New York: Norton, 1976. 318p. index, notes.

A combination of personal experience and painstakingly researched history of child-bearing and mothering in a cultural and historical context, written from a distinctly feminist point of view by one of the leading writers of today. Her journey will touch and inspire you and the book, which is exhaustive and cathartic, will broaden your perspective and enrich your understanding.

Battering

Martin, Del. *Battered Wives*. San Francisco: Glide Publications, 1976. 269p.
Probably the definitive book on the subject and certainly one of the most complete and thoughtful. Very useful for understanding motives.

Russell, Diana E.H. *Rape in Marriage*. New York: Macmillan, 1982. 412p. index, notes, bibliography.
One of the first books to really tackle this subject as serious and important. Using interviews with over 100 women, Dr. Russell carefully analyzes the problem; causes, types, and solutions. There is extensive use of quotes and case studies. When a U.S. Senator can say, in 1979, quite seriously, "If you can't rape your wife, who can you rape?" it is time to examine the issue.

Walker, Lenore. *The Battered Woman*. New York: Harper and Row, 1979. 270p. index.
A really excellent review of the psychology of the battered woman by an obviously sympathetic and widely experienced feminist therapist. You will probably recognize her three-phase cycle of tension building, explosion, and conciliation, even if you have not been physically abused. You'll probably also be fascinated with the "learned helplessness" syndrome, which you have overcome.

Miscellaneous

Arms, Suzanne. *To Love and Let Go*. New York: Knopf, 1983. 228p.
Subtitled "An Intimate View of the Anguish and Joy that is at the Heart of Every Adoption—and Ways to Make the Process More Humane."It is dedicated to "every woman who has given up a child she gave birth to, who did so out of love, and who then suffered the grief in silence and alone." The author maintains that "Giving up a child out of love and respect for its needs is one form of mothering." Many, many parallels between these stories and ours; interesting and moving reading.

Dowling, Collette. *The Cinderella Complex*. New York: Summit Books, 1981. 266p. bibliography.
This book is subtitled "Woman's Hidden Fear of Independence." Based on the author's own experiences but including those of many other women, it outlines the ways in which women refuse to take responsibility for their own lives, how we expect someone else to do it. It will strike many resounding chords, I think, and perhaps make you proud that you have "sprung free," as she calls it. Interesting and well-researched, though certainly controversial.

Faux, Marian. *Childless By Choice: Choosing Childlessness in the 80s*. Garden City, NY: Anchor Press/Doubleday, 1984. 196p. index, notes.
An interesting exploration into the reasons why a woman might choose to forgo motherhood.

Halas, Celia and Matteson, Roberta. *I've Done So Well—Why Do I Feel So Bad?* New York: Macmillan, 1978. 304p.
This was probably my favorite "advice" book, not for the advice in the last chapter,

which was perhaps the least useful, but for its excellent explanations of the paradoxes in women's lives. It is replete with examples of unproductive and ineffective behavior, which the authors then explain and accept. Seeing oneself in the stories of others is a comfort, even when the behavior seems clearly absurd; to know that others have fallen into the same traps and made the same dreary choices is helpful, and in cheering them on to solutions one often finds one's own. Dozens of familiar dirges are treated as understandable and correctable.

Keane, Noel with Dennis L. Breo. *The Surrogate Mother*. New York: Everest House, 1981. 357p. index.
  Written by the well-known lawyer who pioneered such cases, this book details the stories of women who deliberately chose to conceive children they knew they would never raise. It's an interesting aspect of motherhood and one with increasing exposure.

McDonald, Paula and MacDonald, Dick. *Guilt-free*. New York: Grosset and Dunlap, 1977. 330p.
  A husband and wife team explore the multitude of reasons why we feel guilty, and give suggestions on how to overcome the feelings. Chapter Twelve, "I'm a stranger here myself; guilt and the emerging woman," might be paricularly helpful; so might Chapter Eight, "Get me off the pedestal," Chapter Twenty, on friends, and the last chapter, "Yes, I can."

Margolis, Maxine. *Mothers and Such; Views of American Women and Why They Changed*. Berkeley, CA: University of California Press, 1984. 345p. index, notes, bibliography.
  Written by a professor of anthropology, many of this book's ideas and much of its material are available elsewhere, but it is easy and pleasant to read, clear, well researched, and carefully documented. The "they" in the title could refer to either the views or the women. The notes are extensive and the bibliography valuable. A good overview.

Rothman, Barbara Katz. *The Tentative Pregnancy; Prenatal Diagnosis and the Future of Motherhood*. New York: Viking, 1986. 274p. index, bibliography, references.
  A totally absorbing and mind-stretching discussion of the ramifications and implications of modern technology on the nature of childbearing. The author examines the use of amniocentesis and its potential for determining who is and is not born; how serious must a "defect" be to warrant termination of a pregnancy (and is being the "wrong" sex enough of a defect?) and how this power of knowledge and selection affects our views of parenthood. Well worth reading.

Seligson, Marcia. *Options*. New York: Random House, 1977. 290p. bibliography.
  I'd describe this book as hilarious and scatological, relating as it does, in approving and clinical detail, some of the more unusual liaisons of our fellow humans.

Silverzweig, Mary Zenorini. *The Other Mother*. New York: Harper and Row, 1982. 299p.
  An autobiographical account of the adjustments this 28-year-old businesswoman had to make in blending her life with the divorced custodial father of three young girls. I include it as an example of how the other half lives and also because it is not

unkind to the birth mother, a lesbian who lives with her lover and who remains important to the girls even as they chose to live with their father.

Singer, Peter and Wells, Deana. *Making Babies; The New Science and Ethics of Conception*. New York: Scribner's, 1985. 245p. index, bibliography.

A thought-provoking and mind-boggling discussion of the controversial science and technology of "alternative" methods of conception and gestation. It covers *in vitro* fertilization, embryo freezing, surrogate motherhood, as well as ectogenesis, embryo transplants, and other technologies that might very well render the terms "mother" and "father" obsolete.

Triere, Lynette with Richard Peacock. *Learning to Leave; A Womans's Guide*. Chicago,IL: Contemporary Books, 1982. 392p. index, bibliography, notes.

It was astonishing to me that Ms. Triere, who left with only two of her four children, and who sent those two back after less than a year, spent so little time on this aspect of her divorce, and wrote the book geared toward the woman who has custody. It has good solid suggestions, however, useful advice and information, and a good bibliography.

Non-fiction for Children

Bernstein, Joanne. *Books to Help Children Cope with Separation and Loss*. New York: Bowker, 1977. 255p. indexes.

An extensive and generously annotated list of other useful books. There are several indexes in which materials are organized by reading ability and interest level, an interesting chapter on bibliotherapy, and a chapter discussing separation and loss.

Dolmetsch, Paul and Shih, Alexa, eds. *The Kid's Book About Single Parent Families*. New York: Doubleday, 1985. 193p.

Twenty young people are listed as authors. This project was guided by the United Counseling Service in Bennington, Vermont. The families discussed are single-parent for many reasons but the underlying help and support offered by the young authors is sound and valuable.

The Kids' Book of Divorce. by the Unit at Fayerweather Street School, edited by Eric Rofes. Lexington, MA: Lewis Publishing Co., 1981. 123p.

A group of twenty children of divorced parents took two years to put together this discussion of divorce from the children's point of view. It rings true, reads well, and seems very useful. It covers the whole process, from the first announcement through step-parents, growing up (are we different?) and even a chapter called "Loving Your Gay Parent."

Richards, Arlene and Willis, Irene. *How to Get It Together When Your Parents Are Coming Apart*. New York: David McKay, 1976. 170p.

This very practical and completely non-judgmental book is addressed to adolescents who are forced to cope with a marital breakup. It is one of the first of such books and still one of the best.

187

Fiction For Children

<u>Preschool and picture books</u>

Cooper, Susan. *The Selkie Girl*. illus. by Warwick Hutton. New York: McElderry (Macmillan), 1986. unpaged.
A retelling of an old Irish folktale about the capture of a seal during the one night she takes human form. Donallan falls instantly in love and steals the seal's skin, without which she must remain a human and marry Donallan. They have five children. One of them finds the skin and returns it to his mother, who explains that she must return to her five children in the sea. The human children understand her need to leave, declare their love, and visit once a year at "the seventh stream of the flood tide in Spring." A good way to show young children the ambivalence of love and commitment.

Eichler, Margaret. *Martin's Father*. Lollipop Power, 1971. unpaged.
Martin's father cooks, washes, plays, and generally cares for Martin and is obviously the single parent. No mention of mother.

Gelstein, Mordecai. *The Seal Mother*. New York: Dial, 1986. unpaged.
Another retelling of the folktale about the seal who becomes a woman once a year. Her skin is stolen by a fisherman who marries her. Her son, Andrew, finds the skin and returns it, though he knows it will mean she will leave. She takes Andrew all around her undersea home, promising to come back whenever he wants to visit. For all his life, later with his wife and children, Andrew returns every Midsummer Night's Eve, confident of the continuing loving bond with his seal mother. A nice allegory for us.

McAfee, Annalena and Browne, Anthony. *The Visitors Who Came To Stay*. New York: Viking Kestral, 1984. unpaged.
Katy lives happily with her father; their routine is reviewed. "Sometimes" Katy takes the train to visit her mother, on an "occasional weekend." The story is concerned with Katy's feelings about the arrival of Dad's live-in girlfriend, Mary, and her son Sean. The illustrations are marvelous; witty and inventive and surrealistically reflective of Katy's feelings.

Pearson, Susan. *Monnie Hates Lydia*. New York: Dial Press, 1975. unpaged.
Monnie and Daddy plan and run a birthday party for older sister Lydia. Full-page black and white illustrations show a bearded Dad baking a cake, being "it" with Monnie for Hide-and-seek, and especially being nurturing and supportive to a jealous Monnie. No mention of a mother; Dad is obviously the single parent.

Schuchman, Joan. *Two Places to Sleep*. illus. by Jim LeMarche. Minneapolis, MN: Carolrhoda Books, 1979. 28p.
A simple story, beautifully illustrated, about seven-year-old David, who lives with his father, and sees his mother on weekends. Interesting and simple conversations with both mother and father explain the reasons for the divorce and the current arrangement. David is not completely reconciled but he is definitely getting there.

188

Steptoe, John. *Daddy Is A Monster...Sometimes*. New York: Lippincott, 1980. unpaged.
A picture book about two children's view of their father, who is a "monster" when he won't let them have two ice cream cones, objects to too much noise, insists on good behavior in restaurants, etc. No mother is mentioned; these children obviously live with their custodial father.

Tax, Meredith. *Families*. Boston: Little, Brown, 1981. 32p.
Angie, who lives with her mother most of the time and with her father on vacations, describes all the various kinds and configurations of families she has observed. Her friend Willie lives with his father. Basically a picture book; the point is made that it really doesn't matter what your family is like, it's still a family.

Van Woerkom, Dorothy *Something To Crow About*. Niles, IL: Albert Whitman, 1982. unpaged.
A delightful picture book about a rooster who finds himself the single parent of three eggs. He hatches them himself, names them Annabelle, Sarabelle, and Paul, cares for them (with some help from his friend Harriet the Hen), and is well-pleased with them and himself.

Zolotow, Charlotte. *The Summer Night*. New York: Harper and Row, 1974. unpaged.
Father and daughter are alone; he "takes care of her all day," and then helps her get to sleep at night. No mention of mother.

Middle Grades

Alcock, Gundrun. *Duffy*. New York: Lothrop, Lee and Shepard, 1972. 192p.
When 11-year-old Duffy's father is killed in an auto accident, Duffy learns that her "mother," Nan, is really her stepmother and her "real" mother, Ellen, now wants her back. Shifted to several foster homes while Nan is hospitalized, Duffy runs away to find Ellen. In a most realistic denouement, all concerned realize that while they care about each other and are bonded in many ways, the best course is for Duffy to stay with Nan.

Betancourt, Jeanne. *Rainbow Kid*. New York: Avon Camelot, 1984. 108p.
Aviva Granger, sixth grader, learns that her parents are divorcing and that she will alternate weeks living with each of them. This is a very subtle book, moving from Aviva's anger and embarrassment and sorrow to the beginning of acceptance and adjustment.

Carlson, Natalie Savage. *Ann Aurelia and Dorothy*. New York: Harper and Row, 1968. 130p.
Ann Aurelia Wilson, aged nine, is in her third foster home after her mother married and left her with Child Welfare. The story itself is light and amusing, but throughout there are references by Ann Aurelia about her mother's not wanting her. However, the mother returns, without her husband, and wants Ann Aurelia back. The fact that everyone makes mistakes, even mothers, is well handled; the two do get back together.

Cleaver, Vera and Cleaver, Bill. *Ellen Grae*. Philadelphia, Lippincott, 1967. 89p.

Cleaver, Vera and Cleaver, Bill. *Lady Ellen Grae*. Lippincott, 1968. 124p.
Eleven-year-old Ellen Grae Derryberry lives with her father in the summer and with
the MacGruders during the school year. Her mother is very much a part of her
life and the relationship between the mother and father is most cordial. The situation
is best summed up by her father:"You and Grace and I are a family. Right?...We
don't live together but that doesn't make any difference. We're still a family. Right?"
Quite clearly they are. Ellen Grae is a delightful heroine and both these books
are warm and funny and good.

Danziger, Paula. *The Divorce Express*. New York: Delacorte, 1982. 147p.
Fourteen-year-old Phoebe Brooks lives with her artist father during the week and
commutes by bus to Manhattan to be with her designer mother on weekends; her
mother is the wealthier of her parents. Phoebe's friend Rosie also rides the "Divorce
Express" and between them we get a pretty good picture of joint custody from the
child's point of view.

Fairless, Caroline. *Hambone*. Plattsburgh, NY: Tundra Books of Northern New York,
1980. 48p.
Hambone is Jeremy's pet pig. Realities of farm life dictate that he must be slaughtered,
and he is. Jeremy and his sister Stoner bury memorabilia and plant a tomato plant
atop the shrine. The tomatoes grow to huge size, and in such abundance that the
local paper prints a story about them. There are enough copies for Jeremy to send
one to his Mama in answer to her bi-weekly letters, which up until now only Stoner
would read. "Mama didn't like much about the farm. It's not her fault...But I wish
she'd known it before." A strange little story, but upbeat and kind to absent Mama.

Fisher, Lois. *Rachel Vellas, How Could You?* New York: Dodd, 1984. 155p.
Both Cory Matthewson, the book's narrator, and her best friend Rachel Vellas, live
with their fathers—Cory alone and Rachel with her fourth stepmother. The book is a
good one, though ordinary—school upsets, strange teachers, difficult friends—but
Cory's relationship with her mother comes across as positive and acceptable to all.
"I loved the change and having Daddy as my only parent. Even though Mom had been
around all the time I always got the feeling she was a babysitter.... I knew she loved
me in her own way but never knew exactly what to do with me." Mrs. Matthewson
has built a successful dress design business from scratch, a woman who, as Cory
says, had sense enough to realize she "wasn't cut out for raising a kid and eventually
admitted defeat." Cory's custody situation fits very comfortably into the plot as a whole.

Greene, Constance. *The Unmaking of Rabbit*. New York: Viking, 1972. 125p.
Timid 11-year-old Paul, nicknamed Rabbit by unkind schoolmates, lives with his
grandmother and yearns for the day when his mother will be ready for him to live
with her. After a very unsuccessful visit with his mother and her new husband,
Paul realizes that that day will never come, and that it's probably just as well because
his mother has her new husband and not much room for Paul, while his grandmother
does love and need him. In token of that realization he demands of the school bullies
that he be called by his real name, not Rabbit.

Keller, Beverly. *No Beasts! No Children!* New York: Lothrop. Lee, and Shepard, 1983. 124p.
This is a funny book (although there are enough wild mishaps to make it almost irritating) about Desdemona, her twin siblings Antony and Aida, and their father, as they all adjust to life without mother, who has left to "find herself." Good treatment of children's feelings and reactions; fun to read but with a serious underpinning.

Mazer, Harry. *Guy Lenny.* New York: Delacorte Press, 1971. 117p.
Guy has lived for 7 of his 12 years with his father, after his mother left them to marry an Army major. Guy does not get along well with his father's girlfriend Emily, and when his mother returns and wants him back, the adults agree that that would be best. Guy flings himself out into the rain, and after several hours returns with a new "sense of separateness, freedom, and strength." The book ends with no decision being reached but with Guy ready for whatever lies ahead.

Newfield, Marcia. *A Book for Jodan.* New York: Atheneum, 1975. unpaged.
This book is included for its excellent dialogue and for the truly creative project that gives the book its title. Jodan's book is a combination of memories and philosophies put together by her non-custodial father, and might inspire you to attempt something similar.

Pfeffer, Susan Beth. *Marly the Kid.* Garden City, NY: Doubleday, 1975. 137p.
Marly runs away from her mother to live with her father and stepmother. She is warmly welcomed, and hears nothing from her mother, but when Marly is threatened with expulsion from school for insolence, her mother arrives and proves that she does indeed care. There is no big reconciliation here, and no change in the relationship, but it makes a good point nevertheless.

Sachs, Marilyn. *Fran Ellen's House.* New York: E.P.Dutton, 1987. 97p.
In this sequel to *The Bear's House* Fran Ellen and her brothers and sister are reunited after two years of foster homes, and the readjustment to living with their mother again is hard on everyone. I include this title because part of the readjustment is in the realization that three-year-old Flora is so bitterly miserable and so hard to handle that everyone's best interests are served by sending her back to her loving foster home. This happens early in the book and is treated as entirely sensible and acceptable.

Shreve, Susan. *The Nightmares of Geranium Street.* New York: Knopf, 1977. 127p.
The Nightmares, a club with four young members, accepts visitor Amanda as a member and unravels the truth about the mysterious and beautiful "Aunt Tess," who, it turns out, runs a highly successful narcotics ring and is also Amanda's long-lost mother. Tess is caught, jailed, but still much beloved by the children.

Sullivan, Mary W. *Bluegrass Iggy.* Nashville, TN: Thomas Nelson, 1975. 96p.
Fourteen-year-old Iggy has moved into a trailer park with his teamster father, and is finally able to find a place for himself through his music. Iggy's mother is mentioned only twice—once when we learn she has remained behind in Milwaukee with their beloved dog Waggles, and once when Iggy states that she will be so proud when she hears about his band. I include this book because of the matter-

of-fact way in which these references are made; it is also a fairly interesting story.

Teibl, Margaret. *Davey Come Home*. New York: Harper and Row, 1979. 60p.
A rather gloomy and depressing tale, despite a "happy ending," written by an author who is described as a latchkey child herself. Eight-year-old Davey's mother lives in another city and "sometimes...called to talk to him-on his birthday or Christmas, mostly...Davey had a picture of her...but...he still couldn't remember her." The baby-sitter pays no attention to Davey, his father often works late and doesn't do the household chores, and life is pretty depressing until warm, caring, cookie-baking Mrs. Summers comes to keep house, and Davey's fondest wish comes true; there is now someone to call him home for dinner. The mother stays remote and does not figure in the story except as the cause of much misery.

Warren, Mary Phraner. *The Haunted Kitchen*. Philadelphia, PA: Westminster Press, 1976. 124p.
After the divorce Dad and the three children move to a house in Oregon that appears to be haunted. The children solve the mystery of strange voices and disappearing belongings. Mother has moved to Hawaii with her new husband. When Lisa bursts into tears one day her father says,"You needed a good cry...not one of you has shed enough tears since your mother took off to Hawaii." Lisa replies, "I hate her, and Mark does too, and Katie too." Father says, "What all of us needs to do is talk." But they never do, and that is the last we hear of Mother. Rather disappointing.

Junior High School and High School

Adler, C.S. *The Cat That Was Left Behind*. New York: Clarion Books, 1981. 146p.
Chad's new foster family takes him to Cape Cod for the summer, and despite their best efforts Chad remains aloof and wary, much like the stray cat he befriends. Chad still hopes to join his natural mother, but must face the fact that she has released him for adoption because her new husband "has powerful feelings about religion" and doesn't want her illegitimate son. His mother, April Anne, is dealt with fairly gently, as someone who must find her way the best she can, just as Chad must. In the end the foster family decides to adopt him, and he agrees. Well written; sympathetic characters and well-stated values.

Adler, C.S. *Roadside Valentine*. New York: Macmillan, 1983. 185p.
An excellent book on all counts, including the feminist viewpoint. The plot revolves around 17-year-old Jamie and his relationship with his father. His mother left him when Jamie was nine (because "your father needs you," which Jamie believes, and "you'll be better off with your father," which he doesn't) and went off with a Jamaican to live in Jamaica. She is, at the time of the story, dead after an auto accident. Jamie's relationship with her and his feelings about it are beautifully (and painfully) outlined, and the developing independence of all the characters is carefully told.

Alexander, Anne. *To Live A Lie*. New York: Atheneum, 1975. 165p.

The three Henning children now live with their father; bitter and hurt, 12-year-old Noel/Jennifer tells the kids at her new school that her mother is dead. You won't find this one easy to take, but it is realistic and well-written, and makes no bones about the anger, pain, and embarassment felt by children coping with an absent, even though still-loving and involved, mother.

Angell, Judie *What's Best For You*. New York: Bradbury, 1981. 187p.

One of the better "divorce novels" for young people by one of the better known authors (real name Fran Arrick). Realistic emotions and reactions and relationships hold the plot together; its positive tone and upbeat solutions add to its usefulness. This is an unusual story in that the children do not stay together. The heroine, Lee, stays with her father while her brother and sister stay with the mother who, by the way, is a fairly sympathetic character willing to accept this potentially awkward solution to the children's struggles to adjust to the divorce.

Bates, Betty. *It Must've Been the Fish Sticks*. New York: Archway Paperbacks, 1987. 131p.

Twelve-year-old Brian Cobb, son of a college president, discovers by accident that his real mother did not die but is alive in Ohio. She "deserted" Brian and his father when Brian was a baby. Brian is determined to see her, and gets permission to leave school for two weeks to visit (he will be transported by Jamaican Nat, the family retainer). His experience is an unhappy one, due almost entirely to his mother's hard-drinking, abusive, race-car-driving boyfriend Kelsey. The mother is a rather shadowy character, nice, kind, ineffective, who does not really convey the message I sense the author intended—that is, that some women are not cut out to be mothers. Naturally Brian returns home, but plans to visit regularly.

Bauer, Marion Dane. *Shelter From the Wind*. New York: Seabury Press, 1976. 108p.

Fourteen-year-old Stacy runs away from her father and pregnant stepmother with no clear plan except to get away, as her mother had done some seven years before. She finds shelter with an old woman who lives alone with two dogs and her "wedding tree," as her husband left her 25 years before. The value in this book is in Stacy's gradual insights as to why her mother might have chosen as she did; that life is full of painful choices and requires us to accept things as they are.

Branscum, Robbie. *The Girl*. New York: Harper & Row, 1986. 113p.

The cover blurb notes that Ms. Branscum writes to "give other people the joy books gave me." They won't find much in this one. Unnecessarily crude, and written in an irritating dialect, we learn of the bleak existence of The Girl (never named, also annoyingly) and her two brothers, who live in the hills of Arkansas (the author's home ground) with their abusive grandmother and weak grandfather, having been left there by their mother after their father's death. Naturally they dream of their mother's return, and return she does, for one day, to tell them of her remarriage and the birth of their half-siblings. Then she drives off, with The Girl, on the final page, running wildly after the car with "years of tears running out of her...." A definite downer.

Byars, Betsy. *The Pinballs*. New York: Harper and Row, 1977. 136p.

Carlie, Harvey, amd Thomas J. find themselves together in a foster home. Thomas J. had been abandoned by his parents on the doorstep of elderly twin sisters; their illness caused his placement. Harvey's mother had left to join a commune; he still hoped she'd come back for him if she knew his plight. Carlie's stepfather (her third) beat her; her mother refused to intervene or to answer Carlie's pleas to come get her. Excellent characterizations, strong support among the children and the foster parents. These children are survivors despite their dreadful backgrounds.

Byars, Betsy. *The Two-Thousand Pound Goldfish*. New York, Harper and Row, 1982. 153p.

Warren Otis and his sister Weezie live with their grandmother; their mother is a fugitive from the FBI and has not seen them in three years. She calls once a month to a phone booth, a fact Warren has only recently learned. He also learns that his mother was in the city for three months and did not make her presence known, though she watched the children as they left school once or twice. The mother is not a sympathetic character and there is a lot of pain in the children, but it is realistic pain and well decribed. Warren's fantasy movie about a 2000-pound goldfish is wonderful, as are the various other movie scenes he invents.

Calvert, Patricia. *Yesterday's Daughter*. New York: Scribner's, 1986. 138p.

Leenie O'Brien has lived with her grandparents since her unmarried mother left her as an infant in their care. As the book opens, the mother returns to try to "be friends" and Leenie, in spite of herself, realizes she is willing to build a relationship of sorts. Leenie is also introduced to her father, whose new family knows nothing of her existence. Pretty thin plot and very little depth, but worthwhile because of the positive outcome.

Cooney, Caroline. *Among Friends*. New York: Bantam Books, 1987. 169p.

Newcomer Paul "Classified" is the object of curiosity for the "Awesome Threesome," a friendship now disintegrating, and one of their boyfriends, Jared Lowe. While the story deals mostly with the brilliant and talented Jennie, we learn that the cause of Paul's silent anguish is the collapse of his family after his biologial mother returns and takes his very willing sister away. His stepmother has a breakdown, his father, unable to cope, disappears, and Paul is left to cope. Interesting angle.

Crawford, Charles. *Split Time*. New York: Harper and Row, 1987. 185p.

Evan is filled with fury and anguish when his mother leaves him and his father to live with another man. This book covers the first few months of their adjustment. A good exciting story line dominates this background theme.

Fitzhugh, Louise. *The Long Secret*. New York: Harper, 1965. 275p.

This book is a sequel to the author's classic *Harriet the Spy*, but a major focus here is Harriet's friend Beth Ellen. Beth Ellen's flighty mother Zeeny and Zeeny's husband Wallace appear after a seven-year absence to disrupt the peaceful life Beth Ellen and her grandmother have built together. Excellent evocation of the emotions of all characters, some explanation of motivation, but from the start it is clear that Zeeny is not a particularly nice person, that Beth Ellen will decide to stay with her grandmother, and that everyone will be happy and relieved about that decision.

194

Fitzhugh, Louise. *Sport*. New York: Delacorte, 1979. 218p.

A rather absurd and not very good tale of an 11-year-old heir to a fortune and his greedy, grasping, thoroughly disagreeable mother. Sport has lived happily with his father since he was four, and wants nothing to do with his mother, which is no wonder. She reappears when the money changes hands; the story is complete with an attempted kidnapping, which attracts the police, a saintly stepmother; a father who can't remember to shave on his wedding day; and a set of friends that just happens to include a black, an Hispanic, a Jew, and a female. Not particularly useful.

Holl, Kristi. *Patchwork Summer*. New York: Atheneum, 1987. 115p.

This is the sort of book I had in mind when I first started collecting fiction for young people on this subject. It deals almost exclusively with the pain and anger felt by 13-year-old Randi, who was left to manage a household and a little sister when her mother left to "find herself." The book opens with the return of the mother to the household; Randi must overcome her destructive and unhealthy resentment and rage. A revealing encounter between mother and grandmother starts Randi on the way to understanding, though she realizes she has a big job ahead to get rid of her hate. Very good.

Kerr, M.E. *Is That You, Miss Blue?* New York: Harper and Row, 1975. 170p.

Flanders Brown is sent off to the Charles School while her father establishes a new (and offbeat) business; her mother has "run off" to New York with a much younger man. Flanders' anger and embarassment are much in evidence, but at the end she and her mother reconcile. The Miss Blue of the title is a strange but unforgettable science teacher.

Klass, Sheila Solomon. *To See My Mother Dance*. New York: Fawcett Juniper, 1981. 148p.

"My mother, Karen," says 13-year-old Jessica, "isn't dead. She just didn't like being a mother. That happens sometimes, Daddy explained..." So Karen, who "ran out" when Jess was a baby, has not been heard from since. The savvy reader suspects early that Jess's fantasies about her beautiful and successful dancer-mother will prove to be just that, and sure enough, when Jessica's much-resented stepmother arranges a meeting, we discover that Karen is a member of a cult, damaged beyond reach by heavy drug use, and completely uninterested in her daughter, who is then free, we assume, to live happily ever after with her "new" mother. Not a bad story, with some good sub-plots (a friend with an alcoholic mother; a tyranncial grandmother).

Klein, Norma. *Taking Sides*. New York: Pantheon, 1974. 156p.

Twelve-year-old Nell and her younger brother Hugo live with their father and visit their student/writer mother on weekends, an arrangement which Nell prefers, though she worries about what her friends will think. There are several interesting angles in this book; for instance, the mother and father have married and divorced each other twice; the father has a married girlfriend; the mother lives with another woman (one scene has everyone gathering in "Mom and Greta's bedroom") and the maternal grandparents are not pleased about it all. There are a lot of real people in this book, written by a leading author of young adult fiction.

Morgan, Alison. *All Kinds of Prickles*. New York: Elsevier/Nelson Books, 1980. 175p.
Paul Evans has lived with his grandfather since his mother, and then his father, left him. When the grandfather dies, Paul goes to live with his aunt and her family. The police locate his long-absent mother; the book ends with Paul planning to spend a week with her. A tender book, full of sage advice and some hilarious adventures of Paul's pet goat.

Morgan, Alison. *Paul's Kite*. New York: Atheneum, 1982. 113p.
A sequel to the author's *All Kinds of Prickles*, this book takes up as Paul journeys to London to join his mother. She is quite obviously at a loss as to what to do with him, and so ignores him, leaving him on his own to explore London, which he does with great aplomb. Eventually all realize that Paul's place is with his aunt and uncle; no hard feelings. The character of retired judge Mr. Abraham is marvelous; so is the final chapter, as Paul's kite soars over the city, clarifying his world vision.

Naylor, Phyllis Reynolds. *The Solomon System*. New York: Atheneum, 1983. 210p.
This is the story of two teen-aged brothers during the summer of the breakup of their parents' marriage. I include it not only because it is a well-written and rewarding book but because during the custody decision-making process full weight is given to the option of mother as non-custodian, and indeed the solution allows for this choice as a viable one.

Norris, Judy. *The Crazies and Sam*. New York: Viking, 1983. 136p.
Sam lives in Washington, DC with his father; his mother runs a health clinic in Florida and has very little contact. While the book proceeds mainly according to an eventful story line (which is interesting, exciting, and entertaining), it has some excellent sections on Sam's feelings about his mother and his situation ("I don't exactly miss her.... I miss something...sometimes I just forget about her.... It's not that I miss Sheila so much..I miss having a mother.")

O'Neal, Zibby. *A Formal Feeling*. New York: Viking, 1982. 162p.
Sixteen-year-old Anne Cameron is unable to accept the reality of her mother's death and her father's remarriage until she is able to remember the until-then forgotten year when her mother left the family to be on her own. An unusual book, very delicate and serious.

Paterson, Katherine. *Great Gilly Hopkins*. New York: Crowell, 1978. 148p.
An award-winning author gives us another dynamite book. Tough, gutsy, thoroughly engaging 11-year-old Galadriel Hopkins is placed in her third foster home in less than three years, that of large, illiterate Maime Trotter and "freaky" seven-year-old William Ernest. Galadreil's mother, Courtney Rutherford Hopkins, writes postcards now and then but has never visited. Nevertheless, Gilly hopes to be rescued by her. A letter wildly exaggerating Gilly's desperate situation brings her grandmother to the rescue instead—a grandmother who didn't know of her existence until Courtney forwarded the letter to her, but who wants Gilly anyway. By now, Gilly loves her foster home, but must go with the grandmother (from whom, it becomes clear, she has inherited her pluck and grit). Courtney pays

a disappointing visit at Christmas and Gilly realizes that her mother will never want her. Gilly gets some beautiful advice from Maime Trotter as she accepts her new life with her grandmother.

Pearson, Gayle. *Fish Friday*. New York: Atheneum, 1986. 164p.
A gripping, anguished novel about 15-year-old Jaimie and her brother Inky, her father Arthur, and the ways in which they are coping with the absence of their mother/ wife, who has gone to New York to study art. Jaimie's resentment and anger are beautifully detailed, as is Inky's bewilderment and Arthur's denial. The near-drowning of Inky brings the situation into focus, and they all begin to accept reality. Excellent.

Rinaldi, Ann. *But In The Fall I'm Leaving*. New York: Holiday House, 1985. 250p.
Brieanna McQuade has the standard fantasy of how wonderful life would be in California with her mother, who left when Brie was two. Also standard is the denouement, when Brie realizes her true place is with her staunch and upright journalist father. In between is a good yarn complete with a family secret. Discussions with her priest brother, Father Kevin, and with loyal friend Gina, as well as with her father, are realistic, helpful, and absorbing.

Rodowsky, Colby. *H, My Name is Henley*. New York: Farrar Strauss Giroux, 1982. 183p.
Henley's mother Patti drags her from town to town to city to town, searching for the perfect place and the perfect job. They finally land at "Aunt Mercy's" and when Patti gets the inevitable wanderlust, Henley decides to stay put. Patti doesn't hesitate a bit about leaving Henley behind, which is a great relief to Henley, who at last finds peace and stability.

Sargeant, Sara. *Secret Lies*. New York: Crown, 1981. 118p.
Another in the oh-well-she-wasn't-much-of-a-mother-anyway genre. Laureen elopes, leaving a note for 13-year-old Elvira, instructing her to go to relatives in the back woods of Virginia. While Elvira is there, her fantasy father is revealed as a fat, bald, "skirt chaser" and Elvira finds her real roots with Aunt Carrie and Cousin Henry.

Sharmat, Marjorie. *He Noticed I'm Alive...and Other Hopeful Signs*. New York: Delacorte Press, 1984. 145p.
Fifteen-year-old Jody Kline has "a mother who's not around. Two years ago she left a note, friendly and exuberant and vague...and she split.... I felt sad and abandoned when my mother left. But there was something so crazy and so flighty about what she did that it seemed more like a bad joke than a major tragedy." Jody's life proceeds as is usual in teen novels of this sort; handsome boyfriend, father's new girlfriend, school traumas, offbeat older woman friend, etc. Well-written and absorbing, by a popular author. We are left in the end with Jody's mother on her way back home, with the sequel promised.

Sharmat, Marjorie. *Two Guys Noticed Me...and Other Miracles.* New York, Delacorte Press, 1985. 149p.
The sequel to *He Noticed I'm Alive...*, wherein Jody's mother returns after two years

and moves back in. Several story lines weave in and out, and we see Jody beginning to accept her mother and to understand why she left. All convoluted love angles are resolved, including the rift between Jody's parents.

Smith, Doris Buchanan. *Tough Chauncey*. New York: William Morrow, 1974. 222p.
Thirteen-year-old Chauncey Childs lives with his abusive grandfather and docile grandmother, and visits with his ineffective mother from time to time; she lives nearby. This is a poignant story of struggling relationships, with some empathy for everyone, even the grandfather who shoots kittens for sport. The final pages find Chauncey taking brave and definitive action toward bettering his life. He realizes that, while his mother cares for him, she will never be able to make him a home that is permanent and stable, and that he must remove himself from his well-meaning but destructive grandparents, so he plans to find himself a foster home.

Stretton, Barbara. *The Truth of the Matter*. New York: Knopf, 1983. 243p.
The truth of *this* matter is that this is not a very good book. There are entirely too many story lines, none of which are followed in any kind of depth. I include it because 16-year-old Jenny's mother has left six months before, and has written monthly letters, none of which Jenny answers or even reads. She does keep them, and eventually reads them, but little attention is given to her reaction or to her future plans for contact. The book's premise that in six months everything is back to normal makes it even harder to relate to. Not a must.

Tolan, Stephanie. *The Liberation of Tansy Warner*. New York: Scribners, 1980. 137p.
This book offers one of the very best expressions of support and understanding of the absent mother through the words of Vickie Chamberlain, Tansy Warner's best friend. Tansy's mother has disappeared, leaving Tansy, Gwen, and Dennis with their cold and aloof lawyer father. As Tansy tries to cope with the enormity of this change in her life Vickie consistently assures her that her mother left the marriage, not her, that she will reappear someday, that people do need space and are entitled to try to find it. Vickie presents an excellent case for the "drop-out" mother, and assists Tansy in finding her. In a realistic ending, their mother does not come back, the father does not have a sudden change of heart (if anything, he gets worse) and Tansy, her brother and her sister realize they can cope and be happy anyway.

Wolitzer, Hilma. *Toby Lived Here*. New York: Farrar Straus Giroux, 1978. 147p.
Twelve-year-old Toby's mother tries valiantly to carry on after the deaths of her husband and mother, but cannot. Her breakdown and hospitalization make it necessary for Toby and six-year-old Anne to live with foster parents. The book chronicles about six months in their lives, as Toby comes to terms with her anger and resentment, and learns, as her mother recovers and takes them back, to expand her definition of "family" and the circles we draw around people we love.

Wood, Phyllis Anderson. *Win Me and You Lose*. Philadelphia,PA: Westminster Press, 1977. 137p.
When the judge asks 17-year-old Matt Bristow which parent he wants to live with, Matt decides between the "lesser of two evils" on the basis of a ringing telephone and says, "Dad." Virtual strangers, Matt and his father begin to build a relation-

ship as they befriend Rebecca, the girl down the hall. Nice handling of the father's confusion and uncertainty as well as Matt's.

<u>High School</u>

Bridgers, Sue Ellen. *Notes for Another Life*. New York: Knopf, 1981. 250p.
This is one of the best. Wren and Kevin live with their grandparents; their father is in and out of a mental hospital and their mother is deep in her career. She visits only sporadically and then, as she says, never on the right day. The narrative manages to give everyone a turn at center stage, reflecting the conflicts, motivations, emotions and fears of each one of them. The phrase "skillfully woven" certainly applies here; so would words like honest, thoughtful, perceptive, and painful. The only jarring note is the ages assigned to Wren and Kevin; they are supposed to be 13 and 15 but they would be much more believable as 17 and 19 (both, for example, are involved in fairly serious romances). A really excellent offering.

Brooks, Bruce. *Midnight Hour Encores*. New York: Harper and Row, 1986. 263p.
When Sibilance T. Spooner, born Esalen Starness Spooner, was 20 hours old, her hippie mother told her father to take her East and raise her. Sixteen years later Sib, now a world-class cellist, decides it is time to return to her mother. I found Sib an annoying character and the book overloaded with musical references, cliches, similes, and highly unlikely events in the concert world, but buried in the plot is a wonderful strain of why, what next, the enormity of misunderstanding and the conflicting memories of the same event. Good read.

Cookson, Catherine. *Lanky Jones*. New York: Lothrop Lee and Shepard, 1980. 158p.
A good yarn, however far-fetched, with excitement and adventure and a kidnapping by sheep thieves as one plot line, and the relationship of 15-year-old Daniel Jones to his remarried mother and her husband as another. A new friend, Mrs. Everton, provides some positive supportive statements about Daniel's mother and her possible motivation and current feelings. In the end Daniel and his mother are reconciled and he is more understanding of everyone's position. The "Lanky" in the title has next to nothing to do with the storyline.

Francis, Dorothy B. *Captain Morgana Mason*. New York: E.P.Dutton (Lodestar Books), 1982. 127p.
Thirteen -year-old Morgana and her younger brother Seth live in Key West with their grandfather. When he becomes ill they try to continue the family sponging business, to avoid the awful possibility of having to live with their mother, Nikki, in Tarpon Springs (their father has drowned in a diving accident). Some great lines and insights (Morgana: "Deep down I have always had a feeling that something is wrong with me—some mysterious something that made my mother not want me, but later on I sensed a glimmer of hope. Nikki must like us...She hadn't abandoned us because she hated us. That was something new to consider." Nikki: "We are a different sort of family, but we are a family. Remember that. Please remember that."). There is also some fascinating information on sponging. Nikki's "side" is well presented; when grandfather dies, the two children do return to Tarpon Springs and the book ends on a very positive note.

Mazer, Norma Fox. *Downtown*. New York: Avon/Flare, 1984. 207p.

While the basic premise of this book is well outside any situation apt to occur in "real life," the treatment of 16-year-old Pax/Pete's feelings about his mother and hers about him are not. Pax Martin Gandhi Connors is the real name of Pete Greenwood, whose parents have been in hiding for eight years after they bombed a laboratory involved in germ warfare. Two people died in that "accident" and since then Pete has lived with his Uncle Gene. When his mother decides to give herself up Pete must decide where his loyalties lie. The book ends with Pete on his way to prison to visit his mother, and to stay with friends "at least for the summer." He says he "finally understands that there is no ending for [his] story...no perfect ending...no little-Pax-happy-at-last ending."

Murphy, Shirley Rousseau. *Poor Jenny, Bright as a Penny*. New York: Viking, 1974. 174p.

When Jenny Middle's father died, her mother rushed her and her older sister and younger brother through a series of dingy apartments, always on the run from the welfare workers. But Mrs. Middle is arrested for shoplifting and Jenny and the others find themselves in Juvenile Detention Hall. A powerful story of a will to survive despite pressure and problems. The mother is weak and stays weak, and Jenny learns to make a life apart from her.

Orgel, Doris. *Risking Love*. New York: Dial Press, 1985. 185p.

Told mainly as reports on psychiatric sessions with a woman doctor, this book is a sophisticated story of 18-year-old Dinah Moskowitz' love affair with Gray Dawson, mixed with her conflict over having chosen to live with her father instead of her mother, a decision reached in a flip-of-the-coin way (whoever's car arrived first at camp visiting day "won"). No real resolution, but Dinah's relationships with her parents and with Gray improve considerably.

Peck, Richard. *Remembering the Good Times*. New York: Delacorte, 1985. 181p.

The circumstances of Buck Mendenhall's living with his father is very incidental to this novel of friendship and tragedy. It was Buck's choice to move in with his father when his mother remarried, and we learn about the transition in Chapter Two. From then on it is purely background, but presented as just one of many unusual family configurations. An excellent book by a well-known author.

Rodowsky, Colby. *Julie's Daughter*. New York: Farrar Straus Giroux, 1985. 229p.

Here is one that is right on target. Seventeen years after Julie leaves her baby "Slug" at the bus station and takes off, Slug returns to live with her. They befriend an elderly neighbor and see her through a terminal illness. It develops that this neighbor, too, has "abandoned" a baby daughter and Slug, because of her great admiration for this friend, is able to accept, if not forgive and understand, her mother's actions. Much positive character delineation of each of these mothers, without preaching.

Sallis, Susan. *Secret Places of the Stairs*. New York: Harper and Row, 1984. 151p.

Seventeen-year-old Cass says, as narrator, "She grinned at me exuberantly and I couldn't help grinning back. Somehow it was hard to remember she'd walked out on Dad and me." It seems that "Mum" packed up and left with Alan Forest when

Cass was three, and now has a ten-year-old son. Cass's father has married Betty, and Cass lives with them and their year-old twin girls. The plot is fairly wild—Cass discovers the existence of her severely handicapped sister in a nearby home for the terminally ill. We learn that the mother suffered a breakdown after this Dierdre's birth and during her recovery met and fell in love with Alan. "The farm— none of this was right for her, Cass. She met Alan and he was right," says Dad. And Cass's boyfriend, Gideon, observes that "People are just people...they do the best they can. If you expect them to do more you're never going to be able to forgive them." Which is pretty good advice.

Stolz, Mary. *Go and Catch a Flying Fish*. New York: Harper and Row, 1979. 213p.
Taylor, Jem, and B.J. Reddick live rather idyllically in a driftwood-colored house on an island off the Gulf Coast of Florida. Their father, Tony, is a chef and their mother, Junie, is a very reluctant housewife. This book, with few holds barred, relates the reactions and emotions of the three children (13, 11, 6) to the breakup of their family and their mother's flight to New York. An interesting sub-plot concerns their wealthy neighbors, the Howards, whose tyrannical father and alcoholic mother have driven older daughter Amanda to the breaking point. Taylor's friend Sandy Howard, however, has reached some peaceful conclusions about her life, which are helpful to Taylor when Junie leaves. An excellent and perceptive book.

Stolz, Mary. *What Time of Night Is It?* New York: Harper and Row, 1981. 209p.
In this sequel to *Go and Catch a Flying Fish*, the Reddick children and their father begin to rebuild their family without Junie, assisted by their well-meaning but rigid grandmother Reddick, who has given up her home to live with them. Taylor's pain, Jem's denial, and B.J.'s rage are carefully explored; we also learn more about the "normal" and dysfunctional Howard family. At the close of the book, Junie returns, firm in her belief that she had done the right thing, and ready now, as Tony is, to see whether anything can be salvaged. Her return is not in the least a capitulation, and Taylor, after a thrilling sighting of a peregrine falcon, realizes that personal joy comes only from within.

Voight, Cynthia. *Homecoming*. New York: Atheneum, 1981. 320p.
The four Tillerman children are abandoned in a shopping mall by their mother who, we learn later, has completely collapsed mentally. Led by 13-year-old Dicey, they make their painful way to the Virginia home of their maternal grandmother. Wonderful characterizations, beautifully evoked emotions, and a finely crafted plot.

Voight, Cynthia. *Dicey's Song*. New York: Atheneum, 1987. 196p.
Another beautiful book, sequel to the author's *Homecoming* and winner of the Newbery Award for outstanding fiction for young people. This second book is the story of the adjustment of the Tillerman children to life in Virginia. It relates their continuing love for, and belief in, their mother, and recounts the poignant manner in which Dicey brings her home to rest.

Voight, Cynthia, *Solitary Blue*. New York: Atheneum, 1983. 189p.

Another beautiful book from this outstanding author. Jeff's mother Melody left when he was seven years old, to "help people who need me," the poor, the hungry, the ecologically endangered, etc. When she reappears several years later and invites Jeff to visit, he is completely captivated. After the visit, however, she once again ignores him, and he suffers great disillusionment and pain. Eventually he realizes that the fault is in Melody, not in himself. The mother in this book is not a sympathetic character by any means, and the struggle is for Jeff to come to terms with her shallowness and selfishness.

Zalben, Jane Breskin. *Maybe It Will Rain Tomorrow*. New York: Farrar Straus Giroux, 1987. 181p.

Beth Corey's mother has committed suicide, and Beth must adjust to that reality and to life with her father and his new wife and baby. The process of her adjustment (which includes a sexual relationship with a handsome classmate) is portrayed realistically and well. One realizes that she will even forgive her mother for this ultimate abandonment.

Adult Fiction

Adams, Jane. *Good Intentions*. New York: New American Library, 1985. 223p.

An absorbing novel of changing family relationships. Anne Manning, unable to manage and control her teenaged son, agrees to send him to live with his father, who has left them years ago. Much good material on the ambivalence of motherhood (having Billy gone is a huge relief), parenting (Toughlove in action), and acceptance. In the end, Billy must return to his mother (after the death of the father from cancer, also beautifully handled) but everyone is older and wiser.

Chopin, Kate. *The Awakening*. New York: Norton, 1976. 229p. (Also other editions)

Edna Pontellier finds her marriage dehumanizing and seeks what she needs in an extra-marital affair. It all ends badly, and Edna, in the end, walks out into the sea. This book aroused considerabe furor when it was published in 1899, and it is still a very powerful and absorbing story.

Corman, Avery. *Kramer vs. Kramer*. New York: Random House, 1977. 233p.

Interesting differences can be noted between the book and the movie; in the book Joanna leaves her husband and four-year-old son not for a prestigious and well-paying job in design (which factors heavily in the movie custody victory) but to work as a Hertz Rent-a-Car clerk and later as a "girl Friday" at a tennis club. This is a good, reasonsably fair and accurate novel from the father's point of view.

French, Marilyn. *The Women's Room*, New York: Summit Books, 1977. 471p.

A wonderful and absolutely on-target novel about the metamorphoses of the housewives of the fifties into the women of the seventies. You will suspect she was spying on you; there are scenes of suburban house parties and family arguments that are exquisite in their accuracy. Don't miss this one.

Ibsen, Hendrik. *A Doll's House*. In Ibsen, Hendrik. *The Complete Major Prose Plays*. New York: Farrar Straus Giroux, 1978. (Also other editions).

In this classic play, Nora finds her marriage more and more impossible and finally turns and leaves her husband and two children.

Lessing, Doris. *Children of Violence*. New York: Simon and Schuster, 1964. 5 Volumes.

Most pertinent to our subject is Book II, *A Proper Marriage*, which takes heroine Martha Quest through the early days of marriage, the birth of her daughter Caroline, the awakening of her social conscience, and ultimately her decision to leave her husband and child. Much fascinating social and political commentary by a master writer.

Miller, Sue. *The Good Mother*. New York: Harper and Row, 1986. 310p.

Anna Dunlap is the "good mother" who loses custody of her four-year-old daughter Molly because of the alleged "sexual irregularities with minor child" of her lover, Leo. We see how innocent circumstances result in cataclysmic life changes. I am not sure why I wasn't fully sympathetic to Anna; maybe because she seemed such a wishy-washy victim.

Price, Reynolds. *Kate Vaiden*. New York: Atheneum, 1986. 352p.

Kate is a marvelous heroine who loves her children but can't quite settle down with them in the ordinary way.

Prouty, Olive Higgins. *Stella Dallas*. Boston: Houghton Mifflin, 1923. 304p.

Sure you remember Stella Dallas who, in the Ultimate Sacrifice, sent her beloved Lollie to her father to live in High Society so the frowsy Stella (portrayed in the movies by a tragic Joan Crawford) would not "stand in her way." Stella is quite generally understood to be that paragon, the totally sacrificing mother. "Greater love hath no woman than this," murmurs the new stepmother, and the radio/film/reading audience wipes away a tear and agrees. Not exactly the ideal Role Model, but fun to read.

Tolstoy, Leo. *Anna Karenina*. Garden City, NY: Doubleday, 1946. 736p. (Also other editions).

You will remember that when Anna left her husband for the dashing Count Vronsky, she also left her son, and it is this conflict that concerns a great portion of the plot and action. She, of course, comes to a sad end by her own hand, a fate I hope we can all avoid.

Weldon, Faye.... *And the Wife Ran Away*. New York: David McKay, 1967. 182p.

This book is more a commentary on sexual and marital mores than a straight novel, which gives it a wry twist and an interesting perspective. In this story, Esther Wells, a middle-aged woman, leaves her husband and teenaged son and retreats to a dismal basement apartment where she eats steadily and does little else. She spends most of the novel explaining her actions to her friend Phyllis; a series of flashbacks involving several other people in her life illuminate the ironies of her situation. You'll *hate* the ending.

QUESTIONNAIRE

NAME _____

ADDRESS _____

PHONE _____

Are you willing to be interviewed? Quoted? Are you willing to have this questionnaire shared with other researchers, with your name included? Without name?
****

WHO?

The first section of the questionnaire attempts to develop a picture of who you were, and the physical circumstances in which you lived just prior to the separation. Answer all but the first question according to the facts as they existed AT THE TIME OF SEPARATION.

How long have you been living apart from your child/children?
Your age then: Years married: First marriage?
Religion: Active? Race:
Your level of education: Husband's:
Family income per year ($): Own home? Value ($):
Were you employed full time? Part time? Salary ($):
How long had you been employed (at any job)?
Was your husband employed? Salary ($):
What was your job? Husband's job?
Did you have a separate savings account? How much?
Separate checking account? Life and health insurance?
Were most of the family's possessions held jointly?
What assets, if any, were in your name only?
COMMENT:

Did you have your own lawyer before you left?
Were you in therapy? Under medical care?
Did you consult a marriage counselor/a member of the clergy/ friends/other advisor (describe): Alone or together?
How would you describe your physical health then?
How would you describe your mental health?

Did you smoke? (packs per day): Drink? (per day):
Take any drugs? (list, with approximate frequency):
COMMENT:

What were the age(s) and sex(es) of your children? (Note which stayed with you
and which stayed with the father.)

Did any of them have any unusual physical or mental problems?
Were your parents living? mother: father: (Please give ages)
brother(s): sister(s):
Husband's parents? mother: father: brother(s): sister(s):
COMMENT:

HOW?

There seem to be all sorts of ways of leaving—check those that apply to you,
and add your own.

LEFT: Abruptly; children had no warning/after vague hints to children/ after
extensive preparation of children/after full discussion with (husband/parents/
lawyer/friends/professional advisor/other (describe). COMMENT:

WITH: New husband/lover(male)/lover(female)/lived alone as my choice/
friend/parents/other family (describe)/alone through necessity. COMMENT:

WENT: To live in a house/an apartment/a room. Approximate number of miles
from children's home:
COMMENT:

TOOK:
    About half the household belongings.
    All I needed from the household.
    Only a few items of special meaning (list).
    Only my personal belongings.
    Less than I would have liked to have taken.

If you checked the last above, was there a reason for not taking more?
    Didn't want anything more.
    Didn't want to 'strip' children's home.
    Thought I could take more later.
    Husband refused to relinquish more.
    COMMENT:

WHY?

Probably the most commonly asked question, with multiple answers. This section attempts to pinpoint a few that seem fairly common; please check ALL that applied, and add any others, with comments.

Left to (live with, marry) another man.
Left to live with a woman (friend, lover).
Left to live alone as my choice.
Wanted to go back to school, to study:
Wanted to devote myself to a career as:
Husband asked me to leave.
Children asked me to leave.
Did not enjoy mothering.
Did not feel adequate as a mother.
Felt I could be a better mother from outside the marriage.
Mental, physical health deteriorating.
Was unable to care for children, because:
Felt stifled, wanted my own life style.
Felt the child/children would be better cared for without me.
Saw no future.
Felt, from husband, no sense of (stability, support, caring, interest).
No longer loved my husband.
Husband physically abusive/mentally abusive.
Children physically abusive/mentally abusive.
Did not want to undergo a court battle:
    for financial reasons;
    for emotional reasons;
    because of possible publicity involved;
    lawyer advised against it;
    did not think I could win;
    other (describe).

FOR WOMEN IN SAME SEX RELATIONSHIPS:

This is/was my (first, etc.) lesbian relationship.
I (do, do not) live with my partner.
The relationship is (K=known to; S=suspected by; A=assumed by; ?=don't know) former spouse: children: mother: father: siblings: co-workers: friends:

My option was critical to my decision not to take or sue for custody because:
    I did not think I could win.
    I did not want my preference known.
    I wanted to be free to enjoy the relationship without children.

My lover did not want the children.
Thought it would place too much pressure on the children.
Spouse exacted this price in exchange for silence.
Other (describe):
COMMENT:

OTHER FACTORS WHICH AFFECTED MY DECISION:

FINANCIAL ARRANGEMENTS

Did you have a job adequate to support you? If not, describe how you managed.

Was money a major problem? Why or why not?

Did you return to school? How did you finance your schooling?

Alimony: Paid *to* you?   How much ($)?
        Paid *by* you?   How much ($)?
Child support: Paid *to* you?   How much ($)?
        Paid *by* you?   How much ($)?
Reimbursement for your child-related expenses: In full: Part: No:
Indicate who (M=mother; F=father; B=both; O=other) was given or took responsibility for the following expenses: Clothing: medical: camp: college: recreation: allowance: other (describe):
How satisfactory to you was this settlement?
If it was unsatisfactory, why didn't you object?
    Felt too guilty to push for more;
    Knew I had no legal grounds;
    Thought I could change it later;
    Was just glad to get out;
    Other (describe):
COMMENT:

SETTLEMENT AND CUSTODY

This section seeks to discover various types and styles of custody and financial arrangements made AT THE TIME OF THE SEPARATION. Later in the questionnaire there is space for discussion of changes that have been made.

The settlement and custody arrangements were:
    Agreed to (before, after) my departure;
    Agreed to mutually and then given to lawyers to finalize;
    Negotiated primarily by lawyers;

Contested and settled in court;
No formal agreement.
COMMENT:

VISITATION

The visitation schedule was:
Negotiated *by* children/negotiated *with* children;
Agreed to by children/accepted by children;
Resisted by children;
Formally outlined (please describe).
Developed informally; visits and phone calls, etc. (please describe frequency and type of contact).
COMMENT:

REACTIONS

The reactions of those around us seem vital to the success or failure of the venture. On these 1-10 scales indicate the level of support you felt from your various connections DURING THE FIRST THREE MONTHS. Where you have more than one in a category (e.g. sister) put a mark for each.
SAMPLE:

	active criticism	occasional "sniping"	no reaction	occasional encouragement	active support

Husband:
Mother:
Father:
Sister(s):
Brother(s):
Child/ren:
Mother-in-law:
Father-in-law:
Other in-laws:
Clergy:
Therapist:
Friend(s) Female:
Friend(s) Male:
Friends, Couple:
Neighbor(s)
Employer/Boss:
Co-workers:
Acquaintances:

Did you know of other women in a similar situation?
If yes, what was their level of support?

Did any of these reactions surprise you? Which ones, and why?

Would you say that people *changed* their opinions of you as a person as a result of your action? Would you say they remained about the same?
COMMENT:

COPING WITH THE INSIDE

You may have dealt with the outside arrangements very well; the inner arrangements are more difficult, as you know. In this section are listed about 30 possible emotions, each with TWO answer spaces (__ / __: As nearly as possible, give *each* emotion TWO ratings of intensity (1 is low, 10 is high). The first space should reflect how you felt DURING THE FIRST THREE MONTHS. The second reflects HOW YOU FEEL NOW. Discuss each; why you think you experienced them, how you dealt with the negatives, strengthened the positives, and where you are still having difficulties. Add others.

__ / __ RELIEF
__ / __ GUILT
__ / __ JOY
__ / __ FEAR
__ / __ RELEASE
__ / __ SHAME
__ / __ ANGER
__ / __ DISBELIEF
__ / __ STRENGTH
__ / __ CONFUSION
__ / __ IN-TOUCH-WITH-SELF
__ / __ DESPAIR
__ / __ LONELINESS
__ / __ GROWTH
__ / __ LOSS OF IDENTITY
__ / __ SENSE OF PURPOSE
__ / __ MISTAKEN
__ / __ SCORNED
__ / __ FREE
__ / __ UNSTABLE
__ / __ DISCONNECTED
__ / __ BITTER
__ / __ DEFENSIVE
__ / __ SAD

___ / ___ CHEATED
___ / ___ GLEEFUL
___ / ___ CAPABLE
___ / ___ WICKED
___ / ___ ABNORMAL
___ / ___ RIGHT
___ / ___ HAPPY
___ / ___ GOOD
___ / ___ ABANDONED
___ / ___ CONTENT
___ / ___ (OTHER)

AS TIME GOES BY

Circumstances change daily, and adjustments are made as we go along. Review this list of possible changes, check those that apply, add your own, and use the spaces to discuss these changes and rearrangements:

Your remarriage:
Remarriage of former spouse:
Marriage of child(ren):
Birth of grandchildren:
Death of former spouse:
Drastic change of health (yours, former spouse's, child(ren)'s:
Other:

How has your financial situation changed?
How has your housing situation changed?
Did your original custody arrangements work out? If not, why not?
How did you rearrange them?
How do you handle birthdays?
Holidays?
Other "family" events (graduations, weddings, etc.)?
COMMENTS:

IN RETROSPECT

The following are generalizations on the overall situation. Consider the question and put a check mark anywhere along the scale.

My personal preparation at the time I made this move was:
completely inadequate   fair   good   completely adequate

My subsequent judgment has been:
unsuccessful   fair   good   very successful

I believe society in general views me:
negatively   indifferently   positively

I believe my own 'circle' views me:
negatively   indifferently   positively

I view myself:
negatively   positively

I believe my child(ren) view me:
negatively   positively

In general, my decision was:
wrong   right

OTHER COMMENTS:

MOST HELPFUL TO ME WAS:

LEAST HELPFUL TO ME WAS:

I DEALT WITH IT BY:

I WOULD ADVISE OTHER WOMEN:

****

At this point you are probably acutely aware of what the questionnaire did NOT cover. The postage I have included allows for two more sheets of paper, and I hope you will take the time to add what you have not so far been asked, including, if you will, your definition of mother and/or mothering. Several women, after reading the questionnaire, have used it as a discussion guide and have made a cassette tape of their answers to send to me; you might consider that option. If you know of other women who would be willing to participate in this survey I hope you will send me names and addresses.

Again, my deepest thanks.

212